Richard William Church

**Saint Anselm**

Fourth Edition

Richard William Church

**Saint Anselm**
*Fourth Edition*

ISBN/EAN: 9783337335748

Printed in Europe, USA, Canada, Australia, Japan

Cover: Foto ©Lupo / pixelio.de

More available books at **www.hansebooks.com**

# SAINT ANSELM.

By R. W. CHURCH, M.A., D.C.L.,
*Dean of St. Paul's, and Honorary Fellow of Oriel College, Oxford.*

ST. ANSELM'S WINDOW.

*FOURTH EDITION.*

London:
MACMILLAN AND CO.
1879.

# NOTICE.

THE following pages make no pretension to be anything more than a very slight sketch of the history of one who, as a thinker, a Christian leader, and a man, was one of the most remarkable and most attractive characters of the Middle Ages. In him are combined, in a singular degree, with the interest growing out of a pure and noble religious life, governed by an unswerving purpose and fruitful in varied goodness, the scientific and literary interest attaching to one who opened a new line of thought in philosophy, and the historical interest attaching to one who took a leading and decisive part in the events of his time; and what we behold in him is not the less impressive, when it is observed that this prominent part in high affairs of Church and State in a great nation was in the strongest contrast with his plan of life, with his cherished pursuits, and with what seemed to be his special gifts and calling. Others are to be met with in the Middle Ages who were Anselm's equals, or his superiors, in the separate aspects of his character; but it would not be easy to find one who so joined the largeness and daring of a powerful and inquiring intellect, with the graces and sweetness and unselfishness of the most loveable of friends, and with the fortitude, clear-sightedness, and dauntless firmness of a hero, forced into a hero's career in spite of himself, and compelled, by no seeking of his own, to control and direct the issues of eventful conflicts between the mightiest powers of his time.

I have told the story before. I wish I could tell it as it ought to be told—with due justice to one who impressed permanently on the traditions of Christendom fresh and higher conceptions of Christian saintliness, Christian philosophy, and the obligations of a Christian teacher; with a due sense of what is accidental, imperfect, or belonging to a particular and an early social stage, and likewise with due allowance for it; with an adequate and equitable perception of what is rudimentary or uncouth in a character developed in times so far from our own, and so unlike them, but also of what it has of a rare beauty and completeness, which all times must feel and admire and revere; not raising its imperfections into patterns and standards, or giving them an unreal aspect and colour, to recommend them to the judgment of our own time, nor warped by what is of our own time to miss, in what at first sight is uncongenial and strange, the essential notes of goodness, truth, and strength, or, what is worse, to distort and disfigure them. But it is a difficult task, the difficulty of which does not diminish with the increase of our knowledge, for the men of one age to enter into the conditions of another, removed far from them not only by time, but still more by vast revolutions in history, and sweeping changes in society; to catch and understand what is real, with all its surrounding circumstances, in long past times; to be fair to them, and to be fair also to ourselves.

The plan of this series of works allows but few footnotes, or references to authorities. My materials are to be found chiefly in the memoirs of Eadmer, Anselm's friend and companion in days of peace and days of trouble, and in the contemporary chroniclers, Orderic of St. Evroul in Normandy, Florence of Worcester, the English Chronicle, and William of Malmsbury in England. I have made free use, wherever I have found it convenient, of what I have written before. I need hardly say that I have had before me constantly the history which Sir Francis Palgrave, unfortunately, left half finished, and that later one, soon, we may hope, to be complete, in which Mr. Freeman has taught all students of history so great a lesson, and has shown how the most exact care in the use of materials and the most inexorable criticism of evidence may be united with philosophical breadth and boldness, with generous sympathies, with clearness of narrative, and vigorous eloquence. The originality and charm of Anselm's character, and the interest of his history and of his philosophical writings, have been more appreciated on the Continent than in England. He has attracted much notice among scholars in France and Germany; and I have to acknowledge my obligations to several. The essay on St. Anselm by the eminent Roman Catholic Professor Möhler, a short and imperfect but interesting one, was translated into English in 1842. The Protestant Professor Hasse, of Bonn (*Anselm von Canterbury:* Bonn, 1843, 1852), has treated both Anselm's history and his scientific position with the care and knowledge of a German. There is also a work by Professor Franck, of Tübingen (1842), which I do not know. The late Émile Saisset discussed Anselm's philosophy, and, incidentally, his genius and fortunes, in a short paper, marked with his warmth of sympathy, fairness, and temperateness, which was published first in the *Revue des Deux Mondes*, and has since been republished in a volume of Miscellanies (*Mélanges d'Histoire, de Morale et de Critique:* Paris, 1859). Anselm has also been the subject of an admirable work, admirable in its spirit as well as in its ability, by M. Charles de Rémusat (*Saint Anselme de Cantorbéry:* Paris, 1853; 2nd edition, 1868). M. de Montalembert published a short fragment on Anselm (Paris, 1844), which was to be part of an introduction to his history of St. Bernard, and which, like all that he wrote, was written with power and eloquence and bore the marks of the warfare in which he passed his life. There are also two unpretending but very careful and useful studies on Lanfranc and on Anselm, published at Caen in 1853, by M. Charma, a professor in the Faculty of Letters at Caen; it is to be regretted that they have not been reprinted. In English, there are fair notices of him in the *Biographia Britannica Literaria* (London, 1846), by Mr. T. Wright; and by Mr. Scratchley in the *Biographical Dictionary* (London, 1843). I have referred for some local matters to Aubert's *Vallée d'Aoste*, and to a work on St. Anselm by M. Crozet-Mouchet, Professor of Theology at Pignerol (Paris and Tournai, 1859), who writes with the enthusiasm and something of the credulity of one who feels himself St. Anselm's countryman. Anselm's philosophy has of itself been the subject of several elaborate works. The *Proslogion* and *Monologion* were translated into French, and commented on by M. Bouchitté (*Le Rationalisme Chrétien:* Paris, 1842). Other works, German, Italian, and Spanish, will be found referred to in Hasse and De Rémusat. I must add that an entirely different estimate of Anselm's character from what is given in these pages, and an opposite judgment on his career, are to be found in Dean Hook's important contribution to our Church history, his "Lives of the Archbishops of Canterbury."

R. W. C.

WHATLEY, *June* 26, 1870.

# CONTENTS.

## CHAPTER I.
ANSELM OF AOSTA . . . . . . . . . . . . . . 1

## CHAPTER II.
FOUNDATION OF THE MONASTERY OF BEC . . . . . . . . 16

## CHAPTER III.
DISCIPLINE OF A NORMAN MONASTERY . . . . . . . . 43

## CHAPTER IV.
ANSELM AT BEC . . . . . . . . . . . . . . . 69

## CHAPTER V.
ORDERIC THE CHRONICLER . . . . . . . . . . . . 94

## CHAPTER VI.
ECCLESIASTICAL ADMINISTRATION OF WILLIAM . . . . . 115

## CHAPTER VII.
CHANGES AT WILLIAM'S DEATH . . . . . . . . . . 141

## CHAPTER VIII.
ANSELM, ARCHBISHOP OF CANTERBURY . . . . . . . . 169

## CHAPTER IX.

THE MEETING AT ROCKINGHAM . . . . . . . . . . . 195

## CHAPTER X.

THE FINAL QUARREL WITH WILLIAM . . . . . . . . 212

## CHAPTER XI.

ANSELM ON THE CONTINENT . . . . . . . . . . . 227

## CHAPTER XII.

ANSELM AND HENRY I. . . . . . . . . . . . . . 247

## CHAPTER XIII.

ANSELM'S LAST DAYS . . . . . . . . . . . . . 286


# ILLUSTRATIONS.

CANTERBURY CATHEDRAL . . . . . . . . . . . *Frontispiece*

ST. ANSELM'S WINDOW . . . . . . . . *Vignette on title-page*

# ST. ANSELM.

## CHAPTER I.

#### ANSELM OF AOSTA.

"Far off the old snows ever new
With silver edges cleft the blue
    Aloft, alone, divine;
The sunny meadows silent slept,
Silence the sombre armies kept,
    The vanguard of the pine.

In that thin air the birds are still,
No ring-dove murmurs on the hill,
    Nor mating cushat calls;
But gay cicalas singing sprang,
And waters from the forest sang
    The song of waterfalls."
                    F. W. H. MYERS.

DIFFERENT ages have had their different ways of attempting to carry out the idea of a religious life. The aim of such a life, in those who have been true in their pursuit of it, has always been the same,—to know God and His will, to learn to be like Him and to love Him; to understand and realize that law of life of which our Lord is the example; to shake off the yoke of evil, to face temptation and overcome it, and to rise out of it to that service which is perfect freedom. But though the general principles and motives have been the same, the rules and ordering of life have been various. Social conditions, and the level of cultivation and knowledge, have gone through numberless changes; men have found by experience that what was reasonable in one age alters by the alteration of circumstances into what is unwise and mischievous in another; and that which was inconceivable and impossible in an earlier time turns into the natural course of life in a later one. In the eleventh century, as in those immediately before and after it, the natural form of religious life—that which of itself presented itself to the thoughts of a man in earnest, wishing not only to do right, but to do the best he could to fulfil God's purpose and his own calling by self-improvement—was the monastic profession.

So strong a tendency must have had a reasonable cause. Many things of various character had contributed to bring this about. But one thing must ever be borne in mind if we would understand why monasticism in those times so completely appropriated to itself the name of religion. To comprehend the feelings and thoughts that made it so natural, we must keep in view what was the state of society and life in the world at the time. Since the Gospel had been preached and the Church founded, human society had presented, in the main, but two great aspects: there had been the decaying and infinitely corrupt civilization of the Roman Empire; and then, gradually extinguishing and replacing it, the confused and wild barbarism, full of noble germs for the future, which for ages followed the triumph of the new nations in Europe. Thus there was the loftiest moral teaching, based on the most overwhelming doctrines which the world had ever known, confronted with an evil and hopeless condition of things in real life, to which it formed a contrast of which it is impossible for us now even to imagine the magnitude. For eighteen centuries Christianity has been acting on human society; we know but too well how far it is from having really made the world Christian; but though there must always be much question as to degree, no one can seriously doubt that it has done a great deal. But for the first ten of those centuries it can hardly be said to have leavened society at all. Its influence on individuals, so vast and astonishing, was no measure at all of its influence on society at large. It acted upon it doubtless with enormous power; but it was as an extraneous and foreign agent, which destroys and shapes, but does not mingle or renew. It turned the course of events, it changed worship, it built churches, it suppressed customs and institutions, it imposed punishments and penances, it affected language, it introduced powers, it revolutionized policy, it let loose eventful tendencies; but to the heart of society,—to the common life of common men, the ideas, the moralities, the instincts, the assumptions reigning in business or intercourse in the general direction of human activity, to the unpretending, the never-ceasing occupations of family life,— the awful visitant from on high, which had conquered an empire and put a bridle into the mouth of barbarians, and transformed, one by one, sinners into saints, had not yet found its way. That ordinary daily routine of life, in which we have learned to see one of its noblest and most adequate spheres, seemed then beneath its notice, or out of its reach. The household, the shop, the market, the school, the farm, the places of law and conversation and amusement, never, or but seldom, appeared as the scenes and trial places of a Christian life: other traditions kept hold of them, and, good or bad, they were of times when there was no Christianity. Society was a long time unlearning heathenism; it has not done so yet; but it had hardly begun, at any rate it was only just beginning, to imagine the possibility of such a thing in the eleventh century. Thus that combination of real and earnest religion with every-day pursuits of life, which, in idea at least, is so natural and so easy to us, and is to a very real degree protected and assisted by general usages and ways of thinking, was then almost inconceivable. Let a man throw himself into the society of his day then, and he found himself in an atmosphere to which real religion, the religion of self-conquest and love, was simply a thing alien or unmeaning, which no one imagined himself called to think of; or else amid eager and overmastering activities, fiercely scorning and remorselessly trampling down all restraints of even common morality. And in this state of society, the baseness and degradation of Latin civilization, or the lawless savagery of its barbarian conquerors, a man was called to listen to the Sermon on the Mount, and to give himself up to the service of the Son of God, who had died for him and promised him His Holy Spirit; to believe, after this short life of trouble was over, in an immortality of holiness, and now to fit himself for it.

If *we* can see what that contemporary society as a whole was like, and no one has much doubt of its condition, what would be the effect of it on those whose lot was to be born in it, and whose heart God had touched? They could not help the sharp line by which any serious and real religious life in it seemed to be excluded: their natural thought would be that to live such a life they must keep as much out of it as they could. That was the principle of monasticism, the best expedient that then seemed to present itself, by which those who believed in Christ's teaching might be honest in following it: to leave the unmanageable and uncontrollable *sæculum* to follow its own way, and to secure posts of refuge and shelter out of its wild tumult, where men might find the *religion* which the conditions of actual society seemed to exclude. That it was a most natural expedient is shown by the fact that, wherever religious convictions have been unusually keen and earnest in the face of carelessness and scandals in general society, there, even among those who have most hated the monks, as the Puritans of the seventeenth, and the Methodists and Evangelicals of the eighteenth century, the strong disposition to draw a sharp line between religion and the world has shown itself. That such attempts, in the long run, are vain to exclude the evils they fear, and are but very partial means to secure the good they aim at, religious people, in so early a stage of the experience of the Church, were less able to perceive than we who have seen the results of much wider and more varied trials. But we have no right to expect those who had not our opportunities of seeing things worked out to the end to know as much as we do, to whom time and changes and issues then unimaginable have taught so much.

Any high effort, therefore, in those days to be thorough in religion took the shape of monastic discipline and rule. When we call it narrow and imperfect, and when we dwell on its failures and corruptions, we must remember, first, the general condition of society of which this irresistible tendency to monasticism was the natural and not unreasonable result; and next, that if we have learned better, we have come later on the stage of life. When all things are taken into account, it is hard to resist the conclusion that the monks made the best of their circumstances. If they were too sanguine in one direction, not sanguine and trustful enough in another, they had not seen so many illusions dispelled as we have; and, on the other hand, they had not yet come to know the wonderful and unexpected openings for a true service of God, the unthought-of possibilities of character and goodness, which have been shown to men in states of life where of old such service seemed impossible.

In writing of any eminently religious man of this period, it must be taken almost as a matter of course that he was a monk. St. Anselm, one of the most remarkable men and most attractive characters, not only of the Middle Ages but of the whole Christian history, can never be understood or judged of fairly, except it be kept in mind that the conditions under which he lived shaped the forms under which religious effort and earnestness showed themselves, and left no religious life conceivable but the monastic one. The paths of life were then few, sharply defined, and narrow. A man who wanted to be active in the world had little choice but to be a soldier; a man who wanted to serve God with all his heart had little choice but to be a monk.

Anselm, therefore, was a monk throughout, and in all his thoughts and ways, just as a soldier who is loyal to his profession can nowhere be uninfluenced by its rules and habits. But he was much more than a monk. A great teacher, a great thinker, a great kindler of thought in others, he was also an example of gallant and unselfish public service, rendered without a thought of his own convenience or honour, to fulfil what seemed a plain duty, in itself very distasteful, and not difficult to evade, if he had wished to evade it. Penetrated, too, as he was by the unflinching austerity of that hard and stern time, he was remembered among men, less as the great sage who had opened new paths to thought, or as the great archbishop who had not been afraid of the face of kings, or as the severe restorer of an uncompromising and high aiming discipline, than as the loving and sympathizing Christian brother, full of sweetness, full of affection, full of goodness, full of allowances and patience for others, whom men of all conditions liked to converse with, and whom neither high nor low ever found cold in his friendship, or unnatural and forced in his condescension.

There is naturally not much to say about his early life. The chroniclers of those days were not in the habit of going back to a man's first days; they were satisfied with taking him when he began to make himself known and felt in the world. It is a point of more than ordinary interest as regards Anselm, that we have some authentic information about the times when no one cared about him. He had the fortune to have a friend who was much with him in his later life, loyal, affectionate, simple-hearted, admiring, who, more than most of his contemporaries among literary monks, was alive to points of character. Eadmer, the Englishman, a monk of Canterbury, who was Anselm's pupil and then his follower and attendant in banishment, saw something else worth recording in his great archbishop besides the public passages of his life and his supposed miracles. He observed and recorded what Anselm was as a man, and not merely what he was as an ecclesiastic. We owe to him the notice that Anselm was fond of talking about his boyhood to his friends; and we owe to him, on good authority, circumstances about Anselm's first years, which in other cases we only get from later hearsay.

Anselm was born about 1033 at Aosta, or in its neighbourhood. The old cantonment of Terentius Varro, the conqueror, under Augustus, of the wild hill-tribes of the Alps, at the foot of the two famous passes which now bear the name of St. Bernard of Menthon,—still keeping the shape of a camp given to it by the Roman engineers, and still showing many remains of the grand masonry of the Roman builders,—had then become a border city and an ecclesiastical centre in the Alpine valleys which parted the great races of the north and south, and through which the tides of their wars rolled backwards and forwards. In its middle age towers built of the squared ashlar of the Roman ramparts, in the rude crypts of its two churches, in the quaint colonnades of its cloisters, in the mosaic pavements of its cathedral choir, half Pagan half

Christian, in which what looks at first sight like a throned image of our Lord, turns out to be only an allegory of the year and its seasons—nay, in its very population, in which, side by side with keen Italians from the plains and stalwart mountaineers from the Alps, a race diseased in blood for long centuries and degraded to a degeneracy of human organization as hopeless, as in Europe it is without parallel, grins and gibbers about the streets—Aosta still bears the traces of what it was, in its civilization as in its position; the chief place of a debateable land, where Christianity and heathenism, Burgundians and Lombards, Franks and Italians, had met and fought and mixed. The bishopric, founded, it is,-said, in the fifth century from the see of Vercelli, had been at one time a suffragan see of Milan; its name was written on one of the episcopal thrones which were ranged right and left of the marble chair of St. Ambrose, in the semicircle at the eastern apse of the church which bore his name: on the right, the seats and names of Vercelli, Novara, Lodi, Tortona, Asti, Turin, Aosta, Acqui, and Genoa; on the left, those of Brescia, Bergamo, Cremona, Vintimiglia, Savona, Albenga, Pavia, Piacenza, and Como. But later it had followed the political changes of the Alpine valleys; the Bishop of Aosta is found with those of Geneva and Lausanne figuring at the consecration of a Burgundian king at St. Maurice in the Valais; he received the dignity and feudal powers of a count, and even still he is said to bear the title of Count of Cogne, one of the neighbouring valleys. The district had had its evangelizing saints, St. Gratus, St. Ursus, and St. Jucundus, names little known elsewhere, but meeting us still everywhere round Aosta. Eadmer describes it as lying on the confines of Lombardy and Burgundy—one of those many Burgundies which so confuse historians;—at this time, that kingdom of Burgundy or Arles which had ceased to be an independent kingdom the year before Anselm's birth, by the death of Rudolf III., 1032, and had become part of the Empire. It included Provence, Dauphiny, South Savoy, and the country between the Saône and Jura (Regnum Provinciæ), with *Burgundia Transjurana;* North Savoy, and Switzerland between the Reuss and Jura. The valley had formed part of the dominions of the thrice-married Adelaide, the heiress of the Marquises of Susa and Turin, the "most excellent Duchess and Marchioness of the Cottian Alps," as she is styled at the time : her last husband was Odo or Otto, the son of Humbert of the White Hands, Count of Maurienne. From this marriage is descended the house of Savoy and the present line of Italian kings ; and of the heritage of this house Aosta henceforth always formed a part, and its name continues among their favourite titles.

The scenery of Anselm's birthplace, " wild Aosta lulled by Alpine rills," is familiar to the crowds who are yearly attracted to its neighbourhood by the love of Alpine grandeur and the interest of Alpine adventure, and who pass through it on their way to and from the peaks and valleys of the wonderful region round it. The district itself is a mountain land, but one with the richness and warmth of the South, as it descends towards the level of the river, the Dora Baltea, which carries the glacier torrents from the mountains round Mont Blanc and the Matterhorn to the plains where they meet the Po. Great ridges, masking the huge masses of the high Alps behind them, flank its long valley as it runs straight from east to west. Closely overhanging the city on the south, rises rapidly a wall of sub-alpine mountain, for great part of the day in shadow, torn by ravines, with woods and pastures hanging on its steep flanks and with white houses gleaming among them, but towering up at last into the dark precipices of the Becca di Nona and the peak of Mont Emilius. At the upper end of the valley towards the west, seen over a vista of walnuts, chestnuts, and vines, appear high up in the sky, resting as it were on the breast of the great hills, the white glaciers of the Ruitor, bright in sunshine, or veiled by storms: and from the bridge over the torrent which rushes by the city from the north, the eye goes up to the everlasting snows of the "domed Velan," and the majestic broken Pikes of the Grand Combin. It is a region strongly and characteristically marked. The legends of the valley have not forgotten Anselm: they identify the village where he lived, the tower which was the refuge or the lair of his family,[1] the house in the suburbs of the city where he was born ; in the sacristy of the cathedral they show his relics along with those of the local Saints, St. Gratus and St. Jucundus. These legends are not in themselves worthless; there is no reason why tradition should not have preserved real recollections : but no documentary evidence appears for them, and it is quite possible that they grew up only because in regions far distant Anselm became a famous man and a saint of the Church. Aosta and

[1] The village with the ruined tower is Gressan, a few miles S. W. of Aosta.

its scenery after all has little to do with the events of Anselm's life, and had probably little influence in shaping his mind and character. We only know, on his own authority through Eadmer, or from his letters, that his father Gundulf was a Lombard settler at Aosta, and that he married Ermenberga, who was related to the Counts of Maurienne, the upper lords of the valley. Anselm bore a name which was common at that time in North Italy, and is met with three times in the lists of the bishops of Aosta in the tenth and eleventh centuries. His parents were accounted noble, and had property, for which they paid homage as vassals to the Count of Maurienne. His father was an unthrifty and violent man, who on his deathbed took the monastic habit. His mother, a good woman and a prudent housewife, used to talk to her child, as mothers do, about God, and gained his love and reverence. From Anselm's letters we learn that he had uncles who had been kind to him, and an only sister, married in the district, who did not forget, in after-times, that her brother had become the Primate of distant and famous England. We know nothing more of his family.

The only trace of the influence on him of the scenery in the midst of which he grew up is found in the story of a boyish dream which made an impression on him, as it is one of the few details about his life at Aosta which, doubtless from his own mouth, Eadmer has preserved. The story is not without a kind of natural grace, and fits in, like a playful yet significant overture, to the history of his life. "Anselm," it says, "when he was a little child, used gladly to listen, as far as his age allowed, to his mother's conversation; and having heard from her that there is one God in heaven above, ruling all things, and containing all things, he imagined, like a boy bred up among the mountains, that heaven rested on the mountains, that the palace of God was there, and that the way to it was up the mountains. His thoughts ran much upon this; and it came to pass on a certain night that he dreamed that he ought to go up to the top of the mountain, and hasten to the palace of God, the Great King. But before he began to ascend he saw in the plain which reached to the foot of the mountain women reaping the corn, who were the King's maidens; but they did their work very carelessly and slothfully. The boy, grieved at their sloth and rebuking it, settled in his mind to accuse them before the Lord, the King. So having pressed on to the top of the mountain, he came into the palace of the King. There he found the Lord, with only his chief butler: for as it seemed to him, all the household had been sent to gather the harvest; for it was autumn. So he went in, and the Lord called him; and he drew near and sat at his feet. Then the Lord asked him with gracious kindness, who he was, and whence he came, and what he wanted. He answered according to the truth. Then the Lord commanded, and bread of the whitest was brought to him by the chief butler; and he ate and was refreshed before the Lord. Therefore, in the morning, when he recalled what he had seen before the eyes of his mind, he believed, like a simple and innocent child, that he really had been in heaven, and had been refreshed by the bread of the Lord; and so he declared publicly before others."

From his boyhood he seems to have been a student, and he early felt the common attraction of the age for the monastic life. "He was not yet fifteen, when he began to consider how he might best shape his life according to God; and he came to think with himself that nothing in the conversation of men was better than the life of monks. He wrote therefore to a certain abbot who was known to him, and asked that he might be made a monk. But when the abbot learned that Anselm was asking without his father's knowledge, he refused, not wishing to give offence to his father." Anselm then, according to a common idea so often met with in the records of mediæval religion, prayed that he might be struck with sickness, in order that the repugnance of his friends to his proposed change of life might be overcome. He fell sick; but even then the fear of his father hindered his reception, and he recovered. "It was not God's will," says his biographer, "that he should be entangled in the conversation of that place."

Then came the time of reaction; renewed health and youth and prosperity were pleasant, and put the thoughts of a religious life out of his mind: he looked forward now to entering "the ways of the world." Even his keen love of study, to which he had been so devoted, gave way before the gaieties and sports of his time of life. His affection for his mother was a partial restraint on him; but when she died, "the ship of his heart lost its anchor, and drifted off altogether into the waves of the world." But family disagreements sprung up. His biographer, perhaps he himself too in after life, saw the hand of Providence in his father's harshness to him, which no submission could soften, and which at last drove him in despair to leave his home, and after the fashion of his countrymen to seek his fortune in strange lands. Italians, especially Lombards, meet us continually in the records and letters of this time as wanderers, adventurers, monks, in Normandy and even England. He crossed Mont Cenis with a single clerk for his attendant, and he did not forget the risk and fatigue of the passage. He spent three years partly in what was then called Burgundy, the portions of modern France corresponding roughly with the valley of the Saône and Rhone, and the upper valley of the Seine, partly in France proper, the still narrow kingdom of which Paris and Rheims and Orleans were the chief cities; then, following perhaps the track of another Italian, Lanfranc of Pavia, he came to Normandy, and remained for a time at Avranches, where Lanfranc had once taught. Finally, he followed Lanfranc, now a famous master, to the monastery where he had become prior, the newly-founded monastery of Bec. Bec was a school as well as a monastery, and there Anselm, along with other young men whom the growing wish to learn and the fame of the teacher had drawn thither, settled himself, not as a monk but as a student, under Lanfranc. The monastery of Bec was so characteristic a growth of the time, and in its short-lived but brilliant career of glory exercised so unique and eventful an influence, that a few words may be properly given to it.

# CHAPTER II.

### FOUNDATION OF THE MONASTERY OF BEC.

> "There is a day in spring
> When under all the earth the secret germs
> Begin to stir and glow before they bud:
> The wealth and festal pomps of midsummer
> Lie in the heart of that inglorious day,
> Which no man names with blessing, though its work
> Is blest by all the world."
> *The Story of Queen Isabel,* by M. S.

IN the end of the tenth and the beginning of the eleventh century the waste caused by the great invasion which had made Normandy was beginning to be repaired. The rapidity with which the Normans took the impress of their new country, and assimilated themselves to the Latin civilization round them, is one of the most remarkable points in the character of this remarkable race. Churches and monasteries had perished among the other desolations of Rollo's Pagan sea-kings: but the children of Rollo's Pagan sea-kings had become the settled lords of lands and forests and towns; and though the taint of heathenism was still among them, even in their creed, and much more in their morality, the most important portion of them had come to feel about their new faith as if it was the one which all their forefathers had ever held. Churches and monasteries were beginning to rise again. The famous house of Jumiéges, which Hasting the pirate had destroyed, had been restored by Rollo's son, William Longsword, about 940; another of Hasting's ruins, St. Wandrille at Fontanelle, was restored by Richard the Good (1008). Fécamp, Mont St. Michel, St. Ouen, ascribed their foundation or renovation to his father, Richard the Fearless, still, like William Longsword, a "Duke of Pirates" to the French chronicler Richer (943-996). At Fécamp, where he had a palace, he built or rebuilt an abbey and minster in prospect of the sea, from which his fathers had come; minster and palace, as at Westminster, Holyrood, and the Escurial, were in close neighbourhood. The church, one of the first of which we have any details, was costly and magnificent for the time; an architect was carefully sought out for it, and it was "constructed of 'well-squared masonry by a Gothic hand,'—the Goth being unquestionably a master mason from Lombardy or the Exarchate." "It was adorned by lofty towers, beautifully finished without and richly ornamented within." "There was one object, however, which excited much speculation. It was a large block of stone placed right across the path which led to the transept doorway, so close to the portal as to be beneath the drip of the eaves. . . . Fashioned and located by Duke Richard's order, the stone was hollowed out so as to form a huge strong chest, which might be used as a coffin or a sarcophagus. Its present employment, however, was for the living and not for the dead. On the eve of every Lord's-day the chest, or whatever it might be called, was filled to the brim with the finest wheat-corn—then a cate or luxury, as it is now considered in many parts of France. To this receptacle the poor resorted, and each filled his measure of grain." They also received a dole of money, and an almoner carried the gift to the sick. When Richard died, then the purpose of the chest was made clear. "His last instructions were, that the chest should contain his corpse, lying where the foot should tread, and the dew descend, and the waters of heaven should fall."[1] He

> " Marked for his own,
> Close to those cloistered steps, a burial-place,
> That every foot might fall with heavier tread,
> Trampling his vileness."

Richard the Good favoured still more the increasing tendency to church building and the restoration of monasteries; and the Norman barons began to follow the example of their chiefs. They rivalled one another, says Ordericus, the chronicler of St. Evroul, in the good work and in the largeness of their alms; and a powerful man thought that he laid himself open to mockery if he did not help clerks or monks on his lands with things needful for God's warfare. Roger de Toeni built the Abbey of Conches, and brought a monk from Fécamp to be its first abbot (1035). Goscelin, Count of Arques, founded that of the "Trinité du Mont"(1030), on that Mount St. Catherine which looks down on Rouen, and brought a German monk from St. Wandrille to govern it; and from this house, again, William, Count of Eu, or his widow, called another German, Aimard, to be the abbot of their new foundation at St. Pierre sur Dive (1046). About the same time William Fitz-Osbern, soon to be a famous name, founded an abbey at Lire

[1] Palgrave, iii. 21—27.

(1046), and later another at Cormeilles (1060). At Pont Audemer two houses, one for men and another for women, were founded by Humphrey de Vieilles. Two brothers of the famous house of Grentmaisnil began on their lands a foundation which was afterwards transferred, at the instance of their relative, William the son of Geroy, to a site anciently hallowed, then made desolate by war, and lately again occupied for its old purpose in the humblest fashion;—the spot on which arose the important monastery of St. Evroul or Ouche (1056). William, son of Geroy, who had first thought of restoring St. Evroul, was the son of a father who, fierce warrior as he was, is said by Orderic to have "built six churches in the name of the Lord out of his own means" in different parts of his estates. This must have been in the early part of the eleventh century.

But along with the account of this remarkable movement are deep and continual complaints of the character both of clergy and monks. Restoring churches was one thing; having fit men to serve in them was another. The change was so great between the end of the century and the beginning, between the religious feeling of the men who lived with William the Conqueror and Lanfranc, and those who lived when Richard the Good built Fécamp, that some allowance must be made for the depreciating and contemptuous tone in which a strict age is apt to speak of the levity and insensibility of an easier one before it. Such judgments are often unjust and always suspicious. All was not godless and cold in the last century, though the more decided opinions or greater zeal of this often makes it a proverb of reproach.

But still it is clear that the Norman clergy as a whole were rude, ignorant, and self-indulgent, to a degree which seemed monstrous and intolerable fifty years later. The chief ecclesiastical dignity of the duchy, the great Archbishopric of Rouen, was occupied for a hundred and thirteen years by three prelates, of whom the least scandalous part of their history was that two of them were bastards of the ducal house, and who in their turbulence and licence were not to be distinguished from the most unscrupulous of the military barons round them Marriage was common, even among bishops; it may not always have been marriage, but there plainly was a connection which was not yet looked upon, as it came to be at the end of this century, as concubinage; and even a writer like Orderic, who of course condemns it unreservedly in the general, speaks of it incidentally in men whom he respects, and without being much shocked. The clergy were not only easy in their lives; they were entirely without learning; and the habit prevailed of their holding lay fees by military service, and of bearing arms without scruple. The old Danish leaven was still at work. In 1049 a council at Rheims, held under Pope Leo IX., formally forbade clerics to wear warlike weapons or to perform military service The standard was low among churchmen, according to the ideas of the age, both as to knowledge and morality. Attempts were made from time to time to raise it. The example of the great abbeys in France, Cluni and Marmoutier, was appealed to. A colony of monks from one of them was introduced into a Norman house to reform it. Strangers of high character, Frenchmen, Germans, Italians, were placed at the head of abbeys, as Duke Richard invited St. William of Dijon to Fécamp. These things were probably not without their effect. But a real movement of wholesome and solid change, though the stimulus may come from without, must begin and grow up at home. It must spring out of native feelings and thought, and an understanding of necessities on the spot, and it must shape itself amid the circumstances in which it is to act.

And so, in fact, the reform came; influenced by external example, directed by foreign experience, but of home growth in the will to begin it, and in the heart to carry it out. The monasteries which we have read of were founded or restored by great and powerful men; their motives probably were mixed, but among these motives, there is no reason to doubt, was the wish to help the side of goodness and peace; to strengthen it by the efforts of men who undertook to live for it; to give it stability and even grandeur in the world—a grandeur not disproportionate to its own claims, and to the grandeur which was realized in the secular state. But there was one thing which these foundations had not;—the founder was not the occupant of the house which he founded; he founded it for others to live and work in, and not himself. The life and vigour which come when a man throws himself with all his soul into a work or an institution—and nothing less could suffice to give success to an undertaking like the monastic rule —were wanting. The genuine impulse, coming not from patronage, but from enthusiasm, not from the desire to see others do a hard and important thing, but to do it oneself; the impulse, not from above and outside, but from below and from the heart of society itself, was first seen in the attempt, plain, humble, homely, unpretending, without the faintest thought or hope of great results, which led to the growth —its actual foundation was in the last degree insignificant—of the famous abbey of Bec.

It is hardly too much to say that the character of the Abbey of Bec influenced not merely Norman monasticism, but the whole progress of learning, education, and religious thought and feeling in Normandy, more than any other institution. Orderic, the chronicler of Normandy and Norman life, whose praise of other monasteries is very warm, but usually rather vague and undiscriminating, is in the case of Bec, in spite of the exaggeration of his high-flown eulogies, unusually distinct in what he fixes upon as characteristic. It is the intellectual activity of Bec on which he dwells, as marking it out from all other houses. The men of Bec were excellent monks; he praises especially their cheerfulness among one another, and he cannot say enough of their hospitality: "Burgundians and Spaniards, strangers from far or near, will answer for it how kindly they have been welcomed. . . The door of Bec is open to every traveller, and to no one who asks in the name of charity is their bread denied." But the thing which above all strikes him in them, as different from other communities round, is their unique eminence as a school of study and teaching. He dwells at great length and with much satisfaction on the pursuits followed at his own monastery, St. Evroul; he mentions the names of its distinguished members; and he himself is a proof that its cloister was not an idle or care-

## MONASTERY OF BEC.

less one: but the things which were cultivated and were of repute at St. Evroul, were the art of copying books and church music. But what he notes at Bec was a spirit of intellectual vigour in the whole body which does not appear elsewhere. Bec first opened to Normandy the way of learning. "Under Lanfranc the Normans first fathomed the art of letters; for under the six dukes of Normandy scarce any one among the Normans had applied himself to liberal studies, nor was there any teacher found, till God, the Provider of all things, brought Lanfranc to Normandy." There is perhaps a touch of sly half-unconscious banter in the remark that the monks of Bec "seem almost all philosophers," and "from their conversation, even that of those who seem illiterate among them, and are called rustics, even pompous men of letters (*spumantes grammatici*) may learn something worth knowing." It is something like the half-compliment, half-sneer, of the nickname which used to be applied in Oxford to one of its most famous colleges, in days when it led the way in revived religious and intellectual earnestness, and opened the march of university reform. But it is not the less a proof of the way in which Bec was regarded. Yet no monastery in Normandy started from humbler beginnings, or less contemplated what it achieved.

"The tale of the early days of Bec," says Mr. Freeman, "is one of the most captivating in the whole range of monastic history and monastic legend. It has a character of its own. The origin of Bec differs from that of those earlier monasteries which gradually grew up around the dwelling-place or the burial-place of some revered bishop or saintly hermit. It differs again from the origin of those monasteries of its own age, which were the creation of some one external founder. Or rather, it united the two characters in one. It gradually rose to greatness from very small beginnings; but gradual as the process was, it took place within the lifetime of one man; and that man was at once its founder and first ruler. The part of Cuthberht at Lindisfarne, the parts of William and of Lanfranc at Caen, were all united in Herlwin, Knight, Founder, and Abbot."

The Abbey of Bec, or, as it should be properly written, "the Bec" (*Le Bec*), took its name from no saint, from no previously existing designation of place or mountain, but from the nameless rivulet, or *Beck*, which flowed through the meadows where it was at last built, and which washed the abbey wall. These fields were on the skirts of the forest of Brionne: and the Beck, on which were originally two or three mills, flowed through a little valley into one of the streams of eastern Normandy, the Rille. The Rille springs from the high ground where the chief rivers of Normandy all rise near to another, the Eure, the Iton, the Touque, the Dive, the Orne; and it flows from north to south, by Pont Audemer, into the great mouth of the Seine, below Quillebœuf. The map shows us, marked on its course, many names, since become familiar and illustrious in England: Montfort, Harcourt, Beaumont, Romilly. Two castles on its banks were very famous in the history of Normandy—the Eagle's Castle, *Castrum Aquilæ*, *L'Aigle*, in its upper course; and Brionne, half-way to the sea. Brionne, the "noble castle," not the fortress on the rock, of which the ruins remain now, but one on an island in the river, was one of the keys of the land, a coveted trust and possession among the rival lords of Normandy; often exchanging masters, often besieged, won and lost. In the days of Duke Robert, the Conqueror's father (1028-1035), it was held by Count Gilbert, himself of the ducal house; who, when Duke Robert went on the Eastern pilgrimage from which he never came back, was left one of the guardians of his young son. Among Count Gilbert's retainers was Herlwin, a soldier of the old Danish stock, but with noble Flemish blood in his veins from his mother. Herlwin, a brave knight, wise in council, and famous after he became abbot for his thorough familiarity with the customs and legal usages of the Normans, was high in favour and honour both with Count Gilbert and Duke Robert. There was a natural nobleness and generosity too about him, that did not always go together with the stout arm and strong head. His biographer tells that once, when he thought he had been ill-used by his lord, he absented himself from his service; but after a while he heard that Count Gilbert was engaged in a quarrel with a powerful neighbour whom he had challenged, and that a battle was at hand. On the day fixed for the battle, when Count Gilbert was anxiously measuring his strength, a band of twenty men was seen approaching behind him. It was Herlwin, who, with unlooked-for generosity, had come, in spite of his sense of injury, to help his lord at his need. The battle was stopped by the Duke's officers, and the quarrel referred to his court; and Herlwin was reconciled with Count Gilbert. But in this wild society and wild household, Herlwin was a man whose heart was touched with the thoughts and claims of another world. He tried in his way, and with such light as he had, to lead a pure and Christian life ; he tried, in many uncouth and perhaps absurd ways, to be true to his conscience ; he tried, in spite of mockery and jeers from his rough fellows, who in those days, we are told, could not understand any one in a whole skin thinking of religion. The ways of a Norman military family were more and more distasteful to him ; and, in spite of his lord's reluctance to part with so faithful a vassal, his mind was set more and more on getting free in the only way which seemed open to him. A story is told by the chronicler of the neighbouring house of St. Evroul, in introducing his name and foundation, which does not appear in the traditions of Bec, that Herlwin's final resolution was the result of a vow made in a moment of imminent peril in battle. He had accompanied Count Gilbert in a great expedition into a neighbouring land, the Vimeu, the district of the Lower Somme ; but things " fell not out to Count Gilbert according to his desire. For Ingelram, Count of Ponthieu, met him with a strong force, and engaging him, put him to flight with his men, and of the fugitives many were taken, and many slain, and many disabled with wounds. Then a certain soldier there named Herlwin, fearing the danger, and flying with all his might for his life, vowed to God that, if he got off safe from so present a danger, he would henceforth be soldier to none but God. By God's will he honourably escaped, and, mindful of his vow, left the world, and in his patrimony, in a place called Bec, founded a monastery to St. Mary, Mother of God." The story may be true, as it is characteristic of the time, and is not meant to reflect on Herlwin's courage; but it is not inconsistent with the accounts which represent Herlwin's change as arising from deeper and more serious feelings.

Herlwin had no thought of anything but following the leading of a simple and earnest heart, which impressed on him with ever-increasing force that a life of strife, greed, and bloodshed, a life of pride and sensuality—the life which he saw all round him—was no life for a Christian. He knew but one way of escaping from it; and the one motive of all that led to the creation of his monastery was the resolution to escape. No project of foundation, no ideas, however vague, of general reform, crossed his mind. He found himself living where prayer seemed a mockery, where selfishness and hatred ruled, where God was denied at every step; and he sought a shelter, the humblest and most obscure he could find, where he might pray and believe and be silent.' That alone, but that in the most thorough and single-minded earnestness, led him to give up his place, a favoured and honoured one, in the society round him, for the most unpretending form of monastic devotion. He could live with a few companions on his property, where he could build them a humble dwelling and a church, and where they could make it their employment to worship and praise God. He was about thirty-seven years old when his thoughts turned to this change of life. Herlwin was a genuine Norman, resolute, inflexible in purpose, patient in waiting his time, wholly devoted to his end, daunted by no repulse, shrewd, sturdy, and sure of his ground, and careless of appearances in comparison with what was substantial in his object. The time had not yet come for the enthusiasm and the fashion among Normans for the monastic life, the life, as we should call it, of strict and serious religious profession. Priest and bishop still kept up the old Norse habit of wearing arms, and lived very much like their military brethren. Herlwin went through the ordeal of jeers, annoyances, and frowns, which a profession of strictness, probably coarse and rude in its form, was likely to meet with from the coarse and mocking fighting men collected about a powerful Norman chief. It was not easy for a brave soldier and a useful vassal to get leave to quit his lord's service, and it was not safe to offend him by quitting it without leave. Herlwin tried long in vain: at last the tie broke under the strain. Herlwin would not execute some service for his lord which he thought unjust, and his lord's vengeance fell on Herlwin's lands and tenants, and threatened himself. He was summoned to the lord's court; but he only pleaded for his poor tenants, and asked nothing for himself. His lord was touched, and sent for him and asked what he really wanted. "By loving this world," he answered, with many tears, "and in obeying thee, I have hitherto too much neglected God and myself; I have been altogether intent on training my body, and I have gained no education for my soul: if ever I have deserved well of thee, let me pass what remains of my life in a monastery. Let me keep your love, and with me give to God what I had of you." And he had his wish.

He set to work at once to build his retreat, and he sought to gain some knowledge of the practice of monastic discipline. His first attempts led to some rude experiences. "The manners of the time were still barbarous all over Normandy," says his biographer, who tells, with a kind of sly gravity, how while Herlwin was once watching, with the deepest admiration and reverence, the grave order of some monks seated in their cloister, he suddenly found himself saluted by a hearty cuff on the back of his neck from the fist of the custodian, who had taken him for a thief, and who dragged him by his hair out of doors; and how this "solace of edification" was followed at a monastery of greater name, by seeing the monks in their Christmas procession laughing and joking to the crowd, showing off their rich vestments to the bystanders, and pushing and fighting for places, till at last one monk knocked down another, who was hustling him, flat on his back on the ground. But, undiscouraged, Herlwin went on.

He first established his house on his patrimony at Bonneville, a place a short distance from Brionne. He himself dug the foundations for his church, carried away the rubbish, and brought on his shoulders the stones, sand, and lime; and when he had ended the day's work, he learned the psalter at night, which he had not time for by day. At forty years old he learned his letters and taught himself to read. At length his church was built; and in 1034, he, with two companions, was made a monk by the Bishop of Lisieux. Three years after, he was ordained priest, and made abbot of the new house, "because, it being so poor, no one else would take the government." "He ruled most strictly, but in the manner of the pious fathers. You might see the abbot, when the office was done in church, carrying the seed-corn on his shoulder, and a rake or mattock in his hand, going forth to the field. The monks were busy with labour all day; they cleaned the land from thorns and brambles; others brought dung on their shoulders and spread it abroad. They hoed, they sowed; no one ate his bread in idleness; and at each hour of prayer they assembled for service at the church." Herlwin's mother, a lady of noble blood from Flanders, made over all her lands, and served the community as their handmaid, washing their clothes, and fulfilling to the utmost whatever was enjoined her.

The new house had its troubles. It was burned down, and the report, as it first reached Herlwin, was that his mother had perished. Lifting up his eyes with tears to God, he cried out, "Thanks be to Thee, O God, that my mother has been taken away in the work of ministry to Thy servants." The report, however, was a false one. But the place was inconvenient. It wanted the two great necessities of a monastery—wood and water. This, reinforced by a vision, made him change his abode. He removed to a spot about a mile from the castle of Brionne, where he had property called, from the stream that flowed there, "The Beck," *Beccus*. "This place," says the biographer, "is in the wood itself, in the bottom of the valley of Brionne, shut in on each side by wooded hills, convenient for human use, from the thickness of the wood and the refreshment of the stream. It was a haunt of game. There were only the buildings of three mills there, and but a moderate space of habitable ground. What then should he do? In one of the mills he had no interest, and in the other two only a third part, and there was not as much of free space as his house needed. Count Gilbert, too, had nothing that he valued more than that wood. But Herlwin put his trust in God. He began to work, and God evidently to work with him, for his co-proprietors and neighbours, either by sale or free gift, gave up to him each his portion; and in a short time he obtained the whole wood of Brionne which was around." He built in the course of a few years a new church. He settled his brotherhood in a cloister with wooden columns. A great storm, in which the fury of the devil was seen, shattered the work: "The devil deeply grudged these beginnings of good things; he rose with great violence on the roof of the dormitory; thence gathering himself for his utmost effort, he leaped down on the new covering of the new built walls, and overthrew all in ruins to the ground." "But," continues the biographer, "that was not the seed which falls on stony ground and withers away, because it has no moisture, but which, received on good ground, brings forth fruit with patience. In the morning, Herlwin showed to the brethren that '*an enemy hath done this.*' Cheering up their downcast hearts, he began to rebuild the cloister; and this time he built of stone."

"A wooded hill," says Mr. Freeman, "divides the valley of the Risle, with the town and castle of Brionne, from another valley watered by a small stream, or in the old Teutonic speech of the Normans, a *beck*. That stream gave its name to the most famous of Norman religious houses, and to this day the name of Bec is never uttered to denote that spot without the distinguishing addition of the name of Herlwin. The hills are still thickly wooded; the beck still flows through rich meadows and under trees planted by the water-side, by the walls of what was once the renowned monastery to which it gave its name. But of the days of Herlwin no trace remains besides these imperishable works of nature. A tall tower, of rich and fanciful design, one of the latest works of mediæval skill, still attracts the traveller from a distance; but of the mighty minster itself, all traces, save a few small fragments, have perished. The monastic buildings, like those of so many other monasteries in Normandy and elsewhere in Gaul, had been rebuilt in the worst days of art, and they are now applied to the degrading purpose of a receptacle of French cavalry. The gateway also remains; but it is, like the rest of the buildings, of a date far later than the days of Herlwin. The truest memorial of that illustrious abbey is now to be found in the parish church of the neighbouring village. In that lowly shelter is still preserved the effigy with which after-times had marked the resting-place of the founder. Such are all the traces which now remain of the house which once owned Lanfranc and Anselm as its inmates."

Bec would probably have run its course like many other houses, great and small, in Normandy,—perhaps continuing in the same humble condition in which it began, perhaps attracting the notice of powerful and wealthy patrons,—but for an event which shaped its character and history. Herlwin was no scholar; but with the quick shrewdness of his race—a shrewdness which showed itself in his own life by the practical skill which he had brought with him in the legal customs of his land, and which stood him in good stead in resisting the encroachments of greedy neighbours—he understood the value of scholarship. He wished for a companion who knew more than himself; but such men as yet were rare in Normandy. An accident—he looked upon it as God's providence—fulfilled his desire and determined the fortunes of Bec. This was the chance arrival of an Italian stranger, Lanfranc.

Lanfranc was a Lombard from Pavia. He is said to have been of a noble family, and to have taught and practised law in his native city. He was, at any rate, according to the measure of the time, a scholar, trained in what was known of the classic Latin literature, in habits of dialectical debate, and especially in those traditions of Roman legal science which yet lingered in the Italian municipalities. For some unknown reason, perhaps in quest of fame and fortune, he left Italy and found his way northwards. It was a fashion among the Lombards. At Avranches, in the Côtentin, he had opened a sort of school, teaching the more advanced knowledge of Italy among people who, Norse as they were in blood, were rapidly and eagerly welcoming everything Latin, just as the aspiring and ambitious half-civilization of Russia tried to copy the fuller civilization of Germany and France. After a time, for equally unknown reasons, he left Avranches.

The story which was handed down at Bec in after days, when he had become one of the most famous men of his day, was, that he was on his way to Rouen when he was spoiled by robbers and left bound to a tree, in a forest near the Rille. Night came on, and he tried to pray; but he could remember nothing—Psalm or Office. "Lord," he cried, "I have spent all this time and worn out body and mind in learning:

and now, when I ought to praise Thee, I know not how. Deliver me from this tribulation, and with Thy help, I will so correct and frame my life that henceforth I may serve Thee." Next morning when some passers-by set him free, he asked his way to the humblest monastery in the neighbourhood, and was directed to Bec. Another story is told in the Chronicle of Bec of his adventure with the robbers. He was travelling, with a single scholar as his attendant, to Rouen, when he fell among robbers, who stripped him, leaving him only an old cloak. Then he remembered a story in the dialogues of Gregory the Great, of a saint who was robbed of his horse by Lombard thieves, and who, as they were departing, with manifest reference to the words of the Sermon on the Mount, about giving the cloak to him who had taken away the coat, offered them the only thing they had left, his whip—" You will want it," he said, "to drive the horse ;" and then he turned to his prayer. When the robbers came to a rapid river, the Vulturnus, they could in no wise cross it ; and then they bethought them that they had offended by spoiling so completely the man of God, and they went back and restored what they had taken. Lanfranc thought that he would imitate the holy man hoping that the same effect might follow; and so he offered to the robbers what they had left him, his old cloak. But it only brought on him worse treatment : and he deserved it, he used to say : "for the saint did it with one intention and I with another; he did it honestly that they might keep what he gave ; I with cunning and craft, that they might restore and not keep." And so he was punished; for when he offered them the cloak, they turned upon him, thinking themselves mocked, and after beating him well, tied him naked to a tree, and his scholar to another. Then follows the account of his turning to God; and the story ends with his liberation, not at the hands of passers-by, but by a miracle.

To this place, as to the poorest and humblest of brotherhoods, Lanfranc came. The meeting between him and Herlwin is thus told. "The abbot happened to be busy building an oven, working at it with his own hands. Lanfranc came up and said, 'God save you.' 'God bless you,' said the abbot; 'are you a Lombard?' 'I am,' said Lanfranc. 'What do you want?' 'I want to become a monk.' Then the abbot bade a monk named Roger, who was doing his own work apart, to show Lanfranc the book of the Rule; which he read, and answered that with God's help he would gladly observe it. Then the abbot, hearing this, and knowing who he was and from whence he came, granted him what he desired. And he, falling down at the mouth of the oven, kissed Herlwin's feet."

In welcoming Lanfranc, Herlwin found that he had welcomed a great master and teacher. Lanfranc, under his abbot's urging, began to teach; the monastery grew into a school: and Bec, intended to be but the refuge and training-place of a few narrow and ignorant but earnest devotees, thirsting after God and right amid the savagery of a half-tamed heathenism, sprung up, with the rapidity with which changes were made in those days, into a centre of thought and cultivation for Western Christendom. It was the combination, more than once seen in modern Europe, where Italian genius and Northern strength have been brought together; where the subtle and rich and cultivated Southern nature has been braced and tempered into purpose and energy by contact with the bolder and more strong-willed society of the North. Lanfranc supplied to the rising religious fervour of Normandy just the element which it wanted, and which made it fruitful and noble.

It need not be remarked that in the accounts written of these times we meet with endless exaggeration. Every great movement carries with it exaggeration: things, too, were undoubtedly pitched high, and a heroic grandeur was aimed at, in what men thought and attempted in this time when a new spirit seemed to be abroad, and new hopes were stirring in the world and in the Church. And in this case the exaggeration appears the greater, because men wrote not in their own language, but in a foreign one, which they only half knew how to use. But all is in keeping, all is consistent and moves together; grotesque and absurd as these exaggerations appear to us now, they were part of the temporary and accidental vesture of men who, in their rude fashion, with little to help them, and hedged in by limits as yet immoveable, were fighting their way out of ignorance and debasement, and who did great things. Thus Lanfranc's victory over himself, when the lawyer and the scholar cast in his lot with men with whom he had nothing in common but the purpose to know and serve God better, is specially dwelt upon by his biographer in instances which must with us provoke a smile, but in which the homely or childish detail is after all but as the dress of the day, which may disguise or set off the man beneath it. Simple men in that twilight of learning were struck with admiration at the self-command shown by a teacher, famous for what others valued, when he humbled himself before an illiterate Norman abbot, saint as he seemed to be; or when he patiently took the conceited and ignorant rebuke of not so saintly a Prior. "You might see," says the biographer of Lanfranc, "a godly rivalry between Herlwin and Lanfranc. The abbot, a lately made clerk, who had grown old as a layman, regarded with awe the eminence of such a teacher placed under him. Lanfranc, not puffed up by his great knowledge, was humbly obedient in all things, observed, admired, bore witness to the grace which God had granted Herlwin in understanding the Scriptures. 'When I listen to that layman,' he used to say (layman, I suppose, in the sense of one not brought up to letters), 'I know not what to say, but that "the Spirit breatheth where it will."'"

He remained three years in retirement, giving an example of monastic subordination and humility. "He would not, as it is said, read a lesson in church unless the *cantor* had first heard him read it. One day when he was reading at table, he pronounced a word as it ought to be pronounced, but not as seemed right to the person presiding, who bade him say it differently; as if he had said *docēre*, with the middle syllable long, as is right, and the other had corrected it into *docĕre*, with the middle short, which is wrong: for that Prior was not a scholar. But the wise man, knowing that he owed obedience rather to Christ than to Donatus the grammarian, gave up his pronunciation, and said what he was wrongly told to say; for to make a short syllable long, or a long one

short, he knew to be no deadly sin; but not to obey
one set over him on God's behalf was no light transgression."

Again, they tell a story of Lanfranc being met
travelling to an outlying house of the abbey, carrying
a cat tied up in a cloth behind him on his saddle, "to
keep down the fury of the mice and rats" which infested the place. What they mean is the same thing
as people mean now, when they talk of a bishop
going on foot carrying his carpet-bag, or a duke
travelling in a third-class carriage; but the magniloquent and clumsy Latin in which the story is
told gives it an indescribable absurdity of colour, and
we forget that after all it is an instance, proportionate
to the day, of that plainness and simplicity of demeanour which is a common quality where men's
hearts are really great.

But Lanfranc was not to remain in this unnatural
obscurity. Gradually, it is not said how, Bec became a
school, became famous, became the resort of young
men thirsting for instruction, not only in Normandy,
but in the countries round it. It is not easy for us to
understand how, in those difficult and dangerous days,
communication was so extensive, and news travelled so
widely, and the character of a house of monks and its
teacher in the depths of Normandy produced such an
impression in Europe, as was in fact the case. The style
of the time was exaggerated; but exaggeration was
of things that were really great; and it is impossible to
doubt that during the time that Lanfranc taught at
Bec (1045—1063?) he established a name as a reformer of life and a restorer of learning, which made him
seem to the men of his time, at least in the West, as

without an equal; he was to them all that later times have seen in their great reformers and great men of letters. He brought to Bec the secular learning which was possible then; he learned there divine knowledge; and for both, he infused an ardour which was almost enthusiasm in those under his influence. It would be interesting if we knew something more of his method of study and teaching; but, as usual, such details were not thought worth preserving by those to whom they were matters of every day. We have little more than generalities. Latinist (perhaps with some knowledge of Greek) and dialectician, he taught his scholars the best that could then be taught, in rousing thought, in making it exact and clear, and in expressing it fitly and accurately. It is not improbable that his old knowledge of jurisprudence was turned to account in his lecturing at Bec. As a theologian, he was especially a student of St. Paul's Epistles. The only divinity known at the time in the West was contained in the works of the great Latin Fathers; and of this he was master, and his use of it gave a new impulse to the study of it—a study which was to produce results of vast importance both to religion and to philosophy. The value which restorers of learning like Lanfranc set on the Latin Fathers led their successors step by step to raise up the great fabric, so mingled of iron and clay, of the scholastic systems.

Lanfranc, as may be supposed, had a battle to fight to establish his footing in such a community as he would find round Herlwin. Herlwin, with the nobleness and simplicity of a superior nature, recognized the difference between himself and Lanfranc, and saw, without grudging or jealousy, that in all matters of mind,

Lanfranc must be supreme ; and he left to Lanfranc the internal government of the house, while he himself looked after its affairs, and guarded it in the law courts by his intimate knowledge of Norman customs. But the brethren whom Lanfranc had found there "were not very well lettered, nor much trained in religion :" and "seeing their idleness, the frowardness of their ways, their transgressions of the Rule, and the jealousy of some, who feared that he would be put over them" —a curious contrast this to the picture elsewhere given of the devotion of Herlwin's first companions—Lanfranc lost heart, and meditated a second retreat ; a retreat from Bec, into some hermitage in the wilderness. But he was stopped—as usual, it is said by a vision ; and Lanfranc entered on his office as Prior, about 1045. From this time, till he was appointed Abbot of Duke William's monastery of St. Stephen at Caen, Lanfranc was busy, with some intervals of other important work, filling what we should call the place of a great professor at Bec. Gradually, as his name became attached to it, its numbers swelled—its numbers of monks, and also of students not members of the house. Gifts poured in upon it ; for the age was an open-handed one, as ready to give as to take away, and friends and patrons among the lords of Normandy and the conquerors of England endowed the house with churches, tithes, manors, on both sides of the Channel. A saying arose which is not yet out of men's mouths in France :

> "De quelque part que le vent vente
> L'abbaye du Bec a rente."
>
> (" Let the wind blow from where the wind will,
> From the lands of Bec it bloweth still.")

All this had come to pass in the lifetime of Herlwin; and all this had come with Lanfranc. His pupils were numerous, and many of them were famous in their generation: among these was one, an Italian like himself, who became Pope Alexander II. (1061—1073). But the greatest glory of Lanfranc and the school of Bec was to have trained the Italian Anselm to quicken the thoughts and win the love of Normans and Englishmen.

With Lanfranc's position outside of Bec we have here no concern. The great Norman ruler, whose mind was so full of great thoughts both in Church and State, and whose hand was to be so heavy on those whom he ruled and conquered, soon found him out, and discovered that in Lanfranc he had met a kindred soul and a fit companion in his great enterprise of governing and reducing to order the wild elements of his age. Lanfranc, scholar, theologian, statesman, and perhaps also, and not least, Italian, was employed on more than one commission at the court of Rome, which was then rising into new importance and power, under the inspiration of the master-spirit of Hildebrand. He mingled in the controversial disputes, which were once more beginning as the time became influenced by new learning and new zeal; and he was reputed to have silenced and confounded Berengar, both by word of mouth and by his pen. But all this lay without his work as the Prior of Bec—its creator as a school, its director as a teacher; and it is only in this respect that he is here spoken of.

The glory and influence of Bec were great, but they declined as rapidly as they had risen. They depended on the impulse given by great characters; and when these passed away, the society which they had animated gradually sank to the ordinary level. Bec continued a great foundation : in time it became one of the rich and dignified preferments of the Church of France. In the 16th century the abbacy was held by great aristocratic bishops and cardinals, Dunois, Le Veneur, D'Annebaut, Guise ; in the 17th by a Colbert, a Rochefoucault, and a Bourbon Condé. But the "irony of fate" had something more in store. The last abbot of Bec, of the house founded by Herlwin, and made glorious by Lanfranc and Anselm, was M. de Talleyrand.[1]

[1] Émile Saisset, Mélanges, p. 8.

# CHAPTER III.

#### DISCIPLINE OF A NORMAN MONASTERY.

> " And what are things eternal? powers depart,
> Possessions vanish, and opinions change,
> And passions hold a fluctuating seat;
> But by the storms of circumstance unshaken,
> And subject neither to eclipse nor wane,
> Duty exists;—immutably survive,
> For our support, the measures and the forms
> Which an abstract intelligence supplies;
> Whose kingdom is, where time and space are not."
>                         WORDSWORTH, *Excursion*, b. iv.

THE order of life at Bec was modelled according to the strict discipline of the Benedictine order. To enter fairly into its spirit and into the meaning of many of its minute and technical regulations, it has to be remembered that in those ages there was little trust in individual self-management; and it was a fundamental assumption that there was no living an earnest Christian life without a jealous and pervading system of control and rule. Civil life, as we know it, hardly existed: all that was powerful, all that was honoured, was connected with war; the ideas of the time more or less insensibly took a military colour; men's calling and necessity were in one way or another to fight; and to fight evil with effect needed combination, endurance, and practice. The governing thought of monastic life was that it was a warfare, *militia*, and a monastery was a camp or barrack: there was continual drill and exercise, early hours, fixed times, appointed tasks, hard fare, stern punishment watchfulness was to be incessant, obedience prompt and absolute; no man was to have a will of his own, no man was to murmur. What seems to us trifling or vexatious must be judged of and allowed for by reference to the idea of the system;—training as rigorous, concert as ready and complete, subordination as fixed, fulfilment of orders as unquestioning as in a regiment or ship's crew which is to do good service. Nothing was more easy in those days to understand in any man, next to his being a soldier, than his being a monk; it was the same thing, the same sort of life, but with different objects. Nothing, from our altered conditions of society, is more difficult in ours.

The life and discipline of a Norman monastery of the revived and reformed sort, such as Bec, are put before us in the regulations drawn up by Lanfranc, when Archbishop of Canterbury, for the English monasteries under his government. They are based of course on the rule of St. Benedict; but they are varied and adapted according to the judgment of the great monastic reformer, and represent no doubt in a great measure the system carried on at Bec, under which he and then Anselm had lived and worked. They are of course as minute and peremptory as the orders of a book of drill; but what is more remarkable is the recognition in them of the possible desirableness of modifications in their use. There is nothing of stiff blind clinging to mere usage, no superstitious jealousy of alterations, in the spirit in which they are drawn up and imposed. Lanfranc, great man as he was, knew that it was idle and foolish to lay down fixed laws, even for monasteries, without making provision and allowance for the necessities of different circumstances and the changes of the future. "We send you," he says, addressing Henry the Prior of the Cathedral monastery at Canterbury, "the written customs of our order, which we have selected from the customs of those houses which, in our day, are of highest authority in the monastic rule. In these we mean not to tie down either ourselves who are here, or those who are to come after us, from adding or taking away, or in any way changing, if, either by the teaching of reason or by the authority of those who know better, anything is seen to be an improvement. For be a man as far advanced as he may, he can have no greater fault than to think that he can improve no further; for changes in the numbers of the brethren, local conditions, differences of circumstances, which are frequent, varieties of opinions, some understanding things in this way and others in that way, make it necessary for the most part that things which have been long observed should be differently arranged : hence it is that no Church scarcely can in all things follow any other. But what is to be most carefully attended to is, that the things without which the soul cannot be saved should be maintained inviolate; I mean faith, contempt of the world, charity, purity, humility, patience, obedience, sorrow for faults committed, and their humble confession, frequent prayers, fitting silence, and such like. Where these are preserved, there most rightly may the rule of St. Benedict and the order of the monastic life be said to be kept, in whatever way other things vary, as they are appointed according to different men's judgment in different monasteries." And he proceeds to enumerate instances of variety of usage—very small ones, it must be confessed, and somewhat in contrast to the breadth of the general principles laid down : whether on certain occasions the leaders of the choir should chant certain parts of the service in their tunics, or as they call them "frocks," or in albs and copes ; whether albs alone should be used, or, as elsewhere, copes as well ; or whether, on Maundy Thursday, the feet-washing should be by twenties or thirties in a common trough, or each one singly in a basin by himself. But the contrast between general principles and their applications, between the major propositions of our practical reasonings and their minors, is not peculiar to Lanfranc's age. The minors are always the difficulty, and sometimes they are as strange and unaccountable ones for ourselves as any were then. But it is not always that we give Lanfranc's age credit for acknowledging the principle itself, or for stating it so well.

For the objects in view, the organization was simple and reasonable. The buildings were constructed, the day was arranged, the staff of officers was appointed, in reference to the three main purposes for which a monk professed to live—worship, improvement, and work. There were three principal places which were the scenes of his daily life : the church, and in the church especially the choir; the chapter-house; and the cloister ; and for each of these the work was carefully laid out. A monk's life at that period was eminently a social one : he lived night and day in public; and the cell seems to have been an occasional retreat, or reserved for the higher officers. The cloister was the place of business, instruction, reading, and conversation, the common study, workshop, and parlour of all the inmates of the house—the professed brethren ; the young men whom they were teaching or preparing for life, either as monks or in the world ; the children (*infantes*) who formed the school attached to the house, many of whom had been dedicated by their parents to this kind of service. In this cloister, open apparently to the weather but under shelter, all sat, when they were not at service in church, or assembled in the chapter, or at their meals in the refectory, or resting in the dormitory for their mid-day sleep ; all teaching, reading, writing, copying, or any handicraft in which a monk might employ himself, went on here. Here the children learned their letters, or read aloud, or practised their singing under their masters; and here, when the regular and fixed arrangements of the day allowed it, conversation was carried on. A cloister of this kind was the lecture-room where Lanfranc taught "grammar," gave to Norman pupils elementary notions of what an Italian of that age saw in Virgil and St. Augustin, and perhaps expounded St. Paul's Epistles : where Anselm, among other pupils, caught from him the enthusiasm of literature; where, when Lanfranc was gone, his pupil carried on his master's work as a teacher, and where he discussed with sympathising and inquisitive minds the great problems which had begun to open on his mind. In a cloister like this the news, the gossip of the world and of the neighbourhood was collected and communicated : rumours, guesses, and stories of the day, the strange fortunes of kings and kingdoms, were reported, commented on, picturesquely dressed up and made matter of solemn morals or of grotesque jokes, as they might be now in clubs and newspapers. Here went on the literary work of the time; here, with infinite and patient toil, the remains of classical and patristic learning were copied, corrected, sometimes corrupted, ornamented; here, and here almost alone, were the chronicles and records kept year by year, so scanty, often so imperfect and untrustworthy, yet on the whole so precious, by which we know the men and their doings who turned and governed the course of English and European history; here too, when the true chronicles did not speak as people wished, or did not tell enough, were false ones invented and forged. This open-air, sedentary life was a hard one; it was well enough when the weather was fine and warm, but even monks, though they were trained to endure hardness, found their fingers nipped by the frost, and had to give over their work when the winter came round. The indefatigable story-teller Orderic,—like Eadmer, an Englishman, at least by birth, with a Norman training,—who has preserved for us such a profusion of curious touches of his time, and who is so severe on the negligence of his brethren in not committing to writing what they knew of the remarkable events around them, was obliged to confess the numbing effects of winter, and to put by his writing to a more genial season. He breaks off in his account of the quarrels between the sons of William, and lays aside his fourth book for the winter with this reason for the interruption:

"Many disasters are impending over mankind, which, if they should all be written, would fill huge volumes. Now, stiffened with the winter cold, I shall employ myself in other occupations, and, very weary, I propose to finish this present book. But when the fine weather of the calm spring returns, I will take up again what I have imperfectly related, or what yet remains unsaid, and, by God's help, I will fully unfold with a truthful pen the chances of war and peace among our countrymen."

In another place he gives the same reason for the abridged narrative which he inserts of a certain St. William *with the Short-nose,* whose life, in the hands of a pious chaplain, interested and edified the fierce retainers of one of the fiercest of the Conqueror's barons, Hugh the Wolf, Earl of Chester. "The story is not often found," he says, "in this province, and a truthful narrative may be acceptable to some. It was brought to us recently by Antony, a monk of Winchester; we were thirsting to see it, and he showed it to us. There is a ballad about it commonly sung by the minstrels; but the authentic narrative is much to be preferred, which has been carefully drawn up by religious teachers, and reverently recited by serious readers in the common hearing of the brethren. But because the bearer of it was in a hurry to go, and the winter frost hindered me from writing, I noted down a brief but faithful abridgment of it in my tablets, which I will now endeavour to commit succinctly to my parchment."

Certain religious services, but services having reference to those outside the monastery, had their place in the cloister. Thus it was there, that on Maundy Thursday, the *Dies Mandati,* the abbot and his brethren fulfilled the old custom, and, as they considered it, the commandment of the Gospel, by washing the feet of the poor after they washed one another's feet. The ceremony is thus ordered by Lanfranc: "While this is going on, the cellarer, and the almoner, and others to whom it is enjoined, are to bring the poor men into the cloister, and make them sit in order one by another. Before they come into the cloister they are to wash their feet with common water supplied to them by the chamberlains. Everything is to be prepared in its proper place, necessary for performing 'the commandment' (*mandatum*, St. John xiii. 14, 15); as warm water in fitting vessels, towels for the feet, napkins for the hands, cups and drink and such like; and the chamberlain's servants are to be ready to do what is wanted. Then when these things are in order, the abbot shall rise, and the rest of the brethren rising shall make their due obeisance, and, passing forth from the refectory, the children shall go aside into their school with their masters and stand with them before their poor men; and the rest of the brethren shall likewise come and stand before their poor men, each one according to his order before one of them; but the abbot shall have two. Then the prior, at the abbot's command, shall strike the board with three blows, and bowing down on their bent knees to the earth, they shall worship Christ in the poor." Then the abbot is to wash and wipe the feet of the poor men before him, "kissing them with his mouth and his eyes," and so the rest of the brethren; then he is to minister a cup of drink to them; and at the signal given by the prior, by knocking three times on his board, the other brethren are in like manner each of them to give a cup of drink to the poor man before him, and receiving back the cup, to put in his hand twopence, or whatever money the abbot may have ordered. "The brethren also who have died in the course of the year are to have each their own poor for the fulfilment of 'the commandment,' and also those friends of the house for whom the abbot shall order poor men to be set for this 'commandment.'" Then, when all is over, they kneel down and say some versicles and a collect having reference to the commandment and example which have given occasion to the ceremony, and then proceed to the church chanting the *Miserere* Psalm (li.). The *mandatum* is then to be fulfilled by the brethren to one another, but in the chapter-house; and after the feet-washing, a cup of drink, the "loving-cup," the *potus charitatis*, or the *charitas*, as it was technically called, was distributed. And it enjoined on the abbot that he should, if he were able to do so, by himself wash the feet of all his brethren on this day; "for, according to St. Benedict's witness, he bears the part of Christ in the monastery, and especially in this service."

The cloister was the place of ordinary life and work. The chapter-house was the council chamber of the monastery. The word chapter (*capitulum*) denoted both the room of assembly and the assembly itself. It was the place of business for the whole community; and for its members, it was the place for mutual instruction, for hearing advice, maintaining discipline, making complaints, confessing faults, passing judgment, accepting punishment. Every morning, in ordinary seasons, after the prayers of the third hour and the morning mass, the community "held a chapter." A bell rang, and all the brethren, whatever they were doing, gathered in the choir, and proceeded to the chapter-house.

"Every day," says Lanfranc's order, "as soon as the sound of the little bell begins for the chapter, all the brethren who are sitting in the choir are at once to rise, and meanwhile to stand facing to the east; the brethren also, who are elsewhere in the minster, are to come into the choir. No one is to hold a book ; no one is to be reading anything, or to look into a book ; no one is to remain sitting in the cloister on any pretext whatever; and when the bell stops, with the prior going before them, the rest are to follow in the order of their conversion, two and two, the elders first, the children (*infantes*) after them."

The children, too, "held their separate chapter," under their masters, where all matters of discipline were looked after. The brethren having taken their seats on the steps round the wall, the business began by readings and by addresses. Portions of the rule of St. Benedict were read ; and then was the time when the monks received general instruction on religion and their special duties. Scripture was explained and discourses made, more in the way of familiar exposition than of set sermons. When a stranger of note happened to be in the monastery, he would be asked to say something in chapter to the brethren; and what we have of Anselm's homilies, so far as they are genuine, seem to be short sermons of this kind to monks in chapter, such as we read of his addressing to them in his visits to different monasteries in Normandy and England. When this work of instruction and general counsel was done, which of course varied much, the daily inquiry about discipline began, with the formula, "Let us speak touching our order;" (*loquamur de ordine nostro.*) This was the time for the daily reports, and for complaints that were to be made of personal failure of duty. Anyone, it would seem, might complain of any fault that he had observed; and the course of proceeding is characteristic of the stern ideas under which the monastic life grew up and was passed.

"When the words are said, '*Loquamur de ordine nostro*,' if anyone is accused (*clamatur*, the technical word) who has a name common with another or with several, then unless the accuser (*clamans*) makes it so clear who is meant that there can be no doubt, all who are of the same name are to stand up at once, and humbly present themselves to ask pardon, until the accuser (*clamator*) distinctly points out of whom he speaks; and this indication should be, if possible, by the person's order or his office, as *Domnus Eduardus, priest, deacon,* or *secretary, master of the children,* &c., and not '*archdeacon*,' or '*of London*,' or from any surname of the world. The accuser (*clamator*) is not to do judgment on him whom he accuses in the same chapter. The accused, who is prostrate, being asked in the customary way, is at each asking of pardon to say *mea culpa*. . . If he is to receive judgment, he is to be beaten with one larger rod on his shirt, as he lies prostrate, or with several thinner rods as he sits with his body bare, at the discretion of him who presides, according to the character and magnitude of his fault. While corporal discipline is inflicted, all the brethren are to hold their heads down, and to have compassion with him with tender and brotherly affection During this time in the chapter, no one ought to speak, no one ought to look at him, except grave persons to whom it is allowed to intercede for him. The accused may not make a complaint of his accuser in the same chapter. The discipline is to be inflicted by whoever is commanded to do it by the abbot or prior; so that this be never commanded to the children, or the young men, or the novices. No one is to speak in secret to one or more; whatever is said must be said so as to be heard by the person presiding and the whole assembly. All speaking must be about things useful, and things that pertain to the order. When one is speaking, all others are to be silent; no one is to interrupt the speaker's words but the person presiding, who may command the speaker to be silent, if what is said seem to him irrelevant or unprofitable. When the president of the assembly begins to speak, anyone else who is speaking must stop, and perfect silence be observed by all." This discipline of scourging was undergone, as one of the ordinary ways of showing sorrow for having done wrong. It was submitted to in so matter-of-course a fashion by kings and great men, that Anselm in one of his letters lays down a distinction between the monastic scourging inflicted by the judgment of the chapter, and the self-imposed chastisement, which, he says, kings and proud rich men command to be inflicted on themselves, and to which he gives a special name, *regale judicium*, the "royal judgment."

The punishment awarded in chapter might go beyond this. A brother "adjudged to the satisfaction of a light fault" (the expression appears as technical as " being under arrest ") was separated from the rest of his brethren in the refectory, and sat last of all in choir, and he was forbidden to take certain parts in the divine service. One who, after examination before the abbot, was, by the common sentence of the brethren, "ordered to be in the satisfaction of a grave fault," besides the severe corporal chastisement inflicted in chapter, was also adjudged to solitary confinement under the custody of one of the brethren. He was only seen by the rest prostrate, and with his head covered; and when he received pardon, after coming into the chapter, and confessing his fault and asking for mercy, "being ordered to rise, he shall yet frequently prostrate himself, and say again the same or like words, ceasing when the abbot says to him 'it is enough;' and then he shall be commanded to strip, and to submit to the judgment of corporal discipline." Only then was he restored. For rebellious contumacy and resistance to the sentence of the chapter, there was sterner dealing. "Such a person, the brethren who were present were to arise and violently seize, and drag him or else bear him to the prison appointed for such arrogant persons, and being there confined, he was, with due discretion, to be afflicted, until he had laid aside his haughty temper and owned his fault, and humbly promised amendment." Expulsion was the last penalty. The runaway monk was not refused a return, but he was received with the tokens of ignominy upon him, befitting a deserter. He came to sue for pardon, carrying his forsaken monastic dress on one arm, and in the other hand a bundle of rods. All these judgments and vindications of discipline took place in the chapter, in the presence of the whole community, and under the sanction of the whole. In the same way, discipline was administered among the children who formed the school of the monastery. They had their special chapter, in which they received their punishments; "*in capitulo suo vapulent,*" is the concise order, "*sicut majores in majore capitulo,*"—"let them be whipped in their own chapter, as the elders in the older chapter."

In the chapter, all admissions were made of novices, of professing monks, and of strangers who were received into the society and "confraternity" of the house. The novice, on his petition to be received, was warned of the seriousness of what he was undertaking. "Let there be declared to him the hard and stern things which in this order they endure who wish to live piously and according to the rule and then, again, the yet harder and sterner things which may befall him, if he behaves himself unrulily. Which things having heard, if he still persists in his purpose, and promises that he is prepared to bear yet harder and harsher things, let the president of the chapter say to him : '*The Lord Jesus Christ so perform in you what for His love's sake you promise, that you may have His grace and life eternal;*' and all answering, '*Amen,*' he shall add, '*And we for His love's sake by this grant to you what so humbly and so constantly you promise.*'" The rule of the order, according to the common practice, was to be read to him, with the form of warning: "Here is the law under which you desire to serve ; if you can keep it, enter in ; but if you cannot, freely depart." (*Ecce lex sub qua militare vis: si potes observare, ingredere ; si vero non potes, libere discede.*) The novice was kept apart, only associating with his master, or speaking with such of the brethren as might be inflamed with zeal for his improvement. He was fully subject to the discipline of the monastery, and received his judgment and stripes in chapter like the rest. If, "after certain days," he persisted, he was again warned and told of the hard and heavy things which were appointed by the holy fathers for this order of life; and then, if he undertook to bear them humbly and patiently, and yet harder and heavier things still, he was received, and made his profession. His profession was made in writing; the "cantor" was to provide parchment and ink (*membranam et encaustum*), and a writer, if the novice could not write. In this case the novice was to sign his profession with the mark of the cross; but he was to write it out himself, if he could; and then at the mass to read it aloud and lay it on the altar. For three days from his reception and "benediction" he is to observe absolute silence; the cowl with which the abbot covers his head is not to be removed, and he is to sleep in it; and each day he is to receive the communion. Then in chapter his master is to ask leave for him to read and to sing as the rest of the brethren; and the abbot grants it with the words, "Let him do so with the blessing of God." A strange monk asking "confraternity" is to be led into the chapter, and the abbot is to ask him, as he prostrates himself, what he has to say. He is to answer: "*I ask, by the mercy of God, your fellowship and that of all these elders, and the benefit of this monastery;*" and the abbot to answer, " The Almighty Lord grant you what you seek, and Himself give you the fellowship of His elect;" "and then being bidden to rise, he receives from him, by the emblematic delivery to him of the book of rules, the fellowship of the monastery."

Among the various things to be done in the chapter-house, one is worth noticing. On the first Monday in Lent every year, there was to be a general restoring and changing of books. "Before the brethren come into chapter, the keeper of the books is to have the books collected in the chapter-house, and spread on a carpet, except those which have been given out for use during the past year. These last, the brethren coming into chapter are to bring with them, each one having his book in his hand, of which they ought to have had notice from the keeper of the books in the chapter of the day before. The rule of St. Benedict about the observance of Lent is to be read. Then, when there has been a discourse out of it, the keeper of the books is to read a note (*breve*) as to how the brethren have had books in the last year. As each one hears his name mentioned, he is to return the work which was given him to read the last year. And he who is aware that he has not read through the book which he received, is to prostrate himself and declare his fault and ask indulgence. Then again the keeper of the books is to give to each of the brethren another book to read, and when the books have been distributed in order, the keeper is to record in a note (*imbreviet*) the names of the books, and of those who have received them."

The daily service in the church took the first place, and governed all the other arrangements. Lanfranc's regulations go with much detail into the order to be observed for the day's prayers at each season of the ecclesiastical year, for the special ceremonies at the chief solemnities and festivals, and for the various rites and grades of the divine service. They contain an elaborate directory, following what had become by this time the ordinary course of common prayer and the fixed cycle of holy times in the Latin Church; its order exhibits a general agreement with that which is still represented in the breviaries; but this order was not then stereotyped in the degree in which it gradually became fixed, in the usages of the Western Church before the Reformation; and Lanfranc, in this matter as in others, exercises his discretion in his arrangements. The divisions of the year are appointed, and marked by various changes in the order of prayer and living. The festivals of different classes, to be kept in the monastery, are enumerated. The rules, as we have them, were meant by Lanfranc for English monasteries; and the only festivals of more recent saints which he admits into his second class, containing days which come below the highest feasts, days connected with events of the Gospel history like the Epiphany, the Annunciation, and the Ascension, and with the memory of St. John the Baptist, St. Peter, and St. Paul, and of All Saints,—are, with the exception of that commemorative of the great monastic patriarch St. Benedict, days in honour of three persons in whom Englishmen would feel special interest: St. Gregory, "because he is the apostle of our, that is, of the English nation;" St. Augustin, "the Archbishop of the English;" and St. Alfege the martyr—Ælfheah, the Archbishop of Canterbury, slain by the heathen Danes, whose claim to a high place among martyred saints, thus emphatically admitted, was the subject, as we shall find, of a remarkable conversation between Lanfranc and Anselm; and the place which he fills in Lanfranc's monastic calendar was the effect of that conversation. It is worth mentioning that the holy days enumerated are comparatively few: besides the names just mentioned, and those of Scripture personages, the only names found are St. Vincent, St. Lawrence, St. Augustin of Hippo, and St. Martin.

The course of an ordinary day is thus laid out for the autumn season. The community rose for matins, which were sung at night, and then returned to their beds; as the day began to dawn, a small bell gave the signal, and they rose, and, in the dress in which they slept, sang the service for the first hour, with the penitential Psalms and Litanies, and then passed into the cloister, where they sat at their various occupations. The children were employed reading aloud or singing. At the bell which sounded for the third hour, they went to the dormitory and dressed themselves for the day; then they went to the lavatory and washed and combed their hair; and proceeding to the church remained bowing down to the ground, till the children were ready and joined them. Then the third hour service was performed and the morning mass. When it was over, the whole community gathered in the choir, and proceeded two and two to the chapter-house; when the business there was over, they went into the cloister, and might talk till the sixth hour, and the mass which followed it. Twice a week on the fast days, Wednesday and Friday, there was a procession in which all walked barefoot round the cloister. In the summer portion of the year, when the days were longer, the community took a noon-day rest (*meridiana*) in the dormitory; it is especially ordered that during the mid-day rest the children and youths were not to read or write or do any work in their beds, but to lie perfectly still. After the mid-day mass, the brethren were to sit in the choir, and those who would might read, till the service of the ninth hour. As the time of the great festivals came on, from Advent to Whitsuntide, the religious services became much longer and took up more time. After the ninth hour they went to the refectory, and they might speak in the cloister. On ordinary days, they "refreshed" themselves twice a day, after the third hour, and again after the ninth, except on fast days, when all, except the children and the sick, "refreshed" themselves (*reficiunt*) only once; and restrictions as to the quality of the food are laid down for the great solemnities. But little is said about food, compared with the general minuteness of the directions relating to the ceremonial by which the significance and importance of each high service was marked. There appears a sternness and severity running through them, such as there might be in the regulations of a military life, but no privation simply for privations' sake, at least no pushing of privation to extravagant excess. The children, the sick, the weak, and those who, according to the custom of the time, were undergoing their periodical blood-letting, —an operation which was done according to rule, and with a religious service,—were to be treated with indulgence, and all discretion granted to their superiors for this end. Rules were laid down about the time and usage of shaving and washing; before the great festivals there was a general bathing, and much of the washing is ordered to be with hot water. The chamberlain, whose business it was to provide the dress of the brethren, is ordered also to provide razors and napkins for shaving; towels to hang in the cloister; he is to provide and repair glass windows for the dormitory; and once a year he is to have the hay changed in the beds and the dormitory cleaned.

The government of the monastery was arranged with good sense and simplicity according to the habits of the time, and the objects of the institution as a school of discipline. The various offices were laid out with the same distinctness and regularity as, according to an analogy which has already been noticed, and which is continually recurring, in a regiment or a man-of-war. The abbot was elected by the community, or by the majority and "better part." The abbot was often, perhaps more often than not, chosen from some other monastery, where he had already gained reputation for learning or discipline. This was the theory. But in Normandy, in Duke William's time, the election, at least in the larger houses, required the duke's assent and confirmation, if the office was not his direct and sole appointment; and the abbot received from him the investiture of the temporalities of the house by the formal delivery of a pastoral staff. The abbot's authority was, in idea and in terms, absolute and never to be questioned. "Let the whole order of the monastery depend on what he thinks fit." His paramount position was marked by a strict etiquette, and all kinds of marks of exceptional honour; all orders came from him, all power was derived from him; he was the source of pardon and indulgence, and in his presence all other authority was suspended. But he was as much subject as the rest to the regulations and laws of his service; and further, he was controlled and limited directly by acknowledged concurrent rights in the community, as in admission of new members, or in the judgment and sentence of faults, and still more, indirectly, by the opinions and leanings of the body, often an active, and sometimes a troublesome one, over which he presided. A monastery exhibited the mixture, so common everywhere at the time, of great personal and concentrated power with a great amount of real liberty round it; and the force of an abbot's rule depended much less on the despotic supremacy assigned to him by regulations or current ideas than on his own fitness for governing. Under him, and next to him in office and honour, was the prior (a "greater prior," and a "prior of cloister," are specified and distinguished), who was the working hand and head in the interior administration of the house. The servants were specially under his control; he was to "hold the chapter" for the judgment of their behaviour, and for the infliction of necessary punishment. And the police of the house was under his special charge; he was to observe behaviour in choir and in the cloister, and at stated times of day and night—by night with a dark lantern (*absconsa*)—he was to go round the house, the crypt and aisles of the minster, the cloister, the chapterhouse, the infirmary, and the dormitory, to see that there was no idling or foolish gossip. At night he was to take care that all was well lighted in the house. In this work of going his rounds, he was assisted by officers specially appointed for the purpose (*circumitores, quos alio nomine circas vocant*), elected from the more discreet of the brethren, men who would act without favour or malice, who from time to time were to pass through the monastery, observing everything, but never speaking till they made their report in the chapter. "While they are going their rounds they are to make no sign to any one; to no one on any occasion are they to speak, but only watchfully notice all negligence and all offences, and silently passing by, afterwards make their complaint in chapter. If they find any of the brethren talking outside the cloister, one of the speakers is at once to rise up to them, and say, if it be the case that they have leave to be talking. The officers of the rounds are not to answer by word or sign, but quietly passing on, to listen carefully whether the talk is unprofitable and what ought not to be said." All the offices and rooms of the house were under their continual superintendence.

The service of the choir was under the charge of the *Cantor*. He arranged everything relating to the reading and singing. "Every one," it is said,—a necessary precaution where reading was an accomplishment, and right pronunciation more precarious than even now,—"every one who is to read or sing anything in the minster, is bound, if necessary, before he begins, to listen to the passage read or sung by the *cantor*." It was his duty to take care that nothing careless and slovenly was done in any religious service. "If any one from forgetfulness does not begin at his proper place in the responses and antiphon, or goes wrong in it, the *cantor* must be on

his guard and ready without delay to begin what should
be begun, or to set the other right where he has made
a mistake. At his direction the chant is to begin, to
be raised, to be lowered : no one is to raise the chant
unless he first begins." He is to choose those who
are to help him in the choir ; he is to sit among them
on the right side of the choir, on which side the singing is to begin. He also is to have the care of the
books of the monastery. Other officers attended to
the outward or domestic concerns of the house. The
*Secretarius* or *Sacrista* had the charge of the church
ornaments, the bells, and the sacred vessels ; and it
was his business to overlook the making of the "Hosts"
for the Mass, which was done with great solemnity.
The *Chamberlain* was charged with everything relating
to the dress of the brethren and the good order of
their rooms. "He was to have horse-shoes for the
horses of the abbot and prior and their guests, and
to provide the brethren going on a journey with
cloaks, leggings, and spurs;" for whose behaviour while
travelling very careful and elaborate rules are given.
The *Cellarer* looked after the housekeeping. There
is a touch of warmth in the dry, stern rule, in describing his office, which speaks of the feeling with
which he was looked upon even at Bec. "He ought
to be the father of the whole congregation ; to have
a care both of those in health, and also, and especially,
of the sick brethren." On the day on which the rule
of his office was to be read in chapter, he was to take
care that all should be prepared, so that his service
in the refectory to the brethren might be done in an
honourable and festive manner: he was solemnly to
ask pardon in chapter for the imperfect manner in

F

which he had discharged his "obedience," and was to receive forgiveness for it from the community; and then after a recital for him of the *Miserere* Psalm, he was to provide an "honourable refection" for the brethren. There was a separate house for strangers, over which a brother was set who was to provide everything necessary of furniture, firing and food for their entertainment. He was to introduce guests and visitors, and to show the cloister and offices to those who desired to see them; but he was to bring no stranger into the cloister while any of the brotherhood was sitting there, and "no one on any pretence, booted, spurred, or bare-footed." There was an *Almoner*, whose business it was to seek out and relieve the poor and the sick; he had two servants to attend him, and he was to visit the distressed at their houses, and gently comfort the "sick and offer them the best that he had and saw that they needed, and if they needed something that he had not, he was to try and provide it." And there was an *Infirmarius*, who looked after the sick in hospital, with his own separate cook and kitchen for their needs, who was to provide freely for all that could comfort them, and also to take care that no one took advantage of the comparative indulgence of the infirmary. The regulations are minute and lengthy about the treatment of the dying. He was attended with prayers and psalms to the last; when he entered into his "agony," a haircloth was spread, ashes scattered upon it, and a cross made on the ashes, and on this the dying brother was laid. The whole convent was summoned by sharp repeated blows on a board: all who heard it, whatever they were about, except they were at the regular service in church, were to run to the bed of the dying, chanting in a low tone the Nicene Creed; and they were to remain about him, saying the Penitential Psalms and Litanies till he died. So, in the presence of all his brethren, amid their suffrages and supplications, in sackcloth and ashes, the monk gave up the ghost. Such are the descriptions of the last scenes in the lives of men of this time: so Anselm died, and so his friend and pupil Gundulf, Bishop of Rochester, the builder of the Tower of London.

In these regulations, entering frequently into very minute detail as to the observances of times and seasons, it is natural that we should find a great mixture; that with things wise and reasonable, and well adapted to ends deserving of respect, we should find much that is childish, much that is mischievous, much that is simply incomprehensible. So it appears to us now; and probably with our larger experience we are right. But matters which approach to the nature of form and etiquette are always things on which a man who is careful in forming his judgments will be especially cautious in pronouncing a strong opinion. We find them in black and white in a book, and there they look very different from what such things do when we see them in living action, and surrounded by circumstances with which they harmonize; and one age can never expect to understand and feel with the forms of another, just as one class of society is often simply unable to see anything to respect or care for in what is full of gravity and meaning to another, above it, or below it, or even co-ordinate with it. Lawyers, soldiers, doctors, clergymen, are apt to find much that is strange and unintelligible in one another's codes and professional ideas. But with all shortcomings and fantastic usages and misdirection, one thing the monasteries were, which was greatly needed in their day. In an age when there was so much lawlessness, and when the idea of self-control was so uncommon in the ordinary life of man, they were schools of discipline; and there were no others. They upheld and exhibited the great, then almost the original idea, that men needed to rule and govern themselves, that they could do it, and that no use of life was noble and perfect without this ruling. It was hard and rough discipline like the times, which were hard and rough. But they did good work then, and for future times, by impressing on society the idea of self-control and self-maintained discipline. And rude as they were, they were capable of nurturing noble natures, single hearts, keen and powerful intellects, glowing and unselfish affections.

In those days, there were soldiers and soldiers, and no doubt fewer good ones than bad ones. We have no reason to suppose that it was otherwise with monks, or that the general praise which we meet with of monks as such, means more than the corresponding general praise of the military virtues of an army, who are all supposed to be gallant and highminded. But the soldier of knowledge and of religious self-discipline had a noble ideal; and it was not unfulfilled. In Anselm's life we can see how the man filled up the formal life of the monk, as he might have filled up that of the soldier. Through the clumsiness, the simplicity, the frequent childishness of that time of beginnings, the shrewdness and fine sympathies and affection of Anselm's English friend and biographer show us how high and genuine a life could be realized in those rude cloisters.

# CHAPTER IV.

### ANSELM AT BEC.

> "Temperance, proof
> Against all trials; industry severe
> And constant as the motion of the day;
> Stern self-denial round him spread, with shade
> That might be deemed forbidding, did not there
> All generous feelings flourish and rejoice;
> Forbearance, charity in deed and thought,
> And resolution competent to take
> Out of the bosom of simplicity
> All that her holy customs recommend."
>
> WORDSWORTH, *Excursion*, b. vii.

> "Servants of God! or sons
> Shall I not call you? because
> Not as servants ye knew
> Your Father's innermost mind,
> His, who unwillingly sees
> One of His little ones lost—
> Yours is the praise, if mankind
> Hath not as yet in its march
> Fainted, and fallen, and died!
>
> \* \* \* \*
>
> Then in such hour of need
> Of your fainting, dispirited race,
> Ye, like angels, appear,
> Radiant with ardour divine.
> Beacons of hope, ye appear!
> Languor is not in your heart,
> Weakness is not in your word,
> Weariness not on your brow."
>
> MATTHEW ARNOLD.

ANSELM came to Bec, as men later on went to universities, to find the best knowledge and the best teaching of this day. He read indefatigably, and himself taught others, under Lanfranc. Teacher and pupil, besides being both Italians, had much to draw them together; and a friendship began between them, which, in spite of the difference between the two men, and the perhaps unconscious reserve caused by it, continued to the last genuine and unbroken. Lanfranc was a man of strong practical genius. Anselm was an original thinker of extraordinary daring and subtlety. But the two men had high aims in common; they knew what they meant, and they understood each other's varied capacities for their common task. They found themselves among a race of men of singular energy and great ambition, but at a very low level of knowledge, and with a very low standard of morality; illiterate, undisciplined, lawless. To educate and to reform, to awaken the Normans to the interest of letters and the idea of duty, to kindle the desire to learn and to think, and to purify and elevate the aims of life, were the double object of both Lanfranc and Anselm, the key to their unwearied zeal to re-organize and infuse fresh vigour into the monastic system, which was the instrument which they found ready to their hand. Opposite as they were in character, and working in different lines, the great purpose which they had so sincerely at heart bound them together.

When Anselm had, as we should say, followed Lanfranc's lectures for some time, the question presented itself to what use he should devote his life. In those hard days, the life of a monk was not harder than that of a student; each was pinched with cold and want, each could only get through his day's work with toil like that of a day-labourer. What was on the side of the monk's life was its definite aim and its hope of reward. It was a distinct self-dedication to the service of the great Master, and it looked for the great Master's special approval. Anselm had begun to feel his power, and to reflect on the cost of privation and effort at which the fruits of thought and knowledge had been bought. How should he best keep them from being thrown away? The same temper which in those days naturally carried other men to be soldiers, carried him to be a monk; but what sort of monk should he be? Cluni was then the most famous among monastic organizations; but Cluni discouraged learning. Why should he not stay at Bec? He confessed to himself afterwards that he felt that where Lanfranc was so great there was no room for him, and that he wanted, even as a monk, a sphere of his own. "I was not yet tamed," as he said in after times, when he used, in playful mood, to talk over his early life with his friends—"I want a place, I said to myself, where I can both show what I know and be of use to others; I thought my motive was charity to others, and did not see how hurtful it was to myself." But self-knowledge came and an honest understanding with himself, and with it new plans of life opened: if he was to be a monk, he was to be one for God, and at Bec as well as anywhere; if rest and God's comfort were his desire, he would find them there. But with the ever paramount thought came other thoughts, too. His father's inheritance had fallen to him, and he considered the alternative of going back to take it. Should he be a monk at Bec, a hermit in the wilds, or a noble in his father's house, administering his patrimony for the poor? He put himself into Lanfranc's hands. Lanfranc referred him to the Archbishop of Rouen. The archbishop advised him to become a monk. It is hard to see what better advice in those times he could have given to a man consumed by the passion at once for knowledge and for the highest ideal of life. Anselm became a monk at Bec in the twenty-seventh year of his age; in three years' time he succeeded Lanfranc as prior; fifteen years after this Herlwin, the founder, died, and Anselm was chosen abbot; and he governed Bec as abbot for fifteen years more.[1]

Lanfranc had set a high example, and to him belongs the glory of having been the creator of Bec, the kindler of light and force among the Norman clergy, the leader of improvement and efforts after worthier modes of life on a wider stage than Normandy. He was for his day an accomplished scholar and divine, a zealous promoter of learning, of order, of regularity of life, a man of great practical powers, and noble and commanding character, apparently not without a tinge of harshness and craft. He left his scholar Anselm to carry on his work at Bec; his scholar— but it would not be easy to find two more different men. Lanfranc's equal might without much difficulty be found among many of the distinguished churchmen of the Middle Ages. The man who succeeded him was one who, to a child-like singleness and tenderness of heart, joined an originality and power of thought which rank him, even to this day, among the few discoverers of new paths in philosophical speculation. Anselm was one of those

[1] Monk, 1060; Prior, 1063; Abbot, 1078 till 1093.

devout enthusiasts after exact truth, who try the faculties of the human mind to the uttermost, and to whom the investigation of new ideas, pushed to their simplest forms and ultimate grounds, takes the place of the passions and objects of life. He had all that dialectical subtlety and resource which awakening mind in half-barbarous times exacts from and admires in its guides; but he had also, besides this, which was common enough, the daring and the force to venture by himself into real depths and difficulties of thought, such as have been tried by the greatest of modern thinkers, and in which lie the deepest problems of our own times. Fixed at Bec, the philosophic inquirer settled to his toil, and reverently and religiously, yet fearlessly, gave his reason its range. His biographer records the astonishment caused by his attempts to "unravel the darkest, and before his time the unsolved or unusual questions concerning the Divine Nature and our faith, which lay hid, covered by much darkness in the divine Scriptures." "For," adds Eadmer, "he had such confidence in them, that with immovable trust of heart he felt convinced that there was nothing in them contrary to solid truth. Therefore he bent his purpose most earnestly to this, that according to his faith it might be vouchsafed to him to perceive by his mind and reason the things which were veiled in them."

The men of his day, as we see, recognized in him something more than common as an inquirer and a thinker; but it was reserved for much later times to discern how great he was. It needed longer and wider experience in the realms of speculation, and a far higher cultivation than was attainable in his age, to take the true measure of his original and penetrating intellect. His first works written at Bec show his refined subtlety of thought, with the strong effort to grasp in his own way the truth of his subject. They exhibit the mind really at work, not amusing itself with its knowledge and dexterity. They are three dialogues, in which he grapples with the idea of Truth, with the idea of Free-will, and with the idea of Sin, as exhibited in what may be called its simplest form, the fall of an untempted angelic nature. But the fruits of his intellectual activity at Bec are shown on a very different scale in two works, also composed when he was prior, which have gained him his place among the great thinkers of Christian Europe—two short treatises on the deepest foundations of all religion, examples of the most severe and abstruse exercise of mind, yet coloured throughout by the intensity of faith and passionate devotion of the soul to the God of Truth which sets the reason to work. The first of these is the *Monologion*. He originally called it "An Example of Meditation on the Reason of Faith;" and it was meant to represent a person discoursing secretly with himself on the ground of his belief in God. It is an attempt to elicit from the necessity of reason, without the aid of Scripture, the idea of God, and the real foundation of it; and to exhibit it "in plain language and by ordinary argument, and in a simple manner of discussion"—that is, without the usual employment of learned proofs; and he aims, further, at showing how this idea necessarily leads to the belief of the Word and the Spirit, distinguished from, but one with, the Father.

The *Monologion* is an investigation of what reason alone shows God to be; though the inquiry starts from the assumption of the convictions of faith, and finds that reason, independently followed, confirms them. The basis of his method, one of several he says, but the readiest, is the existence of certain qualities in man and nature, moral and intellectual excellences and whatever we call good, which, he argues, to be intelligibly accounted for, presuppose, as the ground of their existence, the same qualities in a perfect and transcendent manner in a Being who is seen, on further reflection, to be the one without whom nothing could be, and who Himself depends on nothing. It is an argument from *ideas*, in the sense in which Plato spoke of them, as grounds accounting to reason for all that is matter of experience. The mode of argument is as old as Plato, and became known to Anselm through St. Augustin. But it is thought out afresh and shaped anew with the originality of genius. A recent French critic, Émile Saisset, remarks on the "extraordinary boldness, which strikes us in every page of the *Monologion*." The clear purpose and the confident grasp of the question, the conduct of the reasoning from step to step, calm and almost impassive in appearance, but sustained and spirited, the terse yet elaborate handling of the successive points, the union in it of self-reliant hardihood, with a strong sense of what is due to the judgment of others, make it, with its companion piece, the *Proslogion*, worthy of its fame, as one of the great masterpieces and signal-posts in the development of this line of thought; though like its great companions and rivals, before and after it, it leaves behind a far stronger impression of the limitations of the human intellect than even of its powers.

But he was not satisfied with the argument of the *Monologion*, a chain consisting of many links, a theory requiring the grasp in one view of many reasonings. Eadmer draws a remarkable picture, which is confirmed by Anselm's own account, of the way in which he was tormented with the longing to discover some one argument—short, simple, self-sufficing—by which to demonstrate in a clear and certain manner the existence and perfections of God. Often on the point of grasping what he sought, and as often baffled by what escaped from his hold, unable in his anxiety to sleep or to take his meals, he despaired of his purpose; but the passionate desire would not leave him. It intruded on his prayers, and interrupted his duties, till it came to appear to him like a temptation of the devil. At last, in the watches of the night, in the very stress of his efforts to keep off the haunting idea, "in the agony and conflict of his thoughts," the thing which he had so long given up hoping for presented itself, and filled him with joy. The discovery, Eadmer tells us, was more than once nearly lost, from the mysterious and unaccountable breaking of the wax tablets on which his first notes were written, before they were finally arranged and committed to the parchment. The result was the famous argument of the *Proslogion*, the argument revived with absolute confidence in it by Descartes, and which still employs deep minds in France and Germany with its fascinating mystery—that the idea of God in the human mind of itself necessarily involves the reality of that idea. The *Proslogion*, a very short composition, is in the shape of an address and lifting up of the soul to God, after the manner of St. Augustin's Confessions, or what in French is termed an *Elévation*, seeking to know the rational foundation of its faith; *fides quærens intellectum.* The "fool who says in his heart, there is no God," in his very negation comprehends the absolutely unique idea of a Being the most perfect conceivable, an idea without a parallel or likeness; but real existence is necessarily involved in the idea of a Being than whom nothing can be conceived greater, otherwise it would not be the most perfect conceivable. He treats the idea of a Being, than which nothing greater can be conceived, and of which existence is a necessary part, as if it were as much an intellectual necessity as the idea of a triangle, or, as Descartes puts it, a mountain which must have its valley; and the denial of the "fool" to be as impossible an attempt as the attempt to conceive the nonexistence of the idea of a triangle. The obviously paradoxical aspect of the argument, in seeming to make a mental idea a proof of real existence, was brought out at the time with some vigour, though with an inadequate appreciation of the subtlety and depth of the question in debate, by a French monk of noble birth, Gaunilo of Marmoutier; and in reply to this, the argument, which is very briefly stated in the *Proslogion* itself, is stated afresh, and Anselm puts forth the full power of his keen and self-reliant mind to unfold and guard it. A curious touch of playfulness occasionally relieves the austere argumentation. To illustrate the absurdity of Anselm's alleged position, that what is more excellent than all things in idea must exist in fact, Gaunilo instances the *Insula perdita* in the ocean, the lost *Atlantis* of poets and philosophers, said to be the most beautiful of all lands, but inaccessible to man. Gaunilo makes merry with his parallel, which Anselm rejects. "I speak confidently," he answers, "*fidens loquor*—if any one will discover for me anything, either existing in fact or in thought alone, *besides That than which nothing greater can be thought*, to which he can fit and apply the structure of this my reasoning, I will find and give him that lost island, never to be lost again." But this is a passing touch which for once he could not resist: in the treatment generally of the argument in this reply, he sacrifices the moral and, so to say, the probable and imaginative aspect of it, to its purely scientific form. Until it is expanded by considerations which Anselm refuses to take in, it seems but a rigorous following out of the consequences, which are inevitably imposed on the reasoner who accepts the definition of God as "That than which nothing greater can be thought." But the argument was one which in its substance approved itself to minds like those of Descartes, and Descartes' great critics, Samuel Clarke, Leibnitz, and Hegel; and these bold and soaring efforts of pure reason, so devout and reverently conscious of what it had accepted as the certainties of religion, yet so ardently bent on intellectual discovery for itself, are the more remarkable when it is considered that in their form and style Anselm had no model, not even in his chief master, St. Augustin. Nor was he imitated. The great Schoolmen followed a different track, and a different method; and it is only on account of their common devotion to abstract thought, and of the impulse which Anselm doubtless gave to a more severe and searching treatment of theology, that he can be classed as one of them, or as their forerunner. It has been observed with justice, that his method is much more akin to the spirit of independent philosophical investigation which began when the age of the Schools had passed, in the sixteenth century. It differs from this in the profound convictions of the certainties of religion, convictions as profound as those of moral duty, from which it starts and with which it is combined, and by the spirit of which it is ever quickened and elevated.

But he was not only a thinker. His passion for abstruse thought was one which craved, not solitude but companionship. He was eminently a teacher. The Middle Ages are full of pictures of great masters and their scholars; but few of them exhibit the connection in its finest form—as a combination of natural authority with affection, of deep personal interest and large public aims, of familiarity and associated labour between the teacher and his circle of pupils, of a guide who does not impose his opinions or found a school, but who shows the way and awakens thought,—so clearly as it is seen in the glimpses which are given, in Anselm's letters and works and in Eadmer's life, of Anselm's monastic school. His chief care, says his biographer, was devoted to the younger men, whose minds were to be formed for work to come, and who were not too old to learn, or to be kindled with high purposes, and quickened into fresh enterprises of thought. "He compared the age of youth to wax fitly tempered for the seal. For if the wax be too hard or too soft it receives but imperfectly the im-

·pression. So is it in the ages of man. You see a man from childhood to deep old age, busy with the vanities of this world, minding only earthly things and hardened in them. Talk to him of the things of the spirit, of the refined thoughts of divine contemplation, teach such a man to search out these secrets of heaven, and you will find that he has not even the power of knowing what you mean. And no wonder—the wax is hardened; he has not spent his life in these things, he has learned to pursue their opposites. Take, on the other hand, a boy of tender age, not able to discern either good or evil, not even to understand you when you talk of such things, and the wax is too soft and melting—it will not retain the impression. The young man is between the two, fitly tempered of softness and hardness. Train up him, and you may mould him to what you will." The turn of hopefulness given to the trite image is characteristic. Gifted with singularly keen insight into men's hearts, and with quick and wide sympathy; instinctively divining, with a sureness which struck even men accustomed, as monks were, to this kind of faculty, the secret wishes, trials, sorrows, perils of each, and exercising that attraction which draws men to those who understand and respect them, Anselm's influence reached to wherever he came in contact with men, inside his monastery or without. The words of Christ and heaven were ever on his lips; but they were words for all.

He was not a preacher; but he was remarkable for his readiness to address or discourse with lay people of all conditions in their own language and on their own ground, as much as to compose Latin homilies for the chapter-house of his monks. His correspondence alone shows how, as time went on, his relations with persons of all classes extended; and he cared for all and willingly worked for all. Whole days, says Eadmer, he would spend in giving advice to those who claimed it; and then the night would be spent in correcting the ill-written copies of books for the library. He was as ready and as unwearied in doing the work of a nurse in the infirmary or at the death-bed, as he was to teach and discuss in the cloister, or to bury himself in contemplation in his cell. His care and his toil were for all within his spiritual household, and flowed over beyond it; but his love and his interest were for the younger men; for minds not yet dulled to the wonders and great ends of living, needing as he did answers to its great questions, eager and hopeful as he was to venture on the "majestic pains" and anxieties of thought needful to meet them. Wearied once with his work, he sought to be relieved of it by the Archbishop of Rouen; but he received the answer usual in those days, that he was to return and prepare for greater and heavier burdens. "So," says Eadmer, "he went back. He behaved so that all men loved him as their dear father. He bore with even mind the ways and the weaknesses of each; to each he supplied what he saw they wanted. Oh, how many given over in sickness has he brought back to health by his loving care! You found it, Herewald, in your helpless old age when, disabled by years as well as by heavy infirmity, you had lost all power in your body except in your tongue, and were fed by his hand, and refreshed by wine squeezed from the grapes into his other hand, from which you drank it, and were at last restored to health. For no other drink, as you used to say, could you relish, nor from any other hand. So it was: Anselm used to be constantly in the infirmary, inquiring after the brethren's sicknesses, and ministering to each what each needed without delay or trouble. So it was: he was to those in health a father, to the sick a mother—rather, to healthy and sick, father and mother in one. And so, whatever secrets anyone had, to Anselm, as to a most sweet mother, he sought to confide it. But it was the young men who were most anxious to do so."

Why the young turned so enthusiastically to one who thus sympathised with them, may be understood from the following conversation, in which Anselm's good sense and freedom of mind appear in contrast with the current ideas of his time, which were not those of the eleventh century only. An abbot, says Eadmer, who was looked upon as a very religious man, was one day deploring to Anselm the impossibility of making any impression on the boys who were brought up in his monastery. "What are we to do with them?" he asked in despair: "do what we will they are perverse and incorrigible; we do not cease beating them day and night, and they only get worse." "And you don't cease beating them?" said Anselm; "what do they turn into when they grow up?" "They turn only dull and brutal," was the answer. "Well, you have bad luck in the pains you spend on their training," said Anselm, "if you only turn men into beasts." "But what are we to do then?" said the abbot; "in every kind of way we constrain them to improve, and it is no use." "*Constrain* them! Tell me, my lord abbot, if you planted a tree in your garden, and tied it up on all sides so that it could not stretch forth its branches, what sort of tree would it turn out when, after some years, you gave it room to spread? Would it not be good for nothing, full of tangled and crooked boughs? And whose fault would this be but yours, who had put such constant restraint upon it? And this is just what you do with your boys. You plant them in the garden of the Church, that they may grow and bear fruit to God. But you cramp them round to such a degree with terrors and threats and blows, that they are utterly debarred from the enjoyment of any freedom. And thus injudiciously kept down, they collect in their minds evil thoughts tangled like thorns; they cherish and feed them, and with dogged temper elude all that might help to correct them. And hence it comes that they see nothing in you of love, or kindness, or goodwill, or tenderness towards them; they cannot believe that you mean any good by them, and put down all you do to dislike and ill-nature. Hatred and mistrust grow with them as they grow; and they go about with downcast eyes, and cannot look you in the face. But, for the love of God, I wish you would tell me why you are so harsh with them? Are they not human beings? Are they not of the same nature as you are? Would you like, if you were what they are, to be treated as you treat them? You try by blows and stripes alone to fashion them to good: did you ever see a craftsman fashion a fair image out of a plate of gold or silver by blows alone? Does he not with his tools now gently press and strike it, now with wise art still more gently raise and shape it? So, if you would mould your boys to good, you must, along with the stripes which are to bow them down, lift them up and assist them by fatherly kindness and gentleness." ... "But," the abbot insisted, "what we try to do is to force them into seriousness and sturdiness of character; what are we to do?" "You do well," said Anselm; "but if you give an infant solid food you will choke it. For every soul, its proportionate food. The strong soul delights in strong meat, in patience and tribulations, not to wish for what is another's, to offer the other cheek, to pray for enemies, to love those that hate. The weak and tender in God's service need milk: gentleness from others, kindness, mercy, cheerful encouragement, charitable forbearance. If you will thus suit yourselves both to your weak and your strong ones, by God's grace you shall, as far as lies in you, win them all for God." "Alas!" sighed the abbot, "we have been all wrong. We have wandered from the way of truth, and the light of discretion hath not shone on us." And falling at Anselm's feet he confessed his sin, and asked pardon for the past, and promised amendment for what was to come.

A strange and touching history in Eadmer—strange, with those ways of thought, which their unquestioned naturalness then render doubly wonderful now,— touching, from that depth of affection which all times know and can understand—shows how Anselm had learned his own lesson. When he was made prior, after only three years' profession, over the head of the older inmates of Bec, a strong feeling of jealousy was shown, and a party formed against him in the monastery. With them was one of the younger monks named Osbern, whose hatred of Anselm was extreme, and who pursued him with the "savageness of a dog" (*canino more*). Anselm, who saw that he had character and talent, began by the most forbearing and immovable good-humour, and by giving him in return the fullest indulgence compatible with the discipline of the house. In time Osbern was softened, and became deeply attached to him. Then, gaining influence over him, Anselm step by step withdrew the early indulgences, and accustomed him to the severities of the monastic life—"punishing him not only with words but with stripes." Osbern stood the test, and was ripening into manly strength. But there came a fatal illness. Then Anselm watched and waited on him like a mother; "day and night was at his bedside, gave him his food and drink, ministered to all his wants, did everything himself that might ease his body and comfort his soul." When the end came and Osbern was dying, Anselm gave him a last charge. He bade him, speaking as friend to friend, to make known after his death, if it were possible, what had become of him. " He promised, and passed away." We need not be surprised that the charge was believed to have been fulfilled. During the funeral Anselm sat apart in a corner of the church, to weep and pray for his friend; he fell asleep from heaviness and sorrow, and had a dream. He saw certain very reverend persons enter the room where Osbern had died, and sit round for judgment; and while he was wondering what the doom would be, Osbern himself appeared, like a man just recovering from illness, or pale with loss of blood. Three times, he said, had the old serpent risen up against him, but three times he fell backwards, and "the Bearward of the Lord (*Ursarius Domini*) had delivered him."

Then Anselm awoke, and believed that Osbern's sins were pardoned, and that God's angels had kept off his foes "as the bearwards keep off the bears." Death did not seem to break the friendship: Osbern's memory was in Anselm's prayers, and his letters show how deep and tender was the surviving affection. He prays his friends to offer for Osbern the prayers and masses which they would offer for himself. "Wherever Osbern is," he writes to his friend Gundulf, "his soul is my soul. Let me, then, while I am alive, receive in him whatever I might have hoped to receive from friendship when I am dead; so that then they need do nothing for me. Farewell! farewell! *mi charissime;* and that I may recompense you according to your importunity, I pray, and I pray, and I pray, remember me, and forget not the soul of Osbern my beloved. If I seem to burden you too much, then forget me and remember him." Whatever the shape in which such feelings clothe themselves, they are not less real for their shape; and to all who feel the mystery and obscurity of our condition, that deep reality will gain their respect and sympathy.

We may trace in such records that remarkable combination of qualities which ultimately made Anselm the object of a love and reverence surpassing even the admiration excited by his rare genius. What is striking is that with so much of his age, so powerful and severe in mind, so stern in his individual life, a monk of the monks, a dogmatist of the dogmatists, he yet had so much beyond his age; he was not only so gentle and affectionate and self-forgetting, but he was so considerate, so indulgent, so humane, so free-spirited, so natural. Austerity was part of the ordinary religious type of the time; it went, indeed, commonly with all loftiness of character and aim; the great Conqueror was austere, and of course a monk with a high estimate of his calling was so. But Anselm's almost light-hearted cheerfulness, his winning and unformal nature, his temper of moderation and good sense, his interest in all kinds of men, and power of accommodating himself to all kinds of characters, his instinctive insight into the substance of questions of truth and justice, his leaning, in an age when all trust was placed in unbending rules, to the side of compassion and liberty, formed a combination with personal austerity with which his age was not familiar. His place of work was among monks, and he must not be regarded as a popular teacher of religion. He had gifts which, perhaps, might have qualified him to exercise a wide popular influence; but he lived in times when there was little thought of direct addresses to the minds of the multitude, and when all serious efforts at ordering life on religious principles were concentrated in a small body of professed ascetics. The days of the great preachers were at hand; but they had not yet come. A certain number of homilies are found among Anselm's works; but they are for the most part of doubtful authority, and those which seem genuine are not sermons, but expositions, meant not for a lay congregation, but for a chapter-house of monks. Yet it is clear that Anselm's influence told on numbers who were not monks; and the vehicle of his influence seems to have been, not preaching, but free conversation. To his passion for abstract and profound thought, he joined a taste for simple and natural explanation, an a homely humour in illustration, which reminds the reader sometimes of Luther or Latimer—more truly, perhaps, of St. François de Sales, and of the vein of quaint and unceremonious amusement running through some of the later Italian works of devotion. Eadmer, or some other of his friends, made a collection of his sayings and comparisons, and his common modes of presenting moral and religious topics, very miscellaneous in selection and unequal in worth, but giving probably an unstudied representation of his ordinary manner of discourse. "He taught," says Eadmer, "not as is the wont with others, but in a widely different fashion, setting forth each point under common and familiar examples, and supporting it by the strength of solid reasons, without any veils or disguises of speech." There is a touch of grim appreciation of the ludicrous in his comparison of himself, peacefully living with his monks or going forth among men of the world, to the fate of the owl which ventures into the day; while she sits still with her "little ones in her cave, she is happy and it is well with her; but when she falls among the crows and rooks and other birds, one attacks her with beak, another with claws, another buffets her with wings, and it goes ill with the owl." There is a deeper touch of sympathy for distress and suffering in the story of the hare, which, when he was riding one day, after he had become archbishop, from Windsor to Hayes, the young men about him started and chased with their dogs. The hare took refuge under the feet of his horse. Anselm reined in his horse, and forbade them to hurt the creature, while, so the story goes, the dogs surrounded the hare and licked it, doing it no harm. When the soldiers crowded round with noisy triumph at the capture, Anselm burst into tears. "'You laugh,' he said, 'but for the poor unhappy creature there is nothing to laugh at or be glad for; its mortal foes are about it, and it flies to us for life, in its own way beseeching for shelter. You see the image of the departing soul of man. It goes forth from the body, and straightway its enemies, the evil spirits, which have hunted it through the doublings of its evil-doings all its life long, cruelly beset it, ready to tear it in pieces, and plunge it into eternal death. But it, terrified and affrighted, looks on this side and on that, longing with desire that cannot be uttered for the hand which shall defend and protect it; and the demons laugh and rejoice if they see it without any aid to help it.' Then he rode on, and with a loud voice forbade that the dogs should touch the hare; and the creature, glad and at liberty, darted off to the fields and woods." The story will remind some readers of Luther's hunting at the Wartburg, and the way in which he "theologized" on it.

In the year 1078, Anselm became abbot, and his connection with England began. Bec, with the other Norman abbeys, had since the Conquest received possessions in England, and the new abbot went over to view the abbey lands and to visit his old master Lanfranc. At Canterbury he was welcomed at the great monastery, and became one with the brotherhood of its monks, most of them probably Englishmen. There he made the acquaintance of Eadmer, then a stripling; and Eadmer's first remembrance of him seems to be of the brotherly way in which he lived with the English monks, and of the original and unusual way in which, in his discourses in cloister or in chapter, he put before them the aims and duties of their state. Lanfranc was then full of the changes which he wished to introduce in the monastic and ecclesiastical organization of England; and Anselm, though he undoubtedly fully sympathised with his master's object, used his influence to temper Lanfranc's sternness and soften his Norman and Latin prejudices. When Lanfranc — *rudis Anglus*, as Eadmer calls him, and inclined to disparage even the saints of the "Barbarians"—disputed the claim of the English Archbishop Elphegè (Ælfheah) to martyrdom, because he had been put to death, not for religion, but for refusing to ransom his life at the expense of his tenants, Anselm, with characteristic but rare generosity and largeness of thought, answered that one who had died rather than oppress his tenants had died for righteousness, and that "he who dies for righteousness dies a martyr for Christ." Anselm, no Norman, and with a larger heart than the Normans, warmed towards the English with something of the love and sympathy which had filled the soul of the great Roman Pope who sent us St. Augustine; and the respect which he showed to the defeated race impressed the foreigners who had become their masters. In his visit, more than once repeated, to the abbey lands about England, he became known. He saw English monasteries and collegiate houses; he was received in the "courts" of some of the nobles; and everywhere his earnest and wise counsels combined, with his frankness and his readiness in meeting all on their own ground, to throw a singular charm about him. "In his wonted manner," says

Eadmer, speaking of these days, "to all he showed himself pleasant and cheerful, and the ways of each, as far as he could without sin, he took upon himself. For, according to the Apostle's word, he suited himself to them that were without law, as if he had been without law, being not without law to God, but under the law to Christ, that he might gain those who were not only without the law, as it was thought, of St. Benedict, but also who lived, devoted to a worldly life, in many things without the law of Christ. So that hearts were in a wonderful manner turned towards him, and were filled with hungry eagerness to hear him. For he adapted his words to each order of men, so that his hearers declared that nothing could have been said to fall in better with their ways. To monks, to clerks, to laymen, according to each man's purpose, he dispensed his words." Eadmer dwells especially on the contrast between his way of teaching and that customary with others, and on his preference for plain reasons, popular illustrations, and straightforward speech which all could understand. He was welcome to old and young, rich and poor; he touched the hearts of English monks, and won the respect of Norman soldiers. "There was no count in England, or countess, or powerful person, who did not think that they had lost merit in the sight of God, if it had not chanced to them at that time to have done some service to Anselm the abbot of Bec." We must remember, of course, that this is the account of a friend, in days when friends were easily satisfied with what made for their friends' credit. But the general account is confirmed by the effect of Anselm's character on William in his later stern and gloomy days. "To all others so harsh and terrible, in Anselm's presence he seemed, to the wonder of the bystanders, another man, so gracious and easy of speech." Years after, when King William was on his forlorn deathbed, Anselm was the man whom he most wished to see.

There is another feature on which Eadmer remarks. The monks who retired from the world found it impossible, after all, to free themselves from the cares and business of the world. They had property; and those who have property must take the chance of lawsuits. Lawsuits were frequent in those days. Even the venerable Abbot Herlwin could not escape them; and one of the excellences for which he was remembered at Bec was the skill with which he used the knowledge he had gained of the customs and rules which then made Norman law, for the protection of his monks in the lords' courts. But even at this time the monks had got a character for knowing and using unscrupulously legal advantages. Eadmer remarks, as if it was something to be remembered, that Anselm steadily set his face against all kinds of chicane. "For he judged it abominable, if in the business of the Church any one made his gain of that which another might lose, by crafty dealing against the rules of justice. So that he never would allow anyone in lawsuits to be taken at advantage by any of his people, through any unfair practice, making a conscience not to do to others what he would not have done to himself." And Eadmer goes on with a picture, quaint, as so many things are in those days, but with touches from the life in it. "So it happened that, sitting among the contending pleaders, while his opponents were taking counsel by what skill or by what trick they might help their own cause or damage his, he, not minding it, was conversing with anyone who wished to address him, either about the Gospel or some other divine Scripture, or some point of right conduct. And often, when he had no one to listen of this kind, quietly at peace in the purity of his heart, he would close his eyes and sleep. And often it came to pass that the cunning devices against him, when they came to his hearing, were at once exposed and torn to pieces, not as if he had been asleep all the while, but as if he had been fully awake and keenly watching. For charity, 'which envieth not, vaunteth not itself, seeketh not her own,' was strong in him, by which he saw at a glance the things that he ought to see ; for the truth was his guide."

The affairs of the house of Bec brought him to England more than once after his first coming over. England became familiar to him, and, according as occasions required it, was repeatedly visited by him." Thus he became well known in England as the great churchman, who, foremost and without an equal in learning, with all his reforming austerity and rigour, showed most signally in word and act the good-will he bore to Englishmen, and whose influence was not less remarkable with the strong and fierce strangers who for the time had become their masters.

# CHAPTER V.

### ORDERIC THE CHRONICLER.

"Oh that our lives, which flee so fast,
　In purity were such,
　That not an image of the past
　　Should fear from Memory's touch!

" Retirement then might hourly look
　Upon a soothing scene ;
　Age steal to his allotted nook,
　　Contented and serene ;

" With heart as calm as lakes that sleep,
　In frosty moonlight glistening :
　Or mountain rivers, where they creep
　Along a channel smooth and deep,
　　To their own far-off murmurs listening."
　　　　　　　　　　　　　WORDSWORTH.

OF course all Norman monasteries were not like Bec, and all their abbots and priors were not like Herlwin, Lanfranc, and Anselm. Monasteries, like colleges, like regiments, like other permanent bodies of men, had each its own spirit, and more or less distinct type ; uniformity of ends, much less of rules, does not necessarily make men alike. These differences of type were not merely differences between good and bad ; they were differences of character, bent, and tastes. And that was a time when, more than ever, a community was apt to reflect the spirit of its leaders. The leaders of the Norman monasteries were of many kinds. The monastic chroniclers, though fettered partly by the etiquette of monastic feelings and respects, partly by the imperfection of their instruments of expression, were not bad observers of character, and let us see, with much distinctness, the variety of men who guided these brotherhoods, and the changes that ensued by the removal of one and the succession of another. A good deal is told when we are informed, for instance, that to Guntard, abbot of Jumiéges, a strict ruler, favourable to the gentle and obedient, but stern to the perverse, succeeded Tancard, prior of Fécamp, "savage as a lion"—*ferus ut leo*. Orderic's pages are full of these vivid touches; and in contrast to the students of Bec, with their spirit of keen and bold speculation, we may set Orderic himself, and the comnunity to which he belonged. Orderic, not a thinker or teacher, but to whom we owe most of what we know of the world in which Anselm and his disciples lived, spent no idle life; and besides preserving the picture of his own times, he has, incidentally and without meaning it, preserved his own portrait—the portrait of a monk who, full of his profession, and made sympathetic, tender-hearted, and religious by it, as well as something of a pedant and a mannerist, looked with curious and often discriminating eye at the scene of life, and contemplated its facts as others inquired into its mysteries.

The monastery of which he was a member, St. Evroul, was situated in a forest near the upper course of the Rille, surrounded by places famous in Norman history, L'Aigle, Breteuil, Séez, on the borders of the dioceses of Evreux and Lisieux. It was, in its new or restored condition, some years younger than Bec; but it was a house which, as much as Bec, represented the new zeal of Normandy, and aimed at carrying out a high religious service. We know about it mainly from Orderic; and his account shows what a stormy existence might be the lot of these places of religious peace. St. Evroul, as has been already said, was founded in part by the great house of Grentmaisnil, one member of which, Robert, a man of some learning, and still more a keen man of business, and a soldier —he had been Duke William's esquire—became a monk in it about 1050. Its first abbot was Theodoric, a monk of Jumiéges, of great piety and zeal, whose holiness imposed awe even on the savage lady, Mabel of Belesme, Countess of Montgomery, the terror of her neighbourhood, and kept her from doing "either evil or good" to his house. He was blameless as a spiritual ruler; he established at St. Evroul a flourishing school of copyists; but in managing the business of the house he was not so successful, and a party of malcontents clamoured against him. "He ought not to be abbot—a man who knows nothing of business and neglects it. How are men of prayer to live, if men of the plough are wanting? (*unde vivent oratores, si defecerint aratores?*) He is a fool, and cares more about reading and writing in the cloister than about providing sustenance for the brethren." The leader of the party was Robert of Grentmaisnil, who had helped to found the house, and was now prior. For a while William of Geroy, one of the co-founders, supported Abbot Theodoric; but William died on a journey to his Norman kinsmen in Apulia, and then the unworldly and simple-minded abbot was driven by sheer worrying and intrigue from his place. He attempted to resign, and retired from the house to one of its dependencies; but Duke William and the Archbishop of Rouen interfered, and a council of eminent churchmen, including Lanfranc, were sent to make peace, who exhorted Robert to "follow the poverty of Christ," and to obey his superior. For a little time there was quiet; then the persecution began again, and the abbot, unable to endure it, fled from the house and from Normandy, and died at Cyprus on his way to Jerusalem. Then Robert was chosen abbot (1059), the monks "reasonably considering his high birth and his ardent zeal in the interests and business of the house." "He was," says Orderic, "much to be praised for purity of life and other sacred gifts; but as nothing, according to Flaccus, is altogether blessed, he was in some points blameworthy. For in the good or evil things which he desired, he was rapid in action and ardent; and when he heard or saw what he disliked, he was swift to wrath; and he liked better to be uppermost than to be under, and to command than to obey. He had his hands open both to receive and to give, and a mouth ready to satisfy his rage with unmeasured words." Robert's way of dealing with troublesome and refractory tenants of the monastery is characteristic: he simply transferred them to their natural feudal lord. "Having taken counsel with the brethren, he handed over the said rebels, for their obstinacy, to his kinsman Arnold, that he might crush *their* stiffneckedness, who would not peaceably endure the mildness of the monks, by a soldier's hand, as long as he lived. Arnold then made their life weary with many and divers services ... so that they earnestly entreated Abbot Robert and the monks that they might be placed again under their power, promising them all subjection and obedience." The members and the possessions of St. Evroul increased under him, and though, as Orderic is fond of repeating, it was founded in a barren and hungry land, yet the Abbot's influence with his friends brought to it the revenues which he needed for his grand designs. But the energetic abbot became involved in the quarrels between Duke William and the house of Grentmaisnil and its friends. He was accused of using mocking words of the Duke. He was cited to appear before the Duke's courts, but he dared not trust himself there, and retired from Normandy. William filled up his place, and the monastery was distracted between partisans of the new abbot Osbern and those who looked on him as an intruder, and could make his place uncomfortable. Robert went to Rome, then to his kinsmen in Apulia. He persuaded the Pope of the goodness of his cause, and returned with letters and two cardinal legates from the Pope, to regain his abbey. When William heard of their coming, he was greatly wroth, and said that "he would gladly receive the Pope's legates, as from the common Father, about faith and Christian religion; but that if any monk of his land brought any complaint against him, he would hang him, without ceremony, by his cowl to the highest oak of the neighbouring wood." Robert hastily took himself off; and after excommunicating his intruding successor, returned to Rome. But the excommunication caused great distress at St. Evroul. The brotherhood broke up: several of the older men followed Robert, as still their rightful abbot, to Rome, where the Pope Alexander, once a pupil of Lanfranc's at Bec, received him hospitably; and the monastery suffered much from its lay neighbours, who took advantage of the quarrel to annoy and plunder the monks. Osbern remained with terrible torments of conscience. He at last made a humble submission to the Pope, and was formally allowed to keep the place into which he had been intruded. "He was from his childhood," says Orderic, "very learned in letters, eloquent of speech, and exceedingly ingenious in all kinds of handicraft: such as carving, building, writing, and the like; he was of middle stature, well grown, with his head completely loaded with black hair or white. He was harsh to the silly and froward, merciful to the sick and poor, fairly liberal to people outside, fervent in discipline, a most skilful provider of all that the brethren needed, spiritually or bodily. He kept the youths in very severe order, and compelled them by word and stripes to read and sing and write well. He himself with his own hands made the writing tablets for the children and the unlearned, and prepared frames, covered with wax, and required from them daily the due portion of work appointed to each. Thus driving away idleness, he laid on their youthful minds wholesome burdens." Robert sought a new home in Apulia among his Norman fellow-countrymen. He founded three monasteries in Italy. He came back afterwards and made his peace with William; but he did not regain his abbey, and found Normandy no place for him. But Orderic rejoices that by his means, "in three monasteries of Italy, the chant of St. Evroul is sung, and its monastic order observed to this day, as far as the opportunity of that country and the love of those who dwell in it allow."

The vicissitudes of St. Evroul are a contrast to the tranquillity of Bec; but they did not prevent St. Evroul from being a flourishing establishment. "The Abbey of Ouche or St. Evroul," says Mr. Freeman, "has its own claim on our respect. It was the spot which beheld the composition of the record from which we draw our main knowledge of the times following those with which we have to deal: it was the home of the man in whom, perhaps more than in any other, the characters of Normans and Englishmen were inseparably mingled. There the historian wrote, who, though the son of a French father, the denizen of a Norman monastery, still clung to England as his country and gloried in his English birth — the historian who could at once admire the greatness of the Conqueror and sympathise with the wrongs of his victims, who, amid all the conventional reviling which Norman loyalty prescribed, could still see and acknowledge with genuine admiration the virtues and the greatness even of the perjured Harold. To have merely produced a chronicler may seem faint praise beside the fame of producing men whose career has had a lasting influence on the human mind; yet, even beside the long bead-roll of the worthies of Bec, some thoughts may well be extended to the house where Orderic recorded the minutest details alike of the saints and of the warriors of his time."

Orderic's picture of himself, as he has incidentally disclosed it, is not unworthy, in its pathetic and simple truthfulness, to stand beside the grander objects of interest in the age to which he belonged.

Orderic was the English-born son of a French father, Odeler of Orleans, who had accompanied one of the most powerful and most trusted of William's barons into England, Roger of Montgomery, the husband of the fierce Countess Mabel of Belesme, heiress of that wicked house of Talvas, from which the sword seemed never to depart. In England, Roger of Montgomery and Belesme had become lord of Arundel and the Sussex shore, and then, in addition, Earl of Shrewsbury; and he guarded the northern marches against the Welsh, whom he "mightily oppressed," after the fashion in which Elizabeth's warriors kept in check the Irish. Of this great lord, Odeler was a confidential and favoured cleric. He was a priest, and he was, or had been, married; and the way in which Orderic, one of his three sons, became a monk of the Norman house of St. Evroul, is a curious example of the habits of the time. Whatever the great earl was to others, to his clerical family he turned a good side; "he was wise and moderate, and a lover of justice," says Orderic, repeating probably the received judgment of his father's house, "and he loved the company of wise and modest men. He kept for a long time three wise clerks with him—Godbald, Odeler, and Herbert—to whose advice he profitably listened." Like others of his time, he was a bountiful benefactor to the religious foundations of France and Normandy, from the spoils of England: St. Stephen's at Caen, Cluni, Troarn, and others received from him English lands; and after having done much mischief to the house of St. Evroul, in the lifetime of his cruel wife, the Countess Mabel, who hunted its founders to death, he afterwards atoned for his ill deeds by large benefactions of rents, churches, and lands on both sides of the Channel. Odeler persuaded his patron to make amends for his offences, and to save something from the perishing goods of time, by founding a monastery near Shrewsbury—"a castle of monks," as Orderic calls it in the quaint speech which he makes his father address to the "glorious consul," to be built for God against Satan, "where cowled champions (*pugiles*) may resist Behemoth in continual battle." He himself offered a site, and half his property; the other half was to be held of the monks by one of his three sons; he offered himself, he offered another son, a boy of five years old; and his eldest child Orderic, a boy at school, he absolutely gave up for the love of the Redeemer, to be separated from him for ever, and sent across the sea, "where, an exile of his own accord, he might be a soldier of the King of heaven among strangers, and, free from all mischievous regard and tenderness of relations, he might flourish excellently in monastic observance and the service of the Lord." "He had provided for him a safe place of abode among the servants of God at St. Evroul in Normandy; and he had given of his substance 30 marks of silver to his masters and companions, as a thank-offering of blessing." "He had long desired thus to devote himself and his family to the service of the Lord, that in the day of account he with his children might be counted worthy to stand among the elect of God."

His proposal was approved by the Earl, and by the Earl's vassals, whose assent was asked: the monastery was built and endowed with gifts from friends; monks from Séez were brought over to start it, and the gift of Earl Roger, comprising a suburb of the town, was offered on the altar to St. Peter by the symbol of the founder's gloves. "This," says Orderic, who long afterwards tells the story, "is a digression, be it of what account it may, about the building of the monastery on my father's land, which is now inhabited by the family of Christ, and where my father himself, as I remember, an old man of sixty, willingly bore to the end the yoke of Christ. Forgive me, good reader, and let it not be an offence to thee, I pray thee, if I commit to record something about my father, whom I have never seen, since the time when, as if I had been a hated step-child, he sent me forth for the love of his Maker, into exile. It is now forty-two years ago, and in those years many changes have been, far and wide, in the world. While I often think of these things, and some of them commit to my paper, carefully resisting idleness, I thus exercise myself in inditing them. Now I return to my work, and speak to those younger than myself,—a stranger, to those of the country,—about their own affairs, things that they know not; and in this way by God's help do them useful service."

In the same strain of perfectly resigned and contented confidence in his lot and his hopes, yet of pensive and affectionate yearning to the now distant days of his boyhood, and to the scenes and men about his father's house where it was passed, and where he had his last sight of his father—the chapel where he was baptized, the altar where he served, the good prior who taught him letters—he concludes the long work of his life; and finishes in a solemn appeal and earnest commendation to the God whom he has served, not unbecoming one whose lifelong study had been the Book of Psalms :—

"Behold, worn out with age and infirmity, I desire to end my work, and for many reasons prudence requires it. For I am now [1141] passing the sixty-seventh year of my age in the worship of my Lord Jesus Christ, and while I see the foremost men of this world crushed by heavy disasters of the most opposite sort, I dance for joy, in the safe estate of obedience and poverty. There is Stephen, king of the English, sighing in prison; and Lewis, king of the French, leading an expedition against the Goths and Gascons, is vexed with many and frequent cares. There is the church of Lisieux, whose bishop is dead, and which is without a pastor; and when it will have one, and of what sort, I know not. What shall I say more? Amid these things, I turn my speech to thee, O Almighty God, and with double force beseech thy goodness that thou wouldest have mercy on me. I give thee thanks, O King most high, who didst freely make me, and hast ordered my years according to thy good pleasure. For thou art my King and my God, and I am thy servant and the son of thine handmaid, who, from the first days of my life, according to my power, have served thee. For on Easter eve I was baptized at Attingesham [Atcham], which village is in England on the Severn, that great river of Severn. There, by the ministry of Ordric the priest, thou didst regenerate me by water and the Holy Ghost, and didst put upon me the name of the same priest, my god-father. Then, when I was five years old, I was delivered over to school in the city of Shrewsbury, and there I offered to thee the first services of clerkship in the Church of the holy apostles, St. Peter and St. Paul. There Sigward, the famous priest, taught me for five years the letters of the Camena Nicostrata,[1] and broke me in to psalms and hymns and other necessary instructions; meanwhile, thou didst exalt the aforesaid church, built on the river Mole, which belonged to my father, and by the pious devotion of Count Roger didst build there a venerable monastery. It did not seem fit to thee that I should longer be thy soldier there, lest with my relations, who often to thy servants are a burden and hindrance, I should suffer some disquiet, or run into some loss in the fulfilment of thy law through the carnal affection of my relations. Therefore, O glorious God, who didst command Abraham to go forth from his country and his father's house and kindred, thou didst put into the heart of Odeler my father, to give up all his claim in me, and to put me absolutely under thy yoke. So he delivered me to Rainald the monk, a weeping father his weeping child, and for the love of thee appointed me to banishment ; and he never saw me afterwards. Young boy as I was I took not on me to dispute my father's wishes, but in everything I willingly assented, for he had promised on his part that, if I would become a monk, I should after my death possess Paradise with the innocent.

---

[1] That is, the alphabet, the invention of the Muse Nicostrata ; a bit of Orderic's erudition. *Vide* Dict. Biog. and Mythol. art. *Camenæ*, and *Hyginus.*

Gladly was this engagement made between me and thee, my father being its minister; and I left behind my native country and my parents and all my kin, and my acquaintance and friends, and they, weeping and bidding me farewell, with loving prayers, commended me to thee, O most high Lord God. Hear their supplications, I beseech thee, and graciously grant what they desired, O merciful King of Sabaoth.

"So being ten years old I crossed the British Sea, and came an exile to Normandy, where, unknown to all, I knew no man. Like Joseph in Egypt, I heard a strange language. Yet by the help of thy favour, among these strangers I found all gentleness and friendliness. In the eleventh year of my age, I was received to the monastic life by the venerable Abbot Mainer, in the monastery of Ouche, and on Sunday, the 21st of September [1085], I was tonsured after the manner of clerks, and for my English name, which sounded harsh to Normans, the name of Vitalis was given me, borrowed from one of the companions of St. Maurice the martyr, whose martyrdom was then celebrated [Sept. 22]. In this house for fifty-six years, by thy favour, have I had my conversation, and by all the brethren and dwellers in it I have been loved and honoured much more than I deserved. Heat and cold and the burden of the day have I endured, labouring among thine own in the 'vineyard of Sorech;'[1] and the 'penny' which thou hast promised I have confidently waited for, for thou art faithful. Six abbots have I reverenced as my fathers and masters, because they were in thy place: Mainer and Serlo, Roger and Guarin, Richard and Ranulf. They were

[1] The vineyard planted with "choice vine" (Isa. v. 2).

the lawful heads of the convent of Ouche; for me and for others they kept watch, as those who must give account; within and abroad they used good husbandry, and, with thee for their companion and helper, provided all things necessary for us. On March 15 [1091], when I was sixteen years old, at the bidding of Serlo, our abbot-elect, Gilbert, Bishop of Lisieux, ordained me sub-deacon. Then after two years, on the 26th of March [1093], Serlo, Bishop of Séez, laid on me the office of deacon, in which grade I gladly ministered to thee fifteen years. Lastly, in the thirty-third year of my age, William, Archbishop of Rouen, on the 21st of December [1107] laid on me the burden of the priesthood. On the same day, he ordained 244 deacons and 120 priests, with whom, in the Holy Ghost, I devoutly approached thy holy altar, and have now for thirty-four years faithfully performed thy service unto thee with a willing mind.

"Thus, thus, O Lord my God, my Maker and the Giver of my life, hast thou through different steps bestowed on me freely thy gifts, and duly ordered my years for thy service. In all the places whither thou hast so far led me, thou hast caused me to find love, not by my deserts but by thy favour. For all thy benefits, O gracious Father, I give thee thanks, with my whole heart I laud and bless thee; and for all my numberless offences, I with tears beseech thy mercy. Spare me, O Lord, spare me, and let me not be confounded. According to thy goodness, which cannot be wearied, look pitifully on thy handiwork, and forgive and wash away all my sins. Give me a will which shall persevere in thy service, and strength that fails not against the craft and malice of Satan, till by thy gift I attain the inheritance of everlasting salvation. And the things which I ask for myself, both here and hereafter, O gracious God, those I wish for my friends and benefactors : those too I earnestly desire according to thy wise ordering for all thy faithful ones. The worth of our own deserts sufficeth not to obtain those everlasting good things, which, with burning desire, the longings of the perfect yearn after. Therefore, O Lord God, Father Almighty, Maker and Ruler of the angels, true hope and eternal blessedness of the righteous, therefore let the glorious intercession help us in thy sight, of the Holy Virgin and Mother Mary and of all the Saints, by the mercy of our Lord Jesus Christ, the Redeemer of all, who liveth and reigneth with thee in the unity of the Holy Ghost, God for ever and ever. Amen."

There is something very touching in the way in which the old man of nearly seventy, broken in and hardened to the stern life of a Norman abbey, cannot help, in the midst of other subjects, going back to the days of boyhood, when he served at the altar and went to school in England by the banks of the Severn, and recalls the bitter days of parting, and his first dreary dwelling in that strange land which had become so familiar to him. There is thankfulness, hearty and sincere, for that ordering of his life, which, hard as had been its conditions, made him a monk ; a thankfulness like that of the patriarch Jacob to his father's God, "which had fed him all his life long;" a thankfulness not perhaps heroic, but simple, genuine, and tender, for having been preserved and fenced round from the storms of a wild and naughty world. But the rigid rule and austere ideas of his profession had left his feelings quick and warm. They had been chastened and brought into subjection; but they kept their place. There was no suppression of natural affection in the old monk whose thoughts dwelt so pathetically on the "weeping" father who had given him up, and "whom he had never seen again;" only a subordination of it to higher purposes, a short parting here for an endless meeting at last. And this warm human interest and power of sympathy mingling, often quaintly enough, with the harshnesses and abrupt severities of his age and of his profession, are the characteristic features of Orderic as a painter of his times. He caught the spirit of work and the horror of idleness which were at this time keen and dominant in the Norman cloisters; and it is curious, and almost affecting, to see how, with such wretched tools as he had in the way of books and language, such an undeveloped stage of intellectual cultivation, such poor and limited possibilities of understanding the world about him and its laws, and what was excellent in the specimens which he had of ancient perfection in thought and expression, he threw himself enthusiastically into the task of setting forth, with life and truthfulness, the state of things amid which he lived, and of connecting with it the story of the world. His superiors found out that he had the power of words and of telling a story, in the learned style fit for clerks who aimed at being lettered men; and they set him to work to record, first the matters of interest to the house, and then other things. Never was there such a mass of confusion as the book, as it grew under his hands for some twenty years or more; it is the torment and despair of historians, who yet find in it some of their best material. Of the style, an English reader may best form an idea by combining the biblical pedantry and doggrel of a Fifth-monarchy pamphlet of the 17th century with the classical pedantry of the most extravagant burlesques of Dr. Johnson's English In Orderic, Greek words play the part which Latin ones play in English bombast. There is no reason to think that he knew Greek; but he had picked up Greek words, partly in the Latin fathers, partly in glossaries and interpretations: he parades them, as a child parades its finery or mock jewels, in his more commonplace Latin; and the effect undoubtedly is inexpressible, though not exactly in the way which he intended. Then, being a man of letters, and having read old Roman authors, he thinks it his duty to express the facts of Norman life as much as he can in the terms of the great days of old: Norman ruffians, whose abominable brutalities he describes, are "heroes;" counts and barons are "consuls and consular men;" a feudal array of Englishmen or Normans is officered by "tribunes and centurions." But every age has its attempts at the grand style; and Orderic's, grotesque as it is, is childishly innocent. For all this, Orderic can see what is before him, and can say what he sees and what he means. He is clumsy, disorderly, full of rambling digressions, with one portion of his account in one place, and the rest of it in another; he does not always remember what he has said, and is by no means to be trusted for accuracy. But he had been, for his opportunities, a zealous and painstaking reader. He had an eye and a care and interest for details and for points of character. And he had a remarkable respect for what seemed to him all the facts of a transaction or a character, whether or not they looked very consistent or compatible when they were put side by side on paper. His sketches of men have sometimes the faithful awkwardness of a bad photograph; the life and expression which reconciled incongruities are not there, but there are the actual things to be seen, ugly and fair together. But there is more than this. Orderic had the Christian—may we say, the English?—spirit of justice. He knew a great man when he saw him; but he saw too what was evil and cruel and mean, even in a great man, and he was not afraid to say it. Profoundly impressed, as most of his contemporaries were, with the awful vicissitudes of human life, and expressing this feeling often in terms which, in their force and simplicity, contrast remarkably with the laboured grandiloquence of the rest of the book, he was more sensible than most about him not only that right was not always with the victorious, but that truth and justice were not always undivided on one side.

From him we get, without fear or favour, the most lively image of what real life seemed to the dweller in a Norman monastery, brought in contact with a great variety of men, with a great and unceasing movement all round him, with great enterprises in the world on foot and in progress, like the Eastern wars, and the gigantic schemes of ecclesiastical policy of the Popes. Sometimes a traveller, Orderic speaks of what he himself saw at Worcester, at Croyland, at Cambray, or at Cluni; more often, hearing the stories or watching the ways of travellers who availed themselves on their journey of the hospitality of St. Evroul, or who sought its shelter for their old age. It is as lively as real life, and also as confused and unassorted. Nothing comes amiss to him—a family history, with the fate of all the members of the house—a great revolution like the conquest and subjection of England—the detailed account, often spirited and vivid, of a deed of arms or a siege; details, equally particular, and though not so vivid yet quite as curious, of the customs and transactions of the time, relating to property, to sales and gifts and rents, and to the various ways in which property was transferred, preserved, or lost; details of the monastic profession, in itself a world of its own, with its vicissitudes, its triumphs, its jealousies, its disasters, its conflicts, its quarrels, its scandals; the manners, the tastes, the occupations, the singularities, the personal appearance, the red hair, or rubicund visage, or short stature, or passionate temper, or shrewd ways, of this or that famous abbot or bishop;—bits of description of natural phenomena, such as remarkable thunderstorms, or flights of falling stars;—repetitions of supernatural and Dantesque legends which had been told in the cloister, or of the stories brought back from the Crusades, bearing on them the mark of the highly excited imagination of the pilgrims who told them;— carefully weighed and balanced summaries of the characters of the great people who pass across his scene, or still better, brief forcible touches, evidently from direct impression, of some leading feature in the abbots or bishops, the barons or knights, and by no means least, the ladies, of that wild time and turbulent society. His great work is a mixture of important history, curious gossip of the country-side, judgments on persons and things, which but for their form would not discredit a professed moralist of sarcastic humour; orations composed with dignity, and put into the mouths of great persons, because the Latin historians did the same; and dry annals from the creation or the flood, down to the current year. He is always in danger of mistaking the true means of producing the real effect of things, as it impresses his own feeling; of expressing his sense of what is great, or eventful, or tragic, by inflated words, or of representing what he intends for picturesqueness and vividness by some ridiculously chosen epithet or some grotesque bit of pedantry. But he is not always on his stilts, and often forgets himself, at least for some sentences; and then he writes with discrimination, clearness, and force; his sense of the absurd and ridiculous gets for a moment, at all risk of indecorum, out of the stiff shell of his erudition; and in the story of some pathetic scene, the last moments, for instance, and the leave-taking of some religious man, or the fate of some former favourite of fortune, he is simple, touching, and impressive. These pictures—though of course there is something conventional in them, and where the occasion seems to demand it, the temptation to be rhetorical is irresistible—are many of them remarkably distinct, unlike in their circumstances to any other, each with its own colour and expression and individual character. He saw great things and great men: not insensible to their greatness, he was still more deeply impressed with the awful contrasts of this mortal state, and the tremendous march and lessons of God's providence; and through the disfigurement of much ignorance, and turgid writing, and bad taste, it is impossible not to discern and recognize the genuine spirit of faith, the profound and overwhelming sense of the living and supreme government and justice of Almighty God.

# CHAPTER VI

### ECCLESIASTICAL ADMINISTRATION OF WILLIAM.

" The vast frame
Of social nature changes evermore
Her organs and her members with decay
Restless, and restless generation, powers
And functions dying and produced at need,—
And by this law the mighty whole subsists:
With an ascent and progress in the main ;
Yet oh ! how disproportioned to the hopes
And expectations of self-flattering minds."
WORDSWORTH, *Excursion*, b. vii.

ANSELM'S life, before he came to England, nearly coincided with the reign of William the Bastard, as Duke of Normandy, and then as King of England. Anselm was born in 1033. In 1035, Robert the Great Duke, Robert the Devil, died on his Eastern pilgrimage far from home, at Nicæa; and left his son of seven years old, with the stain of his birth upon him, to meet the scorn and to tame the anarchy of Normandy. In the same year also, 1035, died the other mighty representative of the Norsemen's victory, the great Cnut, leaving in almost equal confusion the realm which, thirty-one years after, the Norman boy-prince, whose reign began with such dark and threatening signs, was to wrest from its right owner, and unite to Normandy by a conquest the most eventful for good and for evil in the history of Christian Europe. Anselm's life, like the years of the house of Bec, nearly began with the beginning of the Conqueror's reign; and very shortly after the Conqueror's death (1087), the great change in Anselm's fortune came, which transferred him to a new scene, and connected him henceforth with England.

Thus his life, up to the time when he became archbishop, extended almost exactly over the period which saw the moral awakening and the first serious attempts at religious reform and political organization in Normandy. Of these attempts it is too much to say that the impulse came alone from Duke William; but in no one was the improving spirit of the time more powerful, and in no one, according to the measure of the age, did it find a more intelligent and resolute minister. In his latter days, hard and unscrupulous as he was, an honest and large-hearted purpose in favour of order and right directed his government, whenever an irresistible ambition did not overpower every other thought and feeling.

Anselm arrived in Normandy when the poor helpless boy, who had begun to reign just when he himself was born, had grown up, through disaster, treachery, and appalling dangers, into the greatest man of Western Europe, who at nineteen had beaten down domestic rebellion at Val-ès-Dunes (1047), whose hand had been heavy on his neighbours, on Anjou and Maine, who had taught the French invaders and the French king a stern lesson, once and again, at Mortemer (1054) and Varaville (1058). The religious movement which had begun with the century had gained strength with the progress of William's power, and was taking full possession of the Norman Church. William himself was deeply affected by it. The vague position of a royal patron of the Church, fitfully using his power from caprice or temper, had with him passed into that of a jealous and intelligent guardian, watching over all that went on in churches and monasteries, claiming great powers of interference, but interfering with an object and on a system. The interests of religion, as he understood them, were scarcely less a matter of his solicitude than the political affairs of his duchy. To his ambition they, like every moral restraint, were subordinate; sometimes probably they were so to his personal prepossessions: but, on the whole, he had it distinctly in view to raise the tone of feeling, duty, and life, and by his appointments and general policy, as well as by his personal strictness and self-restraint, to check licence and disorder, and to encourage the reality of religious effort. The customs of Normandy, as of other Western countries, allowed him great powers in the Church; and, giving them fresh significance from the edge which he put upon them and the manifest intention with which he used them, he shaped them into a strong weapon for making his authority felt in the fierce and unruly society in which men then had to pass their days.

In the government of mankind at that time, in their religious as well as their political life, three powers may be discerned—law, deliberately settled on some reasonable ground; custom; and personal character and force. Of these three, law, as we understand it, was the weakest, personal action the strongest; but though law was a very small restraint on personal will, custom was a considerable one; and though law was as yet weak, it was the growing element. In various shapes, some very questionable and even disastrous ones, it was beginning to assert its superior claims in contrast with mere custom, and the will, in a good direction or a bad, of individual holders of power. The monasteries with their rules had kept up even in the darkest times the idea of equal and real law, in however confined a range, when the canons of the Church and the laws of the Empire had alike lost their force; the Italian municipalities had also not entirely forgotten the traditions and the use of Roman jurisprudence; and now, both in the political state and in the Church, the statesmen of the age, emperors and pontiffs, were beginning to understand the importance of a system of law, based on principles of universal application, armed with due authority, and enforcing its decisions. The emperors and their adherents looked for it in the civil law of Rome adapted to a feudal state of society; the popes and their partisans had begun to build up the great structure of the Canon Law. Both attempts partook of the coarseness, the mingled rigour and looseness, the inexperience, the necessary ignorance of the time; both, though they were not without much honest purpose to promote and defend right and establish a fixed order for human life, were partial, incomplete, liable to deviate before the prejudices of the many or the selfishness of the strong; both were still fatally influenced by the dominant belief in the claims of personal authority; and one at least was based on forgery and fraud, the parents of a still unexhausted train of mischiefs even to this day. Yet they were the beginnings, perhaps in those times the only possible beginnings, of law. They brought the notion of it prominently before mankind. They furnished examples of it, and with all their shortcomings they excite our interest and deserve our respect, as the forerunners and first essays of those nobler achievements of happier times, the fruit, not yet matured, of the experiments, the mistakes and the late wisdom of so many ages, by which the face of society has been changed.

The impulse, more in its religious than its political character, was approaching Normandy; but there it was still fitful and weak. Custom ruled ordinarily; but when a strong and able man showed himself, his was the influence to which all others bowed or adapted themselves. A reformer and organizer in wild and ignorant days means a man who, with a clearer sight than his brethren, and on the whole higher and wider objects, has a heavy hand and an inflexible will. Such was William. William, accordingly, exercised without question, and as a matter of course, an authority in the Norman Church which in general character differed little from the Tudor supremacy, and which a few years later, and in different hands, was resented as an intolerable grievance, and became the occasion of fierce conflicts. He was the real active head of the government, in the Church as in the State; and no one thought it strange that he should be. He appointed the bishops, not always perhaps in the same manner; sometimes apparently by his sole choice, sometimes with consultation and assent of his chief men. He invested them with their office by the delivery of the pastoral staff, and they became "his men" and owed him service like his military lords: if he had charges against them, they were tried by his council and deposed by his authority. So with the abbots of the chief monasteries: either he appointed them directly himself, or he gave leave to the monks to elect; but in any case their choice had to be confirmed by him, and he conferred the dignity by the pastoral staff. If a monastery was to be founded, his consent had to be obtained; probably not by any distinct law, but because such a foundation would be utterly insecure without the allowance and guaranteed protection of the Duke, who was the general guardian of the peace of his land. If a monastery got into trouble from internal quarrels, the Duke was appealed to, and he sent down a commission to investigate and restore peace. Ecclesiastical as well as civil causes came to his court; over churchmen as well as laymen he asserted his authority, and both equally resorted to his justice. And it was not only as an arbiter and judge, but as a visitor and overseer, acting from himself, and carrying out purposes of his own, that he interposed in Church affairs. He asserted and exercised his right to correct, to reform, to legislate for the Church, and no one thought of contradicting him.

Orderic gives both sides of William's character, and in giving one sometimes forgets the necessary qualifications implied in the other. But undoubtedly there was a real basis of fact in the following judgment, written after William's death:—

"King William was famous and deserved praise for his zeal and love for many sorts of worth in many sorts of men; but above all things he ever loved in God's servants true religion, to which sometimes peace and worldly prosperity minister. This is witnessed by wide-spread notoriety, and proved beyond question by the evidence of deeds. For when any chief shepherd finished his course and passed from this world, and the Church of God in widowhood mourned for its proper ruler, the prince with due care sent prudent delegates to the house which was without its head, and caused all the church possessions to be inventoried, lest they should be wasted by irreligious guardians. Then he called together bishops and abbots and other wise counsellors, and by their advice inquired very carefully who was the best and wisest man, as well in divine things as in worldly, to rule the house of God. Then the person who, for the goodness of his life and for his learning and wisdom, was selected by the judgment of the wise, the gracious king made the ruler and steward of the bishopric or abbacy. This observance he kept for fifty-six years (?), during which he bore rule in the duchy of Normandy or in the kingdom of England; and by this he left a religious custom and example to those who come after. The heresy of simony he utterly abhorred, and therefore in choosing abbots and bishops he considered not so much men's riches or power, as their holiness and wisdom. He set persons approved in excellence over the monasteries of England; by whose zeal and strictness the estate of monastic life, which had somewhat languished, revived, and where it seemed to have failed, rose up again to its former vigour."

Eadmer, writing after the supremacy of the Conqueror had developed into the tyranny of his sons, thus describes the nature of his claims, the "usages" on which he governed.

"Wishing, therefore, to keep in England the usages

and laws which he and his fathers were wont to have in Normandy, he appointed throughout the land bishops, abbots, and other chief men from among persons in whom it would have been judged unseemly, if they did not obey his laws in all things, laying aside every other consideration, or if any of them, by the power of any earthly honour, dared to raise his head against him; for every one knew from whence and for what they were chosen, and who they were. All things therefore, divine and human, waited on his nod. To understand what this came to, I will put down some of the novelties which he caused to be observed throughout England; thinking them necessary to be known, for the understanding of that which I have undertaken to write about. He would, then, suffer no one in all his dominions to receive the Bishop of the city of Rome for the Apostle's Vicar, unless by his command, or in any wise to receive his letters, unless they had first been shown to himself. Further, he would not suffer the Primate of his kingdom, the Archbishop of Canterbury, if he were presiding over a general council of the bishops, to establish or forbid anything, unless what was agreeable to his will, and had first been ordained by him. To none of his bishops, nevertheless, did he permit that it should be allowed to implead publicly or excommunicate any of his barons or servants charged with incest or adultery, or any great crime, except by his precept, or to compel them by any penalty of ecclesiastical severity."

The character of this authority will be best seen in two or three instances—in the part which the Duke takes in the foundation and internal affairs of an abbey, that of St. Evroul; and as regards Church legislation, in the proceedings of two great Norman assemblies, in which he attempted to lay down, in the rude form, familiar to the times, of canons and decrees, the principles of law as opposed to custom or mere will, to which he proposed to make both the clergy and the people generally conform themselves.

In 1050, four Norman nobles, William and Robert, the sons of Geroy, and Hugh and Robert, sons of Robert of Grentmaisnil, having resolved to found a monastery on the spot consecrated by the abode and memory of a saint, St. Ebrulfus or St. Evroul, and to give certain lands for its support, "went to William the Duke of the Normans and opened to him their will, and besought him to help them in their salutary work by his authority as prince. Further, the above-named place they by common consent committed to his guardianship, so that neither to themselves nor to any other should it ever be lawful to exact from the monks or their men any custom or rent, save the benefits of their prayers. The Duke gladly assented to their good wish, and confirmed the disposition of the property which his nobles gave to St. Evroul, and delivered the deed to Malger, the Archbishop of Rouen, and to his suffragan bishops, to be confirmed by their subscriptions. Then Hugh and Robert, having received from the Duke licence to choose an abbot," go to Jumiéges, and ask for a monk of Jumiéges, Theodoric, for the first head of their monastery. Then they present him to the Duke, and the Duke, "receiving him with due reverence, and having given him, as the custom is, the pastoral staff, set him over the Church of Ouche;" and then he is consecrated by the Bishop of Lisieux. That was the customary process in founding a monastic house. In the progress of the history of St. Evroul, the same taking for granted of the Duke's supreme authority to arrange, to sanction, and to redress wrong appears. The Duke grants his privilege that the monastery may be for ever free and exempt from all external authority. The Duke grants to the brethren the right to elect their own abbot, so that they observe the rule of discipline, and are not influenced by friendship or kindred, or love of money. The Duke commands the Archbishop of Rouen and his bishops to confirm his grants, by making excommunication the penalty of violating them. When quarrels arose, and the Abbot Theodoric wishes to get rid of his burdens, he desires "to resign to William Duke of the Normans his pastoral staff." William, acting as a visitor, orders the Archbishop of Rouen to send down a commission, Lanfranc among them, to inquire and make peace. When, in spite of this, the poor old abbot is worried by the quarrels and intrigues of his flock into running away on a pilgrimage to Jerusalem, the newly-elected abbot, his enemy, Prior Robert de Grentmaisnil, is presented to the Duke for approval and confirmation, and receive from the Duke the entire power of the abbacy, by means of the crosier of Bishop Ivo of Séez, and "the care of souls," by the benediction of Bishop William of Evreux. Abbot Robert became mixed up, about 1063, with the factions of the Norman nobles. He fell under William's displeasure, and was cited to appear at the Duke's court to answer for certain crimes of which he was accused—falsely, says the historian of St. Evroul. But Robert, whether guilty or not, preferred to seek his safety by leaving Nor-

mandy, and repaired to Rome to lay his case before
the Pope. On this William, without scruple or hesita-
tion, at once filled up his vacancy. No mention is
made by Orderic of any trial, of any deposition by
ecclesiastical authority. But "the Norman Duke,"
says Orderic, "by the counsel of the venerable
Ansfred Abbot of Préaux, and Lanfranc Prior of
Bec, and other ecclesiastical persons," summoned
Osbern Prior of Cormeilles, and without giving him
any notice, "committed to him the care of the Abbey
of Ouche by the crosier of Maurilius the Archbishop,
in a synod at Rouen. Thence, Hugh Bishop of
Lisieux, by the Duke's order, conducted him to
Préaux, and there, without the knowledge of the
monks of St. Evroul, consecrated him abbot, and afterwards conducted him to Ouche, and by the Duke's
command set him over the sorrowful monks. They
were in trouble, with danger on both sides. For in the
lifetime of their abbot [Robert de Grentmaisnil], who
had founded their church and received them to their
estate of monks, and had been driven out, without
reasonable grounds of charge, not by the judgment
of a synod, but by the tyranny of the angry Marquis"
(a piece of rhetoric of Orderic's, for the more common title of count or duke), "they hesitated to
receive another abbot; and, on the other hand, they
dared not openly refuse him on account of the wrath
of the Duke. At length, by the advice of Bishop
Hugh, they chose to suffer violence, and voluntarily to
show obedience to the master given them, lest, if they
continued without the yoke, they should offend the
power of God, and rouse the ill-will of the Duke to
greater violence, to the destruction of the recently

founded house." The Duke was not able to prevent the grievous tribulation which fell on the unfortunate monks from the harrying of their house and lands by Abbot Robert's kinsmen and friends, or from their internal dissensions and bitter heart-burnings. He was not able to hinder the scruples and troubles of conscience of the new abbot, who felt himself an intruder, and found himself in a nest of hornets. But the Duke kept him there; and his answer when Robert returned, backed by papal legates, to reclaim his abbey, was that straightforward declaration which has already been noticed, that he would gladly confer with the Pope's messengers about religious matters; but that any monk who questioned his authority at home, he would hang without scruple to the highest tree in the next wood. Abbot Robert did not wait to try whether he would be as good as his word. From a safe distance he cited Osbern, who dared not obey, to appear before the Roman cardinals, and excommunicated him. A number of the principal monks left the monastery to join their late head. Osbern would gladly have resigned, if he had dared; but he stayed on in fear, and with an unquiet conscience. The monastery recovered and flourished under him. Robert in after years was reconciled to William, but he could not regain his abbey. And Osbern satisfied his own scruples by addressing a letter of apology and satisfaction to Pope Alexander, "Supreme Head of the Church on earth;" while the Pope, by the advice of Robert himself, made the best of the case, and, absolving Osbern, left him where he was.

And what William did with unsatisfactory or troublesome abbots, he was quite as ready to do with unsatisfactory or troublesome bishops. His uncle Malger, whom William's counsellors in his boyhood had made Archbishop of Rouen, who had held the great see without troubling himself about the Pope's benediction and pall, and who had lived the life of a magnificent noble, given much more to hunting and cock-fighting than to episcopal duties, and caring very little about the canons of the Church, had offended William. In an age of reviving strictness his manner of life was not edifying. Moreover, his brother was the leader of one of the revolts against William, and the archbishop was accused of encouraging the rebellion; finally, in spite of his own laxity, he threw himself strongly into the ecclesiastical opposition to William's marriage, and we even hear of excommunication either pronounced or threatened by him. Nevertheless, though in this matter the Pope was with him, and William had married in spite of the Pope and the alleged canonical impediment, William was too strong for him. Malger was deposed at a council at Lisieux, at which a papal legate was present; and whatever may have been the forms observed, in the natural language of the writers of the time, the act of deposition is ascribed to William. It is one of the puzzles of the confused politics of the Church and State struggle just beginning, and of our incomplete information about them, to find a papal legate presiding in one of William's councils, while William was still defying the Pope's formal prohibition as regards his marriage, and helping or allowing William to depose a great ecclesiastic who, whatever his faults, had, apparently alone, attempted to enforce that prohibition. But there does not seem to have been anything surprising in it to William's contemporaries and chroniclers; they relate without remark, as part of the ordinary course of things, the exercise of his authority in deposing from Church offices as in appointing to them. And, independently of custom, which was, in fact, now beginning to be broken into, the reason is on the surface. William's general policy was thoroughly in harmony with the resolute and austere spirit of reform which was gaining power in the Norman Church, and his own feelings to a great extent sympathised with it. Self-willed, ambitious, and hard as he was, he hated lawlessness and disorder, and with very sincere purpose went along with the efforts of the earnest men round him, to purify and strengthen what the time understood as religion. He set at naught ecclesiastical impediments in the way of his marriage, possibly not very intelligible ones; he cared not the more about them, even when formally declared by a Pope in council; but few royal husbands have loved and honoured their wives as William, in that fierce and licentious age, loved and honoured Matilda. He deposed Archbishop Malger, whose life was scandalous, and who was further personally obnoxious to himself; but he filled his place, once and again, by men who redeemed the great see of Rouen from its long shame, and lived as serious Christian bishops, and not as wild princes of the ducal family, without fear and without law. "A prelate of a very different stamp from Malger," says Mr. Freeman, "succeeded him on the metropolitan throne of Rouen. William had now fully learned that the high places of the Church could not be rightly turned into mere provisions for the younger members of sovereign houses. He determined to give the Norman Church a thoroughly worthy chief pastor, and in his choice he overlooked all prejudices of family, and even of nation. This willingness to recognize the claims of merit in strangers from every land has been already spoken of as one of the marked features of the Norman national character. The new primate, Maurilius, was a man of foreign birth, who had seen much of various parts of the world, and who seems to have made choice of Normandy as his adopted country. His career in many respects reminds us of that of Lanfranc, with this difference, that the earlier years of Lanfranc were spent in a character wholly lay, while Maurilius had first entered the ecclesiastical calling as a secular priest." He had spent his life in seeking, in different lands, new opportunities of religious service ; and, in his last appointment, he left a saintly and venerable name, which did honour to William's choice. A reformer of clerical life, a church-builder and restorer, the friend and adviser of Anselm, he was succeeded by men of the same sort: John, a headstrong and injudicious champion of discipline, and the gentler William "Bonne-âme." Lanfranc, who, on the death of Maurilius, was wished for as his successor by the Church of Rouen, but not apparently by William, was possibly denied to Rouen because he was intended for Canterbury.

William's high prerogative in the Church was no doubt less strange and less unquestioned, because he was so keenly interested in what was supposed to affect its welfare. "Everything," says Mr. Freeman, speaking of the way in which William's part in a council at

Rouen for Church discipline is incidentally noticed in the original account—"everything bears witness alike to the ecclesiastical supremacy of the Norman dukes and of the personal zeal of William in all ecclesiastical matters." There is a kind of indefinite but very vigorous authority implied in respect to his constitutional position, as if Norman lords and Norman bishops were all of one great household, with William at their head, taking a paternal oversight of all its concerns, and keeping every member of it up to his duty. Orderic's way of describing William's relation to two remarkable assemblies shows how natural it was, to those who had known William, to think of him as the foremost figure in them, taking the initiative before archbishops and bishops, tracing out their work, and whether he left it to them to do or joined himself with them, still without rival the chief authority over them. In 1072, a council purely ecclesiastical was held at Rouen. Its canons relate simply to matters of faith and discipline. But it is thus introduced by Orderic. William "assembled the chief men of Normandy and Le Mans, and encouraged them by a king's word to maintain peace and right. The bishops and abbots and ecclesiastical persons he admonished to live well, to consider well and continually the law of God, to take counsel together for the Church of God, to correct the ways of those placed under them, according to the determination of the canons, and all with due care to govern." "*Therefore*," he proceeds, a council was held in the Cathedral of Rouen by the archbishop and his suffragans, in which, after "discussion on the faith of the Holy Trinity," according to the received usage in councils, a number of canons were passed. This was an ecclesiastical assembly. But that this assembly was held, was William's doing; and he assigned its objects. In 1080, another assembly of a more mixed kind—more resembling a parliament—was held at Lillebonne. Orderic thus speaks of it: "In the year 1080, King William had his residence at Lillebonne, at Whitsuntide, and thither he commanded Archbishop William and all bishops and abbots and counts, with other chief men of Normandy, to come together. As the king commanded, so was it done. Therefore, in the eighth year of the Pontificate of our Lord the Pope Gregory VII., a full council was held at Lillebonne, and profitable counsel was taken concerning the state of the Church of God and of the whole realm, by the foresight of the king, with the advice of his barons. But the statutes of the council, as they were faithfully noted down by those present, I will here insert, that those who come after may learn what sort of laws there were in Normandy under William the king." The first thing that strikes a reader in these statutes is their general agreement with the objects of the reforming party in the Norman Church. They enforce the Truce of God. They enforce clerical continence. They guard against lay usurpations. The next thing is, the way in which the king, by himself and his officers, undertakes to guard and give effect to the jurisdiction and claims of the Church. The third thing is, that the king allows neither layman nor churchman to take the law into his own hands; and while he gives the largest and most liberal scope for the exercise of the ecclesiastical powers, and allows full right to custom, he makes all depend upon the king's sanction; he brings all within the king's eye; and, without narrowing or encroaching on the functions and authority of the bishops, he makes all disputed matters depend at last on the authorization of the king's court; he assigns classes of crimes and modes of punishment to be dealt with by the bishops, and traces the order of particular processes. He acts as if the general care of the Church, as well as of the State, was committed to him, and it was his business to give to the authorities in each their duly fenced provinces of work, to draw firmly the lines between their several provinces; and, while granting to each the fullest powers and the amplest countenance, to allow neither to trespass on his neighbour's functions and rights, or to neglect his own.

William's ecclesiastical administration is distinctly characterized by the choice of his chief and confidential adviser. That adviser was Lanfranc, teacher and reformer, restorer of studies, reviver of zeal both for learning and strictness, theologian, administrator, diplomatist, statesman; a man thoroughly in earnest in the cause of religion, but knowing just how far he might go; ready for sacrifices, but only when they were necessary, and not the least inclined to waste them for a trifle: very resolute, and very cautious. In Lanfranc, William had a man who could tell him all that anyone of that age could tell him of what was then known of the history, philosophy, and literature of the Church and the world, and of the actual state of questions, tendencies, and parties in the stirring ecclesiastical politics of the day. He could trust Lanfranc's acquaintance with his proper department of knowledge; he could trust his honesty

and untiring perseverance; he could trust his good
sense and his wise sobriety of mind; he could trust
his loyalty the more, because he knew that it had
bounds, though wide ones. For what seems to have
riveted the connection between William and Lanfranc
was Lanfranc's perilous boldness in siding at first with
the ecclesiastical opposition to William's marriage;
an opposition which probably touched his jealousy as
a ruler, and certainly stung him to rage as a husband.
When he heard that Lanfranc had condemned it, he
ordered not only that the Prior of Bec should be
banished from Normandy at once, but that the house
should be punished also; that the home farmstead of
the abbey, or, as it was called, its "Park," should be
burned and destroyed. The savage order was obeyed.
Lanfranc set out on a lame horse which went on three
legs, for the monks had no better to give him, says his
biographer,—unable, as so often we find it in these
writers, to resist the joke which mixes with their tears
and quotations from Scripture. He met the Duke,
bitter and dangerous in his wrath; he saluted him,
"the lame horse, too, bowing his head to the ground at
every step," as the biographer is careful to add. Lanfranc was sure that if he could only get a chance of
explaining himself, his case was not desperate. The
Duke first turned away his face; then, "the Divine
mercy touching his heart," he allowed Lanfranc to
speak. "Lanfranc began," says the story, "with a
pretty pleasantry," which betrays, as some other stories
do, his astute Lombard humour: "'I am leaving the
country by your orders,' he said, 'and I have to go as if
on foot, troubled as I am with this useless beast; for I
have to look after him so much, that I cannot get on

a step. So, that I may be able to obey your command, please to give me a better horse.'" The joke took. The Duke replied in the same strain, that he never heard of an offender asking for a present from his displeased judge. So, a beginning being made, Lanfranc gained a hearing, and was able to make his position clear. William was too wise a man to throw away lightly an ally like Lanfranc. A complete reconciliation and a closer confidence followed. The dispute about the marriage turned on a matter of Church law which William had broken, but which, according to the doctrine of the time, the Pope could dispense with and condone. Lanfranc would not agree even to William breaking such rules at his pleasure; but he would do his best to repair what could not be undone, and to make peace between him and the Church. He went to Rome as William's representative to plead his cause with Nicholas II.; he urged to the Pope that excommunication and interdict, which, it would seem, had been already pronounced, would only weigh heavy on those who neither had helped the marriage nor could break it; and that it was out of the question that William would ever give up his wife. And he prevailed. William was allowed to keep her; but the foundation of two great monastic houses, St. Stephen at Caen, by William, the Holy Trinity for women, by Matilda, were the satisfaction for their offence, and the monuments of the great compromise, between opponents equally matched in determination and self-reliance, which was the fruit of Lanfranc's mediation. Skilful it undoubtedly was; wise and justifiable in its moderation, —the cause of controversy being what it was, a matter of positive and arbitrary restriction, and not as many of these quarrels were, matters of morality or of important principle,—it may be held to have been with good reason. But it was the achievement of a statesman, a judicious and patriotic one ; it may be that a saint, a hero, or a man of plain and straightforward simplicity might have done differently—perhaps better ; not impossibly worse.

But from this time, Lanfranc, the representative of what was in those days hopeful progress and serious care for higher aims, was everything to William. William let no man be his master. From every grant of his confidence he reserved an ample right to judge for himself, to question the recommendations or the acts of his advisers, to throw on them the burden of making out their case, to put aside their counsel and act in his own way. This self-assertion and inward loneliness of purpose and judgment, in a man who surrounded himself with counsellors and made it all through life his practice to consult them and refer to them, is one of William's striking characteristics. But no one probably had his heart more thoroughly than Lanfranc. Lanfranc was his chosen means of communication with the Roman court. Lanfranc, as Prior of Bec, appears as his commissioner and adviser in the troubles of the monastery of St. Evroul. He goes down there with other churchmen to inquire into the disputes of the house and to restore peace and order. It is by his advice that on the refusal of Abbot Robert to appear before the king's court, and his flight to Rome, a new abbot is appointed by the king's authority and maintained in the face of excommunication and the Pope's legates. To him, on the eve of the invasion, William committed the great Abbey of St. Stephen which he had founded at Caen, his noble and most characteristic monument, the memorial of his marriage, of his love for his wife, of his inflexible will, and of his readiness, when his main point was gained, to pay a large price for gaining it, and to accept judicious accommodations. To Lanfranc he turned, when his sword had done its work in England, for help in quieting it and restoring order, and to be a balance against the lawlessness and licence of his fierce soldiers. The doubtful position of the English Archbishop of Canterbury made it all the easier to do, what William anyhow would have had no scruple in doing. The Pope, the legates, the king's council called Lanfranc to the throne of Canterbury, and the government of the English Church. To Lanfranc was the task committed of doing in the spiritual sphere what William did in the political—a task of mingled good and evil purpose, and good and evil effect; which involved honest efforts to restore order, to raise standards, to curb lawlessness, to promote knowledge; which involved also much plain and undisguised injustice, many harsh and violent measures, the predominance everywhere of foreigners, almost always unsympathising and rude, and often shamelessly greedy. Lanfranc's appointment and administration brought the English Church more fully within the circle of Western Christendom, with its rising spirit of intellectual enterprise; they also brought it more closely within the influence and under the control of the great ecclesiastical monarchy at Rome. To Lanfranc William left large liberty. The archbishop held synods, and introduced the new discipline which Normandy had accepted; replaced English bishops and abbots by Norman ones; drew the strings tight of monastic observance; put down, by force if necessary, monastic mutinies; stiffly and successfully asserted the rights of his see, whether to canonical superiority against the Archbishop of York, or to the possession of lands and manors against one of the strongest of the Norman spoilers, Odo, Bishop of Bayeux and Earl of Kent, William's half-brother. All was in the direction of William's policy, of what was good in it and what was bad; it all helped towards repressing licence, towards giving him an orderly realm, towards keeping in check his turbulent nobles; it also helped to excuse and disguise his hard and unscrupulous rule, to make England more Norman, to crush that English spirit which had greater and nobler elements in it than that of the resolute and crafty race who were lords of the hour. The writers of the time speak of Lanfranc as the depositary of William's thoughts and plans of rule: knowing him well enough to do what at first hearing might offend him, in full confidence of the power of his own well-considered grounds to justify his course to a master who required reasons; trusted by William, as William could not trust his most loyal barons. "When William sojourned in Normandy," says Lanfranc's biographer, "Lanfranc was the chief man and the guardian of England; the other chiefs being subordinate to him, and assisting him in what concerned the defence and the order and the peace of the realm, according to the laws of the land." The expressions may be, perhaps, too broad; but Lanfranc's letters during the rebellion of 1075 show how important was his position, both in watching matters in the king's behalf and in discountenancing the rebels, whom he excommunicated and, even after their submission, refused to absolve without William's leave; and in being a mediator through whom the rebels could approach their lord and seek for reconciliation. Lanfranc, though he felt the dislike and contempt of an Italian turned Norman, for the language and the ways of the conquered English, was not unmindful of what was due from a churchman, and especially from a successor of St. Augustin, to his so-called "barbarian" flock. He took their part, as far as seemed reasonable to him, and in his disputes they were often on his side. But he was too new a ruler, and came too soon after the Conquest, to identify himself heartily with those whom his patron had conquered and ruled so sternly.

Lanfranc was an adviser, a minister, a faithful, calm-judging helper; but the supreme direction, the ultimate sanction, William kept to himself in all things. Thus, respectful, even cordial as he was in his relations with the Holy See, with which he saw it to be important to connect the Norman Church as with the great centre of civilization, and from which he had sought and received benediction on the great enterprise of his life, he had no thought of making his obedience absolute and unconditional. One potentate only of the time knew how to answer Gregory VII. at once with temper and resolution; and that was William. "Hubert your legate," he writes to the Pope, "coming to me on your behalf, admonished me, religious Father, that I should do fealty to you and your successors; and that, touching the money which my predecessors were accustomed to send to the Roman Church, I should take better order. The one claim I have admitted, and the other I have not admitted. Fealty I neither have been willing to do, nor will I do it now, for I never promised it; and I find not that my predecessors did it to yours. The money, for three years while I have been in Gaul, has been carelessly collected; now, however, that by the Divine mercy I am returned to my realm, what has been gathered is forwarded by the aforesaid legate, and the remainder, as soon as there is an opportunity, shall be sent by the envoys of Lanfranc, our faithful Archbishop. Pray for us and for the state of our realm; because we have loved your predecessors, and you above all we desire to love sincerely, and listen to obediently." And Gregory, though angry and contemptuous about the money, had to let the matter pass. Lanfranc himself, who probably was the actual writer of the king's letter, took the same tone of guarded respect, but resolute assertion of rights, to the great and terrible Pope. Gregory wrote to him by the same legate, charging him with having cooled in his regard and duty to the Roman Church since his promotion. Lanfranc "neither wishes nor sought to find fault with the Pope's words," but in his conscience he does not understand how absence or promotion can make him less hearty in his submission to the Pope's commands in all things, "according to the command of the canons;" and insinuates that it is really the Pope who has become cool to him. "The words of your message," he adds, "I, with your legate, to the best of my power, recommended to my lord the king. I urged, but could not persuade. How far he in all points has not assented to your wish, he himself makes known to you both by word and letter." In the great contest between the Pope and the Empire, William, and Lanfranc with him, though far from withdrawing their recognition of Gregory, and refusing to give any countenance to his rival, spoke of him in terms which implied the king's right to form his own judgment and take his own line, if necessary, in the quarrel which had thrown Gregory's claims into dispute. There is a curious letter of Lanfranc's to the representative of the Antipope Guibert, Cardinal Hugo, who had tried to get England on his master's side. " I have received and read your letter, and some things in it have displeased me. I do not approve of your vituperating Pope Gregory, and calling him Hildebrand, and that you give bad names to his legates, and that you praise up Clement so extravagantly. For it is written, that in a man's lifetime he ought not to be praised, nor his neighbour disparaged. It is as yet unknown to mankind what they are now, and what they are to be in the sight of God. Yet I do not believe that the Emperor, without great reason, would have ventured to take so grave a step, nor that without great help from God he could have achieved so great a victory. I do not recommend your coming to England, unless you first receive the king's leave. For our island has not yet disowned the former Pope (Gregory), nor declared its judgment whether it ought to obey the latter. When we have heard the reasons on both sides, if it so happen, we shall be able to see more clearly what ought to be done."

# CHAPTER VII.

#### CHANGES AT WILLIAM'S DEATH.

> " So fails, so languishes, grows dim, and dies
> All that this world is proud of. From their spheres
> The stars of human glory are cast down;
> Perish the roses and the flowers of kings,
> Princes and emperors, and the crowns and palms
> Of all the mighty, withered and consumed."
> WORDSWORTH, *Excursion*, b. vii.

WHILE the Conqueror lived there was government in the State and the Church. There was the strong love of order, the purpose of improvement, the sence of the value of law, the hatred of anarchy and misrule and the firm mind to put them down. William, with his tender and true heart for his wife, and recognizing with the deference of a great mind and spirit the combination of knowledge and power with nobleness of character in men like Lanfranc and Anselm, had little respect and little patience for the people of his time. His own ambition, unscrupulous and selfish as it was, was of a higher order than theirs; it was combined with a consciousness of his fitness for the first place, and the desire of an adequate field for the exercise of his power to rule. To those who put their own ends or their own wishes in the way of his, he was without pity. His great men he would exalt and enrich, and secure to every man his place; for the little folk, he would maintain a due measure of peace and order; bishops and religious men he wished to see zealous for their great objects, and true to their high profession, and there were no limits to his help and countenance when he thought they were fulfilling their calling. Narrow conceptions of government, we may think; but it was much, in those days of beginnings, to have them. But woe to those who thought of thwarting him, or having their own way against his! He knew that he lived in a turbulent and dangerous time, and that there were few to trust; and his hand, to crush or to punish, was swift, heavy, and, in England, relentless. Governing an alien race is the trial and, for the most part, the failure of civilized times; and it was not likely to be easy or successful in his day, and after a great wrong such as he had committed against Englishmen. Hard and stern at all periods of his life, he was cruel and oppressive towards its end, when he became embittered by finding that the race which he had ill-treated, and which he could so little understand, sullenly hated while it feared him. Yet the tyranny of William the king was a light matter to England, if set against the furious insolence of his foreign military lords, which he alone could keep in some order. It was something for the country, vexed as it was by the king's demands for money, and by the greediness of his unscrupulous administration, that these men at least had some one to be afraid of. As his life drew to its close his temper waxed harsher, his yoke heavier, his craving for money more insatiable. An old man's value for a hoard was joined with an old man's increased carelessness for suffering, and the disgust of a conqueror whose ends were but half won and whom success had not made happy. England had become to him what the Indies were afterwards to Spain, a convenient source of wealth to be drawn upon without conscience or mercy. No one can doubt that in the years, dreary and miserable from tempest, murrain and fever, from dearth and famine, just before his death, his inexorable demands for money, searching the country in every corner and racking it to the utmost, made England most miserable. Yet the English writer who with incomparable vigour and pathos describes the wretchedness and humiliation of his country and the fiscal exactions and injustice of her foreign king, is the witness also of the order which he kept; and records, in the form which had become proverbial, that the traveller could pass secure and unharmed through the land with his bosom full of gold, and that no man might raise his hand against his neighbour or harm a woman, without suffering speedy vengeance.

On Thursday, September 9, 1087, William, the "famous Baron," died at Rouen. The impression produced by his death, by the retrospect which it invited of his character and wonderful fortunes, by the contrast between what he had been and what was the end of his greatness, was something deeper and more solemn than that produced by the spectacle of mortality in an ordinary king. In England and in Normandy, it found expression by the pens of contemporary writers, who enable us to understand with more than ordinary distinctness the overpowering feeling of awe and amazement,—partly at his dreadful strength, so irresistible, yet so controlled by purpose and will, partly at the great instance in him of the upshot of the greatest success,—caused by the disappearance of this mighty power from the scene of human life, where he had been so long the foremost object. In England a nameless monk, perhaps a bishop, at any rate one who had been in his court and had seen him close, and whose vigorous words found their way into the monastic chronicles which were yet written in the old English tongue, thus records his feelings at William's death. The passage has been often quoted, but it is difficult to speak of William and his end without quoting it.

"If any one would know what manner of man King William was, or what worship he had, and of how many lands he was lord; then will we write of him as we knew him, who looked on him, and once lived in his court. The King William that we speak of was a very wise man, and very great; and more worshipful and stronger than any of his foregangers. He was mild to the good men who loved God, and beyond all measure stern to those who gainsaid his will. On that selfsame place where God granted him that he might win England, he raised up a great minster, and set monks therein, and enriched it well. In his days was the great minster at Canterbury built, and also very many others over all England. Also this land he filled with monks, and they lived their life after St. Benedict's rule; and Christendom" (the state of Christian religion) "was such in his days that each man followed, if he would, what belonged to his office. Also he was right worshipful: thrice he wore his king's helm (crown) each year, so oft as he was in England. At Easter he wore it at Winchester, at

Pentecost at Westminster, at Midwinter at Gloucester. And there were with him all the great men over all England, archbishops and bishops, abbots and earls, thanes and knights. So he was also a right stern man and a hasty; so that men durst not do anything against his will. He had earls in his bonds who did against his will. Bishops he set off their bishoprics, and abbots off their abbacies, and thanes in prison; and at last he spared not his own brother, called Odo: he was a very great bishop in Normandy: at Bayeux was his see; and he was the chief of men next to the king. And he had an earldom in England, and when the king was in Normandy, he was mightiest in this land. And him did he set in prison. Among other things it is not to be forgotten the good peace that he made in this land; so that any one man, that himself were aught, might fare over his realm with his bosom full of gold, unhurt: and no man durst slay another man, had this one done ever so much evil to the other: and if any man harmed a woman, he was punished accordingly. He ruled over England; and with his craftiness so looked it through, that there was not one hide within England, that he learned not who had it, or what it was worth; and then he set it in his written book. The Britons' land was in his rule, and he made castles therein, and the people of Man, with all authority; so also Scotland he brought under him by reason of his great strength. The Norman land was his inheritance; and over the earldom which is called of Mans he ruled; and if he might have lived yet two years, he had won Ireland by his policy and without any weapons. Surely in his time men had much travail, and very many sorrows; castles he had built, and poor men he made to toil hard. The king was so very stern: and he took of the men under his rule many a mark of gold, and more hundred pounds of silver. That he took, both by right, and also with much unright, of his people, and for little need; he was fallen on covetousness: and greediness he loved altogether. He made great deer-chases, and therewith laid down laws, that whoso slew hart or hind, he should be blinded: he forbad [to touch] the harts and so also the boars; so much he loved the 'high deer, just as if he were their father. Also he appointed concerning the hares, that they might go free. His great men complained of it, and the poor men murmured; but he was so stiff, that he recked naught of them all, and they must altogether

"'Follow the king's will
If they would live, or have land—
—Land or goods, or even a quiet life.
Wala wa! that any man should so be proud,
Should so lift himself up, and reckon himself above all men.
The Almighty God show to his soul mercy,
And grant him for his sins forgiveness.'

This thing we have written concerning him, both the good and the evil: that good men may follow after their goodness, and altogether forsake wickedness; and go in the way that us leadeth to the kingdom of heaven."

In Normandy, Orderic, the man who shared in a remarkable manner both English and Norman feelings, preserved the recollections of Normandy about the end of the greatest of the Normans: what were supposed to be the thoughts of the last hours of his life; how he must have looked back on its strange passages and judged of them then; and how little his greatness could save him from the anguish and bitterness of his mortal condition, and even from its most loathsome humiliations. His account, as usual, is very rhetorical, and full of the pedantry which all ages are apt to mistake for fine writing. He puts a long speech into William's mouth, full of curious bits of history, but as unlike as it well could be, in form and manner, to any discourse that William can be supposed to have held when he was dying. But that he spoke much, and spoke in the same kind of sense as Orderic reports, there is no reason for doubting. Orderic not only represents the tales which went about at the time in the cloisters of the news-loving monks, but probably had heard the story from the mouth of some of the churchmen who were about William's death-bed, such as Gilbert Maminot, the scientific and almost wizard bishop of Lisieux, William's chief physician, and the diocesan of St. Evroul. It is even not improbable that Orderic's long oration represents not merely the general feeling of the dying king, but also, from the way in which Orderic twice dwells on the vigour with which he was able to use his faculties and his speech to the last, that it stands for the full and frequent discourse which he had with his attendants, and that it embodies various portions of what he said to them. It exhibits him going over in memory, from its hard and stormy beginnings, his long and eventful career; his sense of his own offences against God and against those who had suffered from his ambition; his sense of the falseness and ingratitude of men, and his stern will, unshaken by the approach of death, to deal to them their deserts. In its temper, it is at any rate very like William. It is the language of a man awed and humbled, in all severe truth and seriousness, before the supreme goodness and the supreme justice, and, in measure, before those who on earth reflected it: but not afraid, even when feeling himself going to judgment, to pass judgment to the uttermost against the wickedness which he had hated on earth, though his own hands were not clean from it, and not shrinking from calling to mind his counterbalancing good deeds; his care for the cause of religion; his freedom from the great crime of the age, selling the dignities of the Church for money; his desire to put fit persons into her high offices; his love of good men; the houses of prayer and devotion which he had founded or helped. The friend of Lanfranc, the founder of St. Stephen's, is not unlikely to have looked back in this spirit on his chequered course, full of dark passages of wrong and blood, but full also of serious efforts to follow after what he believed to be the light.

To the last, William, in spite of the agony of his disease, was able with clear mind, and with speech that failed not, to communicate his thoughts, his wishes, and his advice to those about him. At early dawn on the 9th of September, from the abbey of St. Gervais outside of Rouen, whither he had been carried to be out of the noise of the city, he heard the great bell sound of the cathedral. He asked what it meant, and he was told that the bell was going for prime in St. Mary's Church. "Then the king raised his eyes to heaven and, stretching out his arms, commended himself to his Lady, Mary the holy mother of God, that she by her holy intercession would reconcile him to her dear Son, Christ; and he at once expired." The physicians who had watched him all night, lying quiet without any sound of pain, were taken by surprise by the suddenness of his passing away, and "became almost out of their mind." Then followed scenes, which showed the change that was coming. His attendants, bishops, and religious men, and probably some of his family and his barons, at once mounted their horses, and hurried off to look to the safety of their lands and houses. The servants, seeing that their betters had gone, stripped the deserted house, and the very corpse of the dead, of all that they could lay hands upon, and made off "like kites" with their prey. The "Justicer" was dead, and the felons took their first revenge and first used their liberty, by despoiling him who had been their chastiser and dread. The story was told and believed that William's death was announced at Rome and in Calabria among those whom he had banished, on the day of his death at Rouen; and Orderic sees in it the joy of the Evil One, conveying the news to the powers of violence and lawlessness, that their great enemy was no more. But at Rouen, for three hours all were thunderstruck, and no one dared to come near the place where the dead king lay, forsaken and almost naked. "O magnificence of the world," cries Orderic, "how worthless thou art, and how vain and frail: like the rain bubbles of the shower, swollen one moment, burst into nothing the next. Here was a most mighty lord, whom more than a hundred thousand warriors just now eagerly served, and before whom many nations feared and trembled; and now, by his own servants, in a house not his own, he lies foully stripped, and from the first to the third hour of morning is left deserted on the bare floor. The townsmen of Rouen, when they heard the news, were amazed, and lost their senses like drunken men; they could not have been more troubled if there had been a host of enemies at their gates. Every one rose up from the place where he was, and sought counsel what to do from his wife or his friend, or the acquaintance he met with on the way. Each man moved, or prepared to move his goods, and in his panic hid them where they might not be found."

The strong king was dead; powerless to guard or to punish; and it was now every man for himself. The clergy of Rouen at last collected their senses, and came in procession to pay the last offices to their king. William Bonne-Ame, the Archbishop, ordered the body to be taken for burial to the minster at Caen. But it seems that William Bonne-Ame, the king's chosen Archbishop, spoken of as a model of goodness, did not feel himself bound to provide the means of transport. Perhaps Orderic only repeats the gossip of the cloister of St. Evroul; but Orderic says that "the king's brethren and kindred had departed from him, and they and his servants had wickedly left him, as if he were but a barbarian. And there was not one of all his vassals to care for his burial." Why not the Primate of Normandy, the Archbishop whom William had honoured and exalted, in his own city? But as the Bishop of Lisieux had deserted his king's corpse and fled to his own house, so it seems that it was no business of the Archbishop of Rouen to transport the body to Caen for burial. It was left to a certain "country knight" named Herlwin, who was "touched with natural goodness, and who, for the love of God and the honour of his race, like a man" took the duty on him. He, at his own charges, hired those who prepared the body for burial and who were to carry it to the grave; and putting it on board a ship, he carried it round to Caen.

To the last, the same dark shadow lowers over the end of the great king. Orderic relates how, as the funeral entered Caen, a terrible fire broke out, and the clergy alone were left to conduct the body to the Minster of St. Stephen. At least the funeral office might be expected to correspond to his greatness. If the lords and captains, and chief estates of Normandy were not there, the leaders of the Norman Church had assembled round the bier of their protector. Orderic recites their names: William of Rouen, Gilbert of Evreux, Gilbert of Lisieux, Michael of Avranches, Geoffrey of Coutances, Gerard of Séez, and, only just released from his captivity on the King's death-bed, and released with the deepest reluctance and misgiving, Odo, the king's half-brother, Bishop of Bayeux and Earl of Kent. There, too, came the abbots of the famous monasteries, almost as great persons as the bishops; Anselm of Bec, William of Fécamp, Gerbert of Fontanelle, Guntard of Jumiéges, Mainer of St. Evroul, Fulk of Dives, Durand of Troarn, Robert of Séez, Osbern of Bernay, Roger of Mount St. Michael in the Peril of the Sea; and those of the great houses of Rouen, St. Ouen, and the Mount of the Holy Trinity. The "Great Gilbert,"

Bishop of Evreux, made an eloquent oration, in which he set forth the magnificence of the king; how he had extended the bounds of Normandy; how he had exalted his nation more than all his predecessors had done; how he had kept peace and justice in all his dominion; how he had chastised thieves and robbers with the rod of law; how, by the sword of valour, he had stoutly guarded clergy and monks and the defenceless folk. He ended with many tears, beseeching the people, in the love of God, that, since no mortal man can live here without sin, they would intercede for him to the Almighty God; and that, if in aught the dead had offended them, they would forgive him. The call was answered. " Then stood up Asceline, son of Arthur, and, with a loud voice in the audience of them all, put forward this complaint : ‚'The ground on which you stand was the place of my father's house, which this man, for whom you make request, when he was yet Count of Normandy, took away from my father by violence, and, utterly refusing justice, he by his strong hand founded this church. This land, therefore, I claim, and openly demand it back; and in the behalf of God I forbid the body of the spoiler to be covered with the sod that is mine, and to be buried in my inheritance.'" On the spot the claim was investigated and acknowledged ; and, before the body could be lowered into the stone coffin, a bargain was struck for the grave, and the ground round it. But the miseries of the scene were not yet ended. " The debt was paid, the price of that narrow plot of earth, the last bed of the Conqueror. Asceline withdrew his ban; but as the swollen corpse sank into the ground, it burst, filling the sacred edifice with corruption. The obsequies were hurried through, and thus was William the Conqueror gathered to his fathers, with loathing, disgust, and horror."[1]

"Behold!" writes Orderic, "I have with care inquired and with truth related what, in the Duke's fall, was pointed out beforehand by God's ordering hand. It is no fancy tragedy that I am palming off; I am not courting the laughter of idlers by the quaint speeches of a comedy; but to thoughtful readers I present the reality of change and chance. In the midst of prosperity, disasters appeared, that the hearts of men on earth might fear. A king once mighty and warlike, the terror of many people in many countries, lay naked on the ground, deserted by those whom he had nourished up. He needed borrowed money for his funeral; he needed the help of a common soldier to provide a bier and bearers of it, he who had, up to that moment, such a superfluity of riches. Past a town in flames, he was carried by frightened men to his minster; and he who had ruled over so many cities and towns and villages, wanted a free spot of earth, that was his own, for his burial. . . . Rich and poor are alike in their lot : both are a prey to death and the worm. Put not, then, your trust in princes, which are nought, O ye sons of men; but in God, the Living and the True, who is the Maker of all. Consider the train of things in the Old and the New Testament, and there take for yourselves examples without number of what to avoid and what to desire. Trust not in wrong and robbery, and desire not the

[1] Sir F. Palgrave.

fruit of violence. If riches increase, set not your heart upon them. For all flesh is grass, and all the glory of it as the flower of the grass. The grass withereth, and the flower thereof fadeth away; but the word of the Lord endureth for ever."

Orderic concludes with a sermon. But had he not indeed a text; and is his sermon more than the thought which would rise of itself in all hearts at such a spectacle?

The reign of strength was over; the reign of insolent lawlessness and brute force began. Robert of Belesme, the head in Normandy of the fierce house of Talvas, the rival of that of Rollo, was entering Brionne on his way to the king's court at Rouen, when the tidings met him. At once he turned his horse, and riding to Alençon, expelled from the castle the garrison which kept it for the king. He did the same at Belesme, and seized or destroyed all the holds of his weaker neighbours. Other lords in the south-east, rivals or enemies, followed his example. William, Count of Evreux, turned out the royal garrison from the "donjon" of the castle. William of Breteuil, and Ralph of Conches, and all the strong hands round, seized each all the fortified posts within reach; that "each might freely carry on his execrable quarrels against his neighbour and the dweller next him. Then the chief men of Normandy drove out all the King's guards from their strongholds, and vied with one another in spoiling with their own hands a country abounding in wealth. And so the riches which they had torn by violence from the English and other nations, they lost, as they deserved, by their own robberies and plunderings among themselves." It was a foretaste of what was coming, though in different ways in England and Normandy. That break-up of society to which military feudalism was always tending—that dispersion of power from a central authority among a crowd of fierce and greedy soldier chiefs, plotting, robbing, destroying, fighting each man for himself; the substitution of arbitrary will not only for law but for custom; the dissolution of all ties of duty and faith, of all restraints which held men back from the wild savageness and appetites of beasts—came upon the lands over which the great Conqueror had ruled. He had kept the anarchy of his generation at bay; he had shamed and cowed its licence. His serious and severe temper, his iron hand, his instincts of kingly greatness, the countenance which he had given so conspicuously to that religion which, hard, narrow, imperfect as it might be, carried with it a weight which the age could understand on the side of self-conquest, of obedience to a rule of life, of peace and industry, of the belief in an ideal of human nature superior to material things, of the conviction of human brotherhood, and faith in divine charity, had for the time accustomed his realms to a state of things in which something was paramount, which, if it was not yet law, was stronger than disorder. Under him turbulence was dangerous and unprofitable, and riot was unfashionable. Now the curb was taken away; and it was soon made evident what the Conqueror's government, uneasy and harsh as it was, had kept down, and from what he had saved his subjects.

The great power which he had founded fell apart, at least for a time, at his death. The succession to

Normandy had long been pledged to his eldest son Robert. Vicious and unruly, he had been his father's enemy and scourge: but he had a strong party in Normandy; Orderic makes William say that the majority of the barons had acknowledged him; his father left him Normandy, to be misgoverned and ruined; but he would not give him England. England, he said, according to Orderic's report, God had *given* to him; it had not come to him by hereditary right in the same way as the Duchy; and as it had been given to him, he dared not *give* it; he only wished and hoped that his second son William might have it: and he sent him away to England bearing a letter to the Archbishop Lanfranc, asking for his aid to make William king. He was without difficulty acknowledged in England, and consecrated by Lanfranc at Westminster before the month was out in which his father died. Henry, the youngest and the ablest, was left with a large treasure in money, to bide his time.

The ungovernable wildness of the old barbarian stock of the Pirate Sea Kings seemed to have revived in the two eldest sons. In Robert it showed itself in alternating fits of fierce energy and lazy torpor and exhaustion, like the succession of wakeful ferocity with slumberous inactivity in a wild animal. In William all was wakefulness. He had all his father's force of character, his father's wary boldness, his father's terrible inflexibility of will, his father's vigour and decision and rapidity in action; but without those perceptions of right, that feeling after something better, that deep though confused respect for goodness, that living though often clouded fear of God, which had given whatever nobleness it had to his father's royalty. Imagine the Conqueror without his aversion to the confusion and anarchy which he made it his task to quell,—imagine him blind to the great intellectual and religious movement in Normandy which was embodied and typified in Lanfranc,—imagine him without his passionate faithfulness to his wife;—and his triumph, supported by ability at the time unequalled, would have been a reign of wickedness and horror to which the actual miseries of his rule, even the laying waste of the North and the murder of Earl Waltheof, would have seemed light in comparison. These makeweights to the Conqueror's unscrupulousness and hardness were taken away in his son; and we have the king who reigned in his stead.

In another point, also, they were a contrast. The Conqueror was austere and his court a grave one. According to a reaction often seen, William the Red turned with revengeful disgust against the solemn ways and speech of his father's household, in which doubtless he had seen many hypocrisies, and broke out into reckless and ostentatious mockery of the restraints and beliefs of the time. The decorum which had been in fashion gave place in him to a new fashion of shameless licentiousness which seemed to aim at affronting and defying what was most sacred and revered. Unmarried, he shocked by his profligacy an age which was accustomed to lawlessness of all kinds; and a noisy openness of speech and boisterous and riotous merriment, which made a very distinct impression on observers round him, partly relieved, and partly masked, as is not seldom the case, the keen shrewdness and craft, and the pitiless selfishness, of the real man beneath.

Yet the difference at first sight seems small between the father's rule and the son's. The father was unscrupulous and oppressive; the son could command like his father. He crushed rebellion as effectually; he hung without mercy thieves and felons; no man, says Orderic, as he might have said in his rhetorical eulogy of the Conqueror, dared mutter a word against him. The crown of England was as safe in the Red King's keeping, and as much feared by its subjects and its neighbours, as it had been in his father's time. What then made the difference between the two royalties, outwardly so like? It was the incipient order, the faint half-conscious preludes of civilization, the sense of something higher than force, the purpose, however dim, of maintaining right, which were present in the Conqueror's notions of kingship, and which disappeared for the time under William the Red. The beginnings of moral elevation under the father went back under the two elder sons to the more naked and undisguised selfishness common in all ages to men who think that power is in their hands to do what they like with, and natural especially to an untaught and untrained stage of political life which is painfully and with many relapses emerging from barbarism. In Normandy all was anarchy under the indolent and reckless Robert; in England all was powerful and vigilant tyranny under his formidable and ambitious brother: but both had lost that which had prevented their father's rule from being confounded with the common self-will and violence of the kings and princes of his time, and had given him his best claim to greatness.

In Normandy, as has been said, the elements of disorder broke loose at once, and there was no hand to check them. But in England, where William the Red had been accepted and consecrated as an English king at Westminster, and had given the solemn promise of an English king to maintain right and peace, turbulence, the turbulence of the foreigners, found its master. There was one keen and decisive trial of strength between William and the fierce Norman lords who looked upon England as their prey. Odo the warrior-bishop of Bayeux was no sooner released from his prison than he was at the head of a great confederacy of the strangers to conquer back England for the Duke of Normandy and his lawless and greedy soldiers. Odo, once the greatest man next the king, had met with a rival in Lanfranc. He had contended with Lanfranc for lands and for influence: to Lanfranc's counsel his imprisonment was ascribed. That Lanfranc had crowned William and was his adviser would be a reason with Odo for urging Robert to invade England. But William could guard his own. The English were with him and fought for him. London was with him, and Kent. He had the hearty support of Lanfranc and Wolfstan; of the foremost of the foreign churchmen, of the saintliest of the English. And his triumph was rapid and complete. He was king at home; not indeed without outbursts of hostility and disaffection in the Welsh and Scottish march-lands, or among the Norman lords in distant Northumberland; but William's rapid energy and decision easily foiled them: his State was never in danger after the first trial of strength; and henceforth his thoughts were given to carrying out his vengeance and extending his power abroad. His reign began with hope. He had promised to be an English king, just merciful, and true: he had fought with Englishmen for his soldiers against insolent and traitorous "Frenchmen," and had triumphed: he had the great Lanfranc, his father's friend and counsellor, from whose hand he had received knighthood and then the crown, the illustrious stranger, who reluctantly, yet with sincerity, had taken part with the English people, to be his adviser and supporter. But the hope soon passed. In the year after the Red King's coronation Lanfranc followed his great master to the grave; and then, what Lanfranc had been to the father, that, to the son — the soul of his counsels, the minister of his policy, the suggester and instrument of his deeds—was the low-born Norman priest, the scandal, amusement, and horror of his age, Ranulf or Ralph, nicknamed Flambard, the Firebrand. The difference between the two reigns is expressed in the contrast between Lanfranc and Ralph Flambard.

Flambard was one of a class of churchmen who were characteristic of a low and imperfect stage of civilization, and who passed away with it. They are not to be confounded with the statesmen-ecclesiastics of the middle and later ages who, whatever we think of them, must be judged of on very different principles, Becket, Wolsey, Ximenes, were statesmen, because to a great churchman all human interests were thought to belong of right, and he was not going out of his high and comprehensive sphere when he handled them. The ideal at least was a great one, however it at last failed in practice, which made those who are charged with man's highest laws and concerns, the companions and yokefellows of kings, the guides of earthly government, the arbiters of the policy of nations, the interpreters of the wants and aims of society. But these men, though they united the priest with the statesman, and often did so to the great hurt of one or other character, and sometimes of both, never forgot their churchmanship. But the other order of men, of whom Ralph Flambard was a typical instance, simply merged and lost their ecclesiastical functions in their secular business, and used their clerkship to make themselves more serviceable instruments of administration and tools of power. The feudal house or *meisney* of the eleventh century had its military family and its clerical family—one for hand-work, the other for headwork; both equally portions of the royal or baronial court, and one as indispensable as the other. The clerics, most of them in orders but not all priests, did all the writing, account-keeping, law business, all that had to do with estate agency or the domestic economy; they furnished, besides the mass-priests and chaplains, the secretaries, chancellors, attorneys, "purveyors," and clerks of the kitchen. They were by no means useless, all of them. The work which is now done in the Exchequer, the Treasury, the offices of Chancery, by the Boards of Revenue and Customs, by the law officers of the Crown, by the departments of Public Works and Crown Domains, the business of public accounts and state correspondence, was mostly in the hands of these men; and their work was by no means always ill done. They had among them the contriving brains, the quick pens, the calculating heads of their time; they had the financial inventiveness, the legal resource, the businesslike coolness, necessary for their work. The finance and the office routine of the age were rude, but they were beginnings; and though much in them was blundering, and, what was worse, corrupt and oppressive, we are even now in many things beholden to these early clerical pioneers of English administration. But of all conceivable employments and functions, it is difficult to imagine any that less suit a man invested with Christian orders.

But there were differences among them, and Ralph Flambard was one of the worst specimens of the worst kind of the class. The accounts which remain of him are so unanimous, so distinct, so consistent, and reflect such deep indignation and scorn, that we feel that we have to be on our guard in judging of a man so detested both in Normandy and in England. Gossip greedily gathers round an unpopular name; about his parents, about his first steps in life, about the early tokens of an evil bent and readiness for mischief, of audacity, craft, servile suppleness; such stories may be but the growth of later hatred, and must be taken with allowance for the feelings of which they are the evidence. There is no reason, however, to doubt the accuracy of the portrait, drawn probably by those who had seen him, of his manners and qualities; of a man without education, but with much mother-wit and boundless fluency of tongue; coarse, impudent, cunning, boisterous, a formidable bully, a ready mocker, free in his loud banter and noisy horse-laughs. But what is certain is this:—that Ralph Flambard being a churchman, and rising to the high dignities of the Church, deliberately set himself not only to plunder but to injure and degrade the Church; that, uniting in his own person the chief management of the revenue and the administration of justice, he was the thorough-going and unscrupulous minister of a policy of fiscal wrong and oppression such as was never in England; that he was the prompter and instrument of a system of barefaced and daring venality which set everything in Church and State to sale. In a reign in which legal chicane was placed at the service of greedy violence, and the land racked to furnish means to the vast ambition of a king who yet seemed to have no other end in ruling but to have all human rights under his feet, Ralph Flambard was the soul of his counsels, the man on whose quick wit and fearless hand, and bold and overbearing tongue, the king relied to outface the opposition and scandal which his outrages provoked, and to find new means to replenish a treasury which his personal manner of life and his ambitious political schemes, in which bribes played as important a part as his warlike qualities, were continually emptying. Of this rule, so ignoble in purpose, and as barren of all wholesome fruit of government as that of a rapacious Roman Prætor or a Turkish Pacha who has bought his province—a rule redeemed from ignominy only (if that be a redemption) by its merciless strength—Flambard was the civil representative. Of what it was in point of law, of what it was in respect for justice and wish to elevate and improve, he is the measure. The charge that Orderic brings against him in his dealing with secular property, of tampering with the measurements and valuations of Doomsday, and subverting the old

English understanding of the quantities and rents of estates for the benefit of the Treasury, might be suspected of exaggeration—the usual exaggeration of the tax-payer when the rights of the revenue are sharply looked after—were it not certain that, in a case where there was no room for mistake, in his treatment of church property, Flambard did not stop at the most flagrant and high-handed wrong. That the king should keep great church offices vacant simply that he might seize and appropriate their revenues, is a proceeding which does not admit of being overcoloured; it is simple and intelligible; it is exactly of the same kind as any other sort of robbery. And this was the great financial invention devised by Flambard. When a bishop or abbot died, the king's officer—Flambard himself when, as at Canterbury, the dignity was great enough—entered on the property, and kept it for the king's use as long as he pleased. After Lanfranc's death the see of Canterbury was vacant for more than three years, and its rents were taken possession of by the king. They were again seized when Anselm left England, and remained in the king's hands for three years more, till his death. When he fell in the New Forest he held, besides the lands of Canterbury, those of Winchester and Sarum, and eleven abbeys besides. The minister of all this iniquity had to go through the ups and downs of such a career of adventure. William the Red made him Bishop of Durham. His brother's first act on succeeding to the crown was to imprison Flambard in the Tower. He escaped by making his guards drunk; and the manner of his escape, and how the "fat prelate," sliding down the rough rope which was not long enough to reach the ground, scraped off the skin from his hands, and finished with a heavy tumble at the end, became one of the good stories of the time. He came to Normandy, and, in the anarchy under Duke Courtehose, quartered himself at Lisieux, where Bishop Gilbert Maninot the astrologer, the Conqueror's old friend and physician, had just died. Flambard got the bishopric for his brother Fulcher; on his death he held it three years for his own son, a child of twelve years old, with the promise from the Duke, that if this boy should die, the bishopric should go to another son; then, when the outcry against this arrangement became too strong, he got the bishopric for one of his creatures, who was turned out of it for his simoniacal bargain with the Duke. Finally, when the battle of Tinchebrai had made it clear which was the winning side, Flambard, who, as Orderic says, was "residing as a prince in the town of Lisieux," made his submission to Henry, recovered his bishopric of Durham, and left the name of a grand prelate and a magnificent builder, dying, it is said, peacefully and a penitent.

It was this brutality and misrule, this detestable and ungovernable sway of selfishness, passion, and cruelty, this treatment of kingdoms and states as a wicked landlord treated his tenants, which roused zeal and indignation in the awakening conscience and awakening intelligence of Christian Europe. The opposition to it came from the clergy; primarily, and as to the origin of the impulse, from the monasteries— places where the search after peace and light and purity, the forgiveness of sin, and the conquest of evil, were, in however imperfect and mistaken a way, made the objects of human life; where the new learning of the time disclosed more and more what men were made for, and might be; where prayer and charity opened a spiritual world for them; where self-discipline made them know what those, who would, could do. From the monasteries the impulse was communicated, not to the secular clergy, as a body, but to their leaders, to the bishops, who carried with them the ideas of the monasteries into public life; at last to the heads of the hierarchy, the popes. By the mouth of the clergy, spoke the voice of the helpless, defenceless multitudes, who shared with them in the misery of living in a time when law was the feeblest and most untrustworthy stay of right, and men held everything at the mercy of masters, who had many desires and few scruples, quickly and fiercely quarrelsome, impatient of control, superiority, and quiet, and simply indifferent to the suffering, the fear, the waste, that make bitter the days when society is enslaved to the terrible fascination of the sword. In the conflict which ensued, there was much of a mixed character, much that was ambiguous. Those who were on the right side were not always right, those on the wrong side not always wrong. The personal interests of the clergy were involved in their efforts against military insolence and self-will, as well as the interests of justice and the interests of the poor. Doubtless they had much to lose by the uncontrolled reign of the sword; but they had also much to lose by opposing it. To resist and counterbalance it, they brought in another kind of power, which in the course of things worked great mischief and had to be taken away. What is worse, they based this power, not always consciously, indeed, yet, in fact, upon ideas and documents which were false. Their great lever was a belief in a divine universal theocracy, appointed by God and assigned by Christ to the Pope; a belief which, springing out of the natural growth of traditions, utilities and claims, and encouraged by the necessity of the times, was at last boldly founded on gross forgeries, and has developed into the pretensions of the later Popes, which to this day astonish a world which has seen many wonders. But this is all easy to say after the event, and the experience of nearly nine centuries. Before the event, in the darkness and perplexity of the eleventh century, things looked very different. Then, in those days of armed and lawless power, it was no unnatural thing for a great Pope to match his moral and spiritual power against the cruel forces which seemed to be amenable to no other check. Then it was most natural for Christians, hating the pride that defied God's law and the licence which trod its sanctities under foot, to rally round the conspicuous and traditional centre of Christendom, and seek there a support which failed them at the extremities. They must be judged by what they knew, and what they could see. It is unjust, as well as unphilosophical, to import into the disputes of the Hildebrandine age the ideas and axioms which belong to later times. Pride, arrogance, falsehood, of course, are the same in all ages, and wherever we meet them deserve our condemnation. But it is a fallacy to carry back, in our thoughts and associations, what a thing has become, to what it was under earlier and different conditions. We all acknowledge this rule of caution in judging of philosophical and religious development. It is equally true of institutions, government, and policy. It is a mistake, in comparing two different and remote stages of the same thing, to make a later false and corrupt direction the measure of a former natural and innocent one. A thing may even turn out in the long run, and under altered conditions, mistaken and mischievous, while yet at the first it was the best and wisest—perhaps the only course to accept with unreserved earnestness.

Of such a nature was the contest which has made Anselm's name famous in English history: a contest in which, as Archbishop of Canterbury, he carried to extremity his opposition to two kings of England; a contest in which he threw himself on the support of the popes, and the result of which did much to confirm their power in England; a contest in which the part he took has made the most illustrious name of his age a byword with English historians, and an object of dislike to some who, but for that, would not be insensible to the power of one of the most perfect examples of middle-age saintliness; a contest in which what he did conduced in the end to results which bore evil fruit in England, but in which, notwithstanding, according to all that he could judge by then, he was right.

# CHAPTER VIII.

ANSELM, ARCHBISHOP OF CANTERBURY.

> " Who is the Happy Warrior? Who is he
> That every man in arms should wish to be?
>  * * * * * *
> 'Tis he whose law is reason ; who depends
> Upon that law as on the best of friends ;
> Whence, in a state where men are tempted still
> To evil for a guard against worse ill,—
> And what in quality or act is best
> Doth seldom on a right foundation rest,—
> He labours good on good to fix, and owes
> To virtue every triumph that he knows ;
> —Who, if he rise to station of command,
> Rises by open means ; and there will stand
> On honourable terms or else retire ;
> Who comprehends his trust, and to the same
> Keeps faithful with a singleness of aim ;
> And therefore does not stoop, nor lie in wait
> For wealth or honour, or for worldly state ;
> Whom they must follow ; on whose head must fall,
> Like showers of manna, if they come at all."
>      WORDSWORTH'S *Happy Warrior.*

THERE can be no doubt that towards the end of the Conqueror's reign the fame of the school of Bec was pre-eminent in his dominions, above all other places of religion and learning ; and that next to the illustrious name of its creator Lanfranc, was that of Anselm, his pupil and successor at Bec. There can be little doubt, either, that when Lanfranc died, the thoughts of all who looked upon him as the great ecclesiastical leader of his day turned to Anselm, as the man to carry on his work. Anselm was known in England as well as in Normandy; known as Lanfranc's friend; known in the cloister of Canterbury as the sharer of his counsels; known at the Conqueror's court; known as even more full of sympathy for the native English than even Lanfranc himself. Everything pointed him out as the fittest man that Normandy could furnish to take the great place which Lanfranc had left vacant. He would probably have been the Conqueror's choice; and by all who desired, for whatever reason, that the see of Canterbury should be filled in a way suitable to its eminence and importance, he was marked at once as the person whom it would most become the Conqueror's son to choose.

But for such appointments, which had been a matter of great consequence with his father, William the Red had little care. Lanfranc was gone, and Ralph Flambard was the king's new counsellor; and even that age of violence was shocked when, instead of naming an Archbishop of Canterbury, the King of England seized the possessions of the see, and that he might rack its revenues, refused to fill it up. For nearly four years this lasted; and the patience with which the scandal was endured,—keenly felt as it was even by the rough barons of William's court,—is the measure of what a bold bad king could do, who knew how to use his power. A contemporary picture of the actual state of things in a case like this is valuable. Eadmer was a monk at Canterbury, and describes what passed before his eyes. "The king," he says, "seized the Church at

Canterbury, the mother of all England, Scotland, and Ireland, and the neighbouring isles; all that belonged to it, within and without, he caused to be inventoried by his officers; and after fixing an allowance for the support of the monks, who there served God, he ordered the remainder to be set at a rent and brought into his domain. So he put up the Church of Christ to sale; giving the power of lordship over it to any one who, with whatever damage to it, would bid the highest price. Every year, in wretched succession, a new rent was set; for the king would allow no bargain to remain settled, but whoever promised more ousted him who was paying less; unless the former tenant, giving up his original bargain, came up of his own accord to the offer of the later bidder. You might see, besides, every day, the most abandoned of men on their business of collecting money for the king, marching about the cloisters of the monastery, regardless of the religious rule of God's servants, and with cruel and threatening looks, giving their orders on all sides; uttering menaces, lording it over every one, and showing their power to the utmost. What scandals and quarrels and irregularities arose from this I hate to remember. The monks of the church were some of them dispersed at the approach of the mischief, and sent to other houses, and those who remained suffered many tribulations and indignities. What shall I say of the church tenants, who were ground down by such wasting and misery; so that I might doubt, but for the evils which followed, whether with bare life they could have been more cruelly oppressed? Nor did all this happen only at Canterbury. The same savage cruelty raged in all her daughter churches in England which, when bishop or abbot died, at that time fell into widowhood. And this king, too, was the first who ordained this woful oppression against the churches of God; he had inherited nothing of this sort from his father: he alone, when the churches were vacant, kept them in his own hands. And thus wherever you looked, there was wretchedness before your eyes; and this distress lasted for nearly five years over the Church of Canterbury, always increasing, always, as time went on, growing more cruel and evil."

The feeling of the time was against fiscal oppression carried on in this wholesale way against the Church. The rough and unscrupulous barons had a kind of respect for the monks, who in peace lived as hard lives as soldiers in a campaign, and seemed so much better men than themselves; and though in passion or quarrel they themselves might often use them ill, they looked with a disapproving eye on a regular system for insulting and annoying them, and for enriching the king out of lands which benefactors had given for the benefit of their souls, and in hope of sharing in the blessings of perpetual prayers. And in the case of Canterbury the pride was touched both of Englishmen and of Norman barons. For Canterbury was a see of peculiar and unmatched dignity in the west, and its archbishop was a much greater person in court and realm than any archbishop of Rouen or Lyons. He was a spiritual father to the whole kingdom; the most venerable among its nobles, the representative and spokesman of the poor and the humble; the great centre of sacred and divine authority, without whose assent and anointing the king's title was not complete, and who was the witness between the king and his people of the king's solemn promises of righteous government, of mercy, mildness, and peace. The king's council was imperfect while no Archbishop of Canterbury was there to be his adviser. The honour of the English crown and realm suffered, when the archbishopric lay vacant year after year, in the hands of Ralph Flambard and his men; and people talked among themselves that the place which Lanfranc had filled so worthily, there was now Lanfranc's friend to fill.

Whether or not with any thought of this kind, and it probably was so, in the year 1092 Hugh of Avranches, Earl of Chester, an old friend of Anselm's, invited him over to England to organize a house in which he had substituted monks for seculars, St. Werburg's at Chester. Hugh the Wolf, one of the Conqueror's march lords on the Welsh border, is painted for us with much vividness in one of the rude but vigorous portraits which Orderic liked to draw, —a violent, loose-living, but generous barbarian, honouring self-control and a religious life in others, though he had little of it himself; living for eating and drinking, for wild and wasteful hunting, by which he damaged his own and his neighbours' lands; for murderous war against the troublesome Welsh; for free indulgence, without much reference to right or wrong; very open-handed; so fat that he could hardly stand; very fond of the noise and riotous company of a great following of retainers, old and young, yet keeping about him also a simple-minded religious chaplain, whom he had brought with him from Avranches, and who did his best, undiscouraged, though the odds were much against him, to awaken a sense of right in his wild flock, and to prove by the example of military saints like St. Maurice and St. Sebastian, that soldiers might serve God. It is one of the puzzles of those strange days, what there could have been in common between Earl Hugh and Anselm to have been the foundation of the mutual regard which from old date seems to have been acknowledged between them. Anselm, however, declined the earl's invitation. It was already whispered about, that if he went to England he would be archbishop. Such a change was, in truth, entirely against his own inclination and habits of life, and he had made up his mind against accepting it; but he would not give room to suspicions by seeming to put himself in the way of it. Again Earl Hugh sent for him; he was sick, and wanted the help of an old friend. If the fear of the archbishopric kept Anselm away, "I declare," he said, "on my faith, that in the reports which are flying about there is nothing;" and it would ill become him to be hindered by such misgivings from succouring a friend in necessity. Again Anselm refused, and again Earl Hugh repeated his pressing message. "No peace that Anselm could have in eternity, would save him from regretting for ever that he had refused to come to his friend." Anselm's sensitive conscience was perplexed; to refuse to go seemed like putting the care of his own character for disinterestedness above the wishes and perhaps the real needs of one who had been from old time his familiar friend. So, commending his intention and purpose to God, he went to Boulogne and crossed to Dover. Eadmer adds, that others among the chief men of England who had chosen him as the "comforter and physician" of their souls, pressed his coming over; and when once he had come over, the community of Bec, which possessed property in England which no doubt needed looking after, made it a matter of command to their abbot that he should remain till he had put their affairs in order. He came to Canterbury, meaning to remain there the next day, which was a festival; but he was met with cries of welcome, as the future archbishop, and he hurried away at once. At the court, which he passed on his way to Chester, he was received with great honour even by the king. There he and the Red King had their first experience of one another. At a private interview Anselm, instead of entering, as the king expected, on the affairs of the monastery, laid before him, in the unceremonious fashion of those times, the complaints and charges which were in every one's mouth against his government. "Openly or secretly, things were daily said of him by nearly all the men of his realm which were not seemly for the king's dignity." It is not said how William received the appeal, and they parted. Anselm went to Chester, and found Earl Hugh recovered. But the affairs of Bec, and the ordering of the Chester monastery, had still to be arranged; and Anselm was kept on nearly five months in England. The talk about the archbishopric dropped, and he ceased to think about it. But when he wished to return to Normandy, the king refused to give him the necessary leave to go out of the realm.

Why William detained him is one of the unexplained points in Eadmer's otherwise clear and distinct narrative. It seems as if William felt that if there was to be an Archbishop of Canterbury, he, like the rest of the world, would rather have Anselm than anyone else; but that he saw no reason for the present to make up his mind to surrender so convenient a possession as the archbishop's heritage. So he kept Anselm in England, on the chance of his being necessary. The nobles and bishops who had perhaps hoped that Anselm's being on the spot might bring matters to a point, and were disappointed at the king's showing no signs of relenting, had recourse, in their despair of any direct influence, to a device which, even to Eadmer, seemed a most extraordinary one, and treated their fierce king as if he were an impracticable child who could only be worked upon by roundabout means. By one of the quaintest of all the quaint and original mixtures of simplicity and craft of which the Middle Ages are full, it was proposed at the meeting of the court at Gloucester at Christmas 1092, that the king should be asked by his barons and bishops, who were troubled and distressed at the vacancy of Canterbury, to allow prayers to be said in all the churches of the realm that God would put it into the king's heart to raise up the widowed see from its scandalous and unprecedented desolation. He was "somewhat indignant" at the suggestion when it was first laid before him, but he assented to it; adding, as his view of the matter, "that the Church might ask what it liked, but he should not give up doing what he chose." The bishops took him at his word, and the person to whom they applied to draw up the form of prayer was Anselm. He objected to do, as a mere abbot, what properly belonged to bishops to do. But they persisted:

prayers were accordingly ordered throughout all the churches of England, and the court broke up. When the king's temper was sounded, he was as obstinate as ever. One of his chief men in familiar talk spoke of the Abbot of Bec as the holiest man he had ever known; "he loved God only, and, as was plain in all his ways, desired nothing transitory." "Not even the archbishopric?" rejoined William with his characteristic scoff. The other maintained his opinion, and said that there were many who thought the same. "If he thought that he had but the least chance of it," said the king, "would he not dance and clap his hands as he rushed to embrace it? But," he added, "by the Holy Face of Lucca," (his usual oath,) "neither he nor any one else at this time shall be "archbishop except myself."

The king was still at Gloucester, when, in the beginning of 1093, he was seized with a dangerous illness. The times were so unsettled, that the anxiety caused by it brought back the bishops and great men who had just dispersed. William thought himself dying, and he looked back and looked forward with the feelings so common in those days, when men were reckless in health and helpless in the hour of need. The victims of his rapacity and injustice, the prisoners in his dungeons, the crown debtors ground down and ruined by fiscal extortion, the churches which he had plundered and sold, and kept without pastors, all rose up before his mind: above all, the flagrant and monstrous wrong to the nation as well as to religion, of the greatest see of the realm, treated with prolonged and obstinate indignity and left unfilled. His barons as well as his bishops spoke their minds plainly, and pressed for reparation and amendment. And now, as was natural, the influence of a spiritual counsellor like Anselm was at once thought of. In those times, sick men thought nothing of sending across the sea for a comforter whose knowledge and goodness they trusted, to aid and advise them in their ignorance and terror: and Anselm had the greatest name of all of his time for that knowledge which heals the soul. He was staying, ignorant of the king's illness, somewhere not far from Gloucester, when he was summoned in all haste to attend upon the dying man. He came; "he goes into the king," as Eadmer tells the story; "he is asked what advice he thinks most wholesome for the soul of the dying. He first begs to be told what had been counselled to the sick man by his attendants. He hears, approves, and adds—'It is written, *Begin to the Lord in confession*, and so it seems to me that first he should make a clean confession of all that he knows that he has done against God, and should promise that, if he recovers, he will without pretence amend all; and then that without delay he should give orders for all to be done which you have recommended.' The purport of this advice is approved, and the charge assigned him of receiving this confession. The king is informed of what Anselm had said to be most expedient for his soul's health. He at once agrees, and with sorrow of heart engages to do all that Anselm's judgment requires, and all his life long to keep more fully justice and mercifulness. He pledges to this his faith, and he makes his bishops witnesses between himself and God, sending persons to promise this his word to God on the altar in his stead. An edict is written, and sealed with the king's seal, that all prisoners whatsoever should be set free in all his dominion; all debts irrevocably forgiven; all offences, heretofore committed, be pardoned and forgotten for ever. Further, there are promised to all the people good and holy laws, the inviolable upholding of right, and such a serious inquiry into wrong-doing as may deter others." "The king," says Florence, with the Peterborough Chronicle, "when he thought himself soon to die, promised to God, as his barons recommended to him, to correct his life, to sell no more churches, nor put them out to farm, but to defend them by his kingly power, to take away unrighteous laws, and to establish righteous ones."

There was one more matter to be settled: the king, who believed himself and was believed by others to be dying, was dying with the vacant archbishopric in his possession and on his conscience. There could be no question now with him about getting free from the perilous load. But who was to be archbishop? All waited for the king to name him. He named Anselm. Anselm, he said, was most worthy of it.

And now followed a scene, which we read with different feelings, according as we are able to believe that a great post like the archbishopric may have had irresistible terrors, overwhelming all its attractions or temptations, to a religious mind and conscience in the eleventh century. If Anselm's reluctance was not deep and genuine, the whole thing was the grossest of comedies; if his reluctance was real, the scene is one of a thousand examples of the way in which the most natural and touching feelings may be expressed in shapes, which by the changes of times and habits come to seem most grotesque and unintelligible. But if it was a comedy, or even if he did not know his own mind, then the whole view which was taken of Anselm in his own time was mistaken, and the conception of his character on which the present account is written, is fundamentally wrong. His writings, the picture of the man shown in his letters, and the opinion of those who knew him by reputation and of those who knew him best and wrote of him, have conspired to lead us wrong.

When the king's choice was announced to Anselm, he trembled and turned pale. The bishops came to bring him to the king, to receive the investiture of the archbishopric in the customary way, by the delivery of a pastoral staff. Anselm absolutely refused to go. Then the bishops took him aside from the bystanders, and expostulated with him. "What did he mean? How could he strive against God? He saw Christianity almost destroyed in England, all kinds of wickedness rampant, the churches of God nigh dead by this man's tyranny; and when he could help, he scorned to do so. Most wonderful of men, what was he thinking about! Where were his wits gone to? He was preferring his own ease and quiet to the call which had come to him to raise up Canterbury from its oppression and bondage, and to share in the labours of his brethren." He insisted, " Bear with me, I pray you, bear with me, and attend to the matter. I know that the tribulations are great. But consider, I am old and unfit for work :

how can I bear the charge of all this Church? I am a monk, and I can honestly say, I have shunned all worldly business. Do not entangle me in what I have never loved, and am not fit for." But they put aside his plea. Only let him go forward boldly and be their guide and leader, and they would take care of the temporal part of his work. No, he said, it could not be. There was his foreign allegiance, his foreign obedience to his archbishop, his ties to his monastery, which could not be dissolved without the will of his brethren. These matters, they answered naturally enough, could easily be arranged; but he still refused. "It is no use," he said; "what you purpose shall not be." At last they dragged him by main force to the sick king's room: William, in his anguish and fear, was deeply anxious about the matter, and entreated him with tears, by the memory of his father and mother, who had been Anselm's friends, to deliver their son from the deadly peril in which he stood. The sick man's distress moved some of the bystanders, and they turned with angry remonstrances on Anselm. "What senseless folly this was! The king could not bear this agitation. Anselm was embittering his dying hours; and on him would rest the responsibility of all the mischiefs that would follow, if he would not do his part by accepting the pastoral charge." Anselm in his trouble appealed for encouragement to two of his monks, Baldwin and Eustace, who were with him. "Ah, my brethren, why do not you help me?" "Might it have been the will of God," he used to say, speaking of those moments, "I would, if I had the choice, gladly have died, rather than been raised to the archbishopric."

Baldwin could only speak of submitting to the will of God; and burst, says Eadmer, into a passion of tears, blood gushing from his nostrils. "Alas! your staff is soon broken," said Anselm. Then the king bade them all fall at Anselm's feet to implore his assent; he, in his turn, fell down before them, still holding to his refusal. Finally, they lost patience; they were angry with him, and with themselves for their own irresolution. The cry arose, "A pastoral staff! a pastoral staff!" They dragged him to the king's bed-side, and held out his right arm to receive the staff. But when the king presented it, Anselm kept his hand firmly clenched and would not take it. They tried by main force to wrench it open; and when he cried out with the pain of their violence, they at last held the staff closely pressed against his still closed hand. Amid the shouts of the crowd, "*Long live the Bishop,*" with the *Te Deum* of the bishops and clergy, "he was carried, rather than led, to a neighbouring church, still crying out, It is nought that ye are doing, it is nought that ye are doing." He himself describes the scene in a letter to his monks at Bec. "It would have been difficult to make out whether madmen were dragging along one in his senses, or sane men a madman, save that they were chanting, and I, pale with amazement and pain, looked more like one dead than alive." From the church he went back to the king: "I tell thee, my lord king," he said, "that thou shalt not die of this sickness; and hence I wish you to know how easily you may alter what has been done with me; for I have not acknowledged nor do I acknowledge its validity." Then, when he had left the king's chamber, he addressed the bishops and nobles who were escorting him. They did not know, he said, what they had been doing. They had yoked together to the plough the untameable bull with the old and feeble sheep; and no good could come of the union. The plough was the Church of God; and the plough in England was drawn by two strong oxen, the king and the Archbishop of Canterbury: the one, by his justice and power in things of this world; the other, by his teaching and governance in things divine. One, Lanfranc, was dead; and in his room, with his fierce companion, they had joined the poor sheep, which in its own place might furnish milk and wool and lambs for the service of the Lord, but now could only be the victim of violence which it was helpless to prevent. When their short satisfaction at the relief which they had gained had passed, they would find that things would become worse than ever. He would have to bear the brunt of the king's savage temper: they would not have the courage to stand by him against the king; and when he was crushed, they would in their turn find themselves under the king's feet. Then dismissing them, he returned to his lodging. He was almost overcome and faint with distress; they brought him holy water and made him drink it. This happened on the First Sunday in Lent, March 6, 1093. The king immediately ordered that he should be invested with all the temporalities of the see, as Lanfranc had held them.

There was plainly no escape. His acceptance was the one chance open for better things. If there was to be an archbishop, it must be Anselm. On cooler thoughts, he recognized what had happened as the will of God; though, as he said, whether in mercy or wrath, he could not tell: and he bowed to it. There were still many steps between him and the archbishopric. The consents of the Duke of Normandy, of the Archbishop of Rouen, and of the monks of Bec were necessary, in order to release Anselm from his existing obligations. From the Duke and the Archbishop the requisite consent was easily obtained. The monks of Bec were more difficult. It is a curious feature in the monastic discipline, that while the abbot was supreme over the monastery, the monastery as a body had the right to command the abbot on his obedience to bow to their claims on his service. At Bec, they were disposed to insist on this right. They did not like to lose their famous abbot. Some were deeply attached to him. There were some who whispered complaints of his ambition and self-seeking. They refused at first to set him free. At the solemn chapter held to decide on the matter, there was an obstinate minority which refused to concur in relieving him from his duties to Bec. Their discontent was shared by others. Duke Robert spoke disrespectfully of Anselm's motives. Gilbert, Bishop of Evreux, the diocese in which Bec was situated, who had given to Anselm the consecration of abbot, expressed himself unfavourably to Anselm's honesty in taking the archbishopric. It is plain that, as was natural enough, there was a good deal of talk in Normandy and the neighbourhood about the motives which had drawn away the Abbot of Bec to England.

Anselm was in the position, always a difficult one to act in, and for others to judge about, of a man long marked out for high and difficult office, who has at first violently shrunk from the appointment which seemed almost called for, and has then made up his mind to take it.  There is indecision in such a situation; and he has to bear the consequences.  He can but throw himself on his character, on the imperious necessities of the call, on the equitable interpretation of circumstances.  There certainly was a cause.  "If you knew," he writes to the monks at Bec, "what mischief the continuance of this long vacancy (of Canterbury) has done both to souls and bodies, and how hateful it is, and they, too, by whom it is caused, to all the better and wiser sort, yes, and to the English people, I think if you had the feelings of men you too would detest its prolongation."  "There are some, I hear," he says in another letter,—"who they are God knows,—who either spitefully fancy, or through misunderstanding suspect, or are stung by unruly vexation to say, that I am rather drawn to the archbishopric by corrupt ambition, than forced to it by a religious necessity.  I know not what I can say to persuade them of what is in my conscience, if my past life and conversation do not satisfy them.  I have lived for thirty-three years in the monastic habit: three without office, fifteen as prior, as many as abbot; and those who have known me have loved me, not from care of my own about it, but by God's mercy; and those the more, who knew me the most intimately and familiarly; and no one saw in me anything from which he could gather that I took delight in promotion.  What shall I do then?  How shall I drive away and quench this false and hateful suspicion, that it may not hurt the souls of those who once loved me for God's sake, by chilling their charity;

or of those to whom my advice or example, be it worth what it may, might be of use, by making them think me worse than I really am; or of those who do not know me and hear this, by setting before them an evil example. . . . . Thou God seest me; be thou my witness, that I know not, as my conscience tells me, why the love of anything, which thy servant as a despiser of the world ought to despise, should drag and bind me to the archbishopric to which I am suddenly hurried." "Here," he proceeds, "is my conscience, about my wish for the archbishopric or my dislike to it. If I deliberately lie to God, I don't know to whom I can speak the truth." He goes on, after warning those who were busy in fostering suspicion, "whether many or one," to notice some of the forms in which the claim of the monastery to keep him was put. " Some of you say that I might have reasonably held out against the election; they say, ' When he was compelled to be an abbot, he delivered himself as a servant to us in *the name of the Lord.*' . . . But what did I give you in '*the name of the Lord?*' Surely this: that I would not of my own will withdraw myself from your service, nor seek to withdraw myself, except under the obligation of that order and obedience of which I was before, according to God's will, the servant.' He ought, they said, to have put forward this previous surrender of himself to Bec as a bar to any other office. He had been given to the brethren at Bec, "according to God;" and after the analogy of marriage, no one ought to take away him whom God had given. They reminded him that he had been used to say, that he desired not to live except for them; that he never would have any other government except that of Bec. The answer is that God's will has overruled it all. "I trusted to my strength and wit to keep myself where I wished to be; God has been stronger and craftier than I, and my confidence has come to nothing." The reluctance of the monks to part with him, notwithstanding the shapes which it took, and the irritation which the change created, are remarkable proofs of what Anselm had been at Bec. "Many of you," he writes, "nearly all, came to Bec because of me; but none of you became a monk because of me: it was for no hope of recompense from me that you vowed yourselves to God; from Him to whom you gave all you had, from Him look for all you want. Cast all your burden upon Him and He will nourish you. For myself I pray that you will not love me less, because God does His will with me; that I may not lose my reward with you, if I have ever wished to do your will, because now I dare not and ought not and cannot resist the will of God, nor up to this time see how I can withdraw myself from the Church of the English, except by resisting God. Show that you have loved me, not only for yourselves, but for God's sake and my own."

All these difficulties caused delay. The king meanwhile got well, and with health came regrets for the engagements made on his sick-bed. Eadmer says that his public promises were without scruple broken. The amnesty to prisoners was recalled; the cancelled debts were again exacted; the suits and claims of the crown, which had been abandoned, were revived. "Then arose such misery and suffering through the whole realm, that whoever remembers it cannot remember to have seen anything like it in England. All the evil which the king had done before he was sick seemed good in comparison with the evils which he did when restored to health." He seemed to look back on his illness with fierce bitterness. Gundulf, Bishop of Rochester, an old pupil and friend of Anselm's at Bec, and the king's chief architect, remonstrated. "Be assured, Bishop," was the answer, perhaps in half-jest to people who understood no jesting on such matters, "that, by the Holy Face of Lucca, God shall never have me good for the ill that He has brought on me." But he had shown no wish to revoke Anselm's appointment. Anselm received the formal consent to his election from Normandy before it reached the king. Anselm, however, was not yet bound. At Rochester, where he met William in the course of the summer, he set before the king three conditions on which only he would accept the archbishopric. All the possessions of the see, as Lanfranc had held them, must be granted to him without trouble; and if the see had claims for lands which had been taken from it, the king must do him right. Then, in things pertaining to God and Christian religion, the king must give special weight to his counsel; and as he took the king for his earthly lord and defender, so the king must have him for his spiritual father and ghostly adviser. Lastly, he reminded the king that in the quarrel that was going on between the rival Popes, Urban and the Anti-Pope Clement, who was recognized by the Emperor, he, with the rest of the Norman Church, had acknowledged Urban, and that from this allegiance he could not swerve. The caution was necessary, because England as yet had been

neutral, and had acknowledged neither. Let the
king, he said, declare his mind on these points, that
I may know what my course is to be. The king
summoned two of his advisers, William de St.
Carileph Bishop of Durham, and Robert Count of
Meulan, or, as it was then written, Mellent, and asked
Anselm to repeat his words. He did so; and the
king by his council answered, that as to the see
property, Anselm should have all that Lanfranc had,
but that about any further claim he would make no
promise. And as to this and other points he would
trust Anselm as he should find that he ought. A few
days after he also received from Normandy the letters
releasing Anselm. He summoned Anselm to Windsor, where the court was staying, and invited him to
acquiesce in the choice made by himself and the
whole realm; but he went on to beg of Anselm, as
a personal favour to himself, that he would agree that
the grants of Church lands made by the king since
Lanfranc's death to military vassals of the Crown, on
tenure of service to himself, should stand. This meant
that these lands were to be withdrawn for good
from the see. To this Anselm would not agree. He
would not bargain to spoil a church office which was
not even yet his. His view, repeated more than once
in his letters, was clear and simple. It was a time
when reckless giving was followed by unscrupulous
encroachment; and his successor, he foresaw, would
have just as much as, and no more than, he himself
should have on the day when he died. If other people
robbed Church lands, or connived at the robbery, the
wrong might be repaired. "But now as the king is
the advocate of the Church, and the Archbishop the

trustee, the answer hereafter will be, to any claim of restitution, that what the king has done, and the archbishop confirmed by allowing, must hold good." The king was so irritated by this refusal that the whole matter was suspended. Anselm, says Eadmer, began to hope that he should escape the burden. "I said and did for six months," he says to his friend the Archbishop of Lyons, "all that I could without sin that I might be let off." But the complaints of the ruin of the Church began again, and were, after what had passed, too much for the king. The monks of Canterbury assailed Anselm with eager and angry appeals. At last he consented. At Winchester he was, "according to the custom of the land, made the king's man, and ordered to be seised of the whole archbishopric as Lanfranc had been." On the 5th of September he came to Canterbury, and was enthroned. On the very day of the solemnity Ralph Flambard appeared there, with his airs of insolence and his harshness, to disturb the festivities by a suit in the king's name against some of the archbishop's tenants. The people's minds were deeply wounded at the insult; that "a man like Anselm should not be allowed to pass the first day of his dignity in peace." He himself took it as a presage of what awaited him.

On the 4th of December, 1093, he was consecrated by the Archbishop of York, in the presence of nearly all the English bishops. According to the old ritual, the Book of the Gospels, opened at random, was laid on the shoulders of the newly consecrated prelate, and the passage at which it opened was taken as a sort of omen of his episcopate. The passage which turned up was, "He bade many, and sent his servant

at supper-time to say to them that were bidden,
Come; for all things are now ready. And they all
with one consent began to make excuse."

His first intercourse with the king was friendly;
but it was soon clouded. William was in the midst
of his projects against his brother Robert, and money
was his great want. Among others who offered their
presents, Anselm, urged by his friends, brought 500
marks. The king at first received it graciously.
But the men round him represented to him that he
might reasonably expect a much greater sum from
one to whom he had done such honour. Accordingly,
as his practice was when he was dissatisfied with a
present, Anselm's 500 marks were refused. He went
to the king and expostulated. "It was his first
present, but not his last; and a free gift was better
than a forced and servile contribution." His words
implied a reproof to the king's system of extortion;
and William answered angrily, that he wanted neither
his money nor his scolding, and bade him begone.
Anselm thought, says Eadmer, of the words of the
Gospel which had been read on the day when he first
entered his cathedral—"No man can serve two
masters." But the refusal was a relief. A sum of
money in the shape of a free gift, after a man was
consecrated, was one of the ways in which church
offices were sold and bought. Implacable opposition to
this system was one of the main points in the policy of
the reforming party with whom Anselm sympathised.
He congratulated himself that he was saved even from
the appearance of a corrupt bargain for the archbishopric. He was urged to regain the king's favour
by doubling his present, but he refused; he gave away

the money to the poor, and left the court when the Christmas festival was over.

He soon met William again. With the rest of the great men of England he was summoned in February 1094, to meet the king at Hastings, where he was waiting for a fair wind to carry him over to Normandy. The bishops were to give their blessing to the expedition, and to help the king by their prayers against the perils of the sea. There was a long delay from contrary winds, and Anselm now made his appeal to the king for help in the work which the king had forced upon him. The points on which he insisted were two. He wanted some check to the unbridled licence of manners to which the contemporary chronicles bear ample and detailed evidence; and he wanted important religious posts, like those of the abbots of the monasteries, to be filled up. The customary remedy for disorders, well known in England as in Normandy, was a council of bishops, meeting with the king's sanction, whose regulations were to be backed by his authority. Anselm asked for such a council, "by which Christian religion, which had well-nigh perished in many men, might be restored," and the influence of its teachers revived and strengthened. William demurred. He would call a council only at his own time—when he pleased, not when Anselm pleased; and, with a sneer, he asked what the council was to be about? "The whole land," said Anselm, "unless judgment and discipline are exercised in earnest, will soon be a Sodom." William was not pleased, and answered shortly, "What good would come of this matter for you?" "If not for me, at least, I hope, for God and for you." "Enough," said the king; "talk to me no more about it." Anselm left the subject, and spoke of the vacant abbeys, representing the ruin caused to the monks themselves, and the great danger to the king's soul, of leaving all this evil unredressed. William could no longer contain his anger. "What are the abbeys to you? Are they not mine? Go to; you do what you like with your farms, and am I not to do what I like with my abbeys?" "Yours," was the answer, "to protect as their advocate, not to waste and destroy and use for the expense of your wars." The king expressed again his great displeasure. "Your predecessor," he said, "would not have dared to speak thus to my father. I will do nothing for you." And they parted.

Anselm thought that in these ungracious answers the old anger about the money might be working; and he resolved to send a message by the bishops asking for the king's friendship. "If he will not give it me, let him say why; if I have offended, I am ready to make amends." "No," the king answered, "I have nothing to accuse him of; but I will not grant him my favour, because I do not hear any reason why I should." The bishops brought back the reply, and Anselm asked what he meant by "not hearing why he should." The bishops saw no difficulty in understanding him. "The mystery," they said, "is plain. If you want peace with him, you must give him money."—"Give him the five hundred pounds you offered," was their advice, "and promise as much more; and he will give you back his friendship. We see no other way of getting out of the difficulty; and we have no other for ourselves." "Far be it from me," said Anselm, "to take this way out of it." To such a precedent for extortion he could never lend himself. Besides, his tenants had been racked since Lanfranc's death; and was he "to strip them in their nakedness, or rather flay them alive?" It was unworthy to think of buying the king's favour, as he would a horse or an ass, for money. What he asked was to have as archbishop his love, and to give himself and all he had to his king's service. His business-like brethren remarked, that "at any rate he could not refuse the five hundred marks already offered." "No," he said, "he would not offer what had been rejected; and besides, the greater part of it was gone to the poor." When William was told of this, he sent back the following answer:—"Yesterday I hated him much, to-day still more; to-morrow and ever after he may be sure I shall hate him with more bitter hatred. As father and archbishop I will never hold him more; his blessings and prayers I utterly abhor and refuse. Let him go where he will, and not wait any longer for my crossing to give me his blessing." "Anselm departed with speed," says Eadmer, who appears from this time as the archbishop's constant companion, "and left him to his will." William crossed to Normandy, for what seemed at the time an inglorious summer war, in which all that was clear was that it had cost him vast sums of money, wrung from the English people, the English churches, and the English monks. Normandy was not yet his. But it was soon to be, and his was money not spent for nothing.

# CHAPTER IX.

### THE MEETING AT ROCKINGHAM.

> " O happy in their souls' high solitude
> Who commune thus with God and not with earth !
> Amid the scoffings of the wealth-enslaved
> A ready prey, as though in absent mood
> They calmly move, nor hear the unmannered mirth."
>
> *Lyra Apostolica*, xxiv.

THE signs of the approaching storm had shown themselves. William had found that the new archbishop was not a man to be frightened by rough words into compliance with arbitrary and unreasonable demands. Anselm had found what he had anticipated, that the king, once more in health, with his political objects before him and his need of money pressing him, would not listen to remonstrances, nor change his ways. Naturally enough, the king thought he had made a great mistake in forcing the archbishopric on Anselm. He began to think how he could force it from him. Occasions for attempting this were not likely to be wanting.

On his return from Normandy a new cause of difference was opened between him and Anselm. The rule had been established by the Popes, and accepted by Western Christendom, that a metropolitan must go to Rome to get from the Pope his *Pallium*, the white woollen stole with four crosses which was the badge of his office and dignity, and is still the special blazon in the armorial bearings of Canterbury. The usage was an acknowledged one at this time: Lanfranc himself had gone to Rome for the purpose. But the chair of St. Peter was now claimed by two rivals, Urban and Clement. Anselm had foreseen a difficulty in the matter. France and Normandy had acknowledged Urban; England had acknowledged neither. Anselm, before his final acceptance, had given fair warning that to him Urban was the true Pope; the king had evaded the subject. Anselm now asked leave to go to Rome for his *Pallium*. William was at Gillingham, a royal residence near Shaftesbury, on the borders of the Forest of Selwood. "From which Pope?" asked the king. Anselm had already given the answer to the question, and he could but repeat it—"From Pope Urban." "Urban," said the king, "I have not acknowledged. By my customs, by the customs of my father, no man may acknowledge a Pope in England without my leave. To challenge my power in this, is as much as to deprive me of my crown." Anselm reminded him of the warning given at Rochester. The king broke forth in anger, declaring that Anselm could not keep his faith to the king, and his obedience to the Apostolic See, without the king's leave. The question thus raised could not be left unsettled. Was that indeed the rule for the Churchmen of England? Anselm demanded that it should be answered by the great council of England. The demand could not be refused, and an assembly was summoned to consider the whole matter, and to give the king advice upon it.

Accordingly a great meeting of the chief men in Church and State was held at the Castle of Rockingham. "The tangled forest of Rockingham," says Sir F. Palgrave, "a continuation of the Derbyshire woodlands, was among the largest and most secluded in the kingdom. At a much later period, this dreary weald measured thirty miles in length. The castle, raised by the Conqueror, had been planned by the cautious sovereign quite as much for the purpose of coercing the inhabitants, as for the protection of the glowing furnaces. Echoes of facts and opinions, the mediæval traditions, represent the forgemen as a peculiarly barbarous class; had Anselm been faint-hearted, he might have dreaded placing himself in a spot where the executioners of any misdeed or cruelty might be so readily found." But he had no reason for such fears. Fierce as the age was, and fierce as William was, such an end to his quarrel with Anselm was never thought of. Roughness, insult, treachery, high-handed injustice, were weapons to be used without scruple; but it is not enough to say that the murder of an opponent like Anselm, judicial or secret, would have shocked everybody: it never presented itself to the king's mind. Anselm all along was quite safe of his life, and felt himself to be so.

The great council—we might almost call it a parliament—met on Mid-Lent Sunday, March 11, 1095, probably in the church of the castle. There were the bishops, abbots, and nobles; and besides a numerous throng, watching and listening, of "monks, clerics, and laymen." The king did not appear; he had his private council sitting apart, from which messages passed to and fro between him and the archbishop in the larger public assembly. The proceedings are reported in great detail, day by day, by Eadmer, who was present, and who probably heard what passed on the king's side from Gundulf, the one bishop who did not take part against Anslem. Anslem stated his case, and the reasons why he invoked their judgment and arbitration. It was the same question which was to be put by the king, and answered so emphatically by bishops and parliament, four centuries later; but it was put under very different circumstances, and under very different conditions at this time. "The king," said Anslem, "had told him that he had not yet acknowledged Urban as Pope, and that he therefore did not chose that Anslem should go to Urban for the Pallium." He had added, "if you receive in my realm Urban or any one else for Pope, without my choice and authority, or if having received him you hold to him, you act against the faith which you owe to me, and offend me not less than if you tried to deprive me of my crown. Therefore be assured that in my realm you shall have no part, unless I have the proof by plain declarations that, according to my wish, you refuse all submission and obedience to Urban." Anselm went on to remind them that it was by no wish or seeking of his own that he was archbishop; that he had been driven to it; that he had known his own infirmities, and urged them; further, that on this point he had from the first given fair notice that he had acknowledged Urban, and would not swerve from his obedience for an hour. "They knew," he said, "how much he had desired the burden, how attractive he had held it, what pleasure he had found in it." He declared once more that he would rather, with all reverence to the will of God, have been cast into the fire than have been exalted to the archbishopric. "But," he said, "seeing that you were importunate, I have trusted myself to you, and taken up the load you put upon me, relying on the hope of your promised assistance." Now the time had come to claim the promise. The question had been adjourned to this assemblage, that they all might by joint counsel inquire whether, saving his faith to the king, he could keep his obedience to the Apostolic See. He especially appealed to his brethren the bishops, that "they would show him how he might neither do anything contrary to his obedience to the Pope, nor offend against the faith which he owed to the king. For it is a serious thing to despise and deny the Vicar of St. Peter; it is a serious thing to break the faith which I promised to keep, according to God, to the king: but that, too, is serious which is said, that it is impossible for me to keep the one without breaking the other."

It was a fair question to men with the inherited and unbroken convictions of the religion of that age. The claim which William maintained had come down to him from his father, who had insisted on it resolutely, with Lanfranc's sanction or acquiescence, even against Gregory VII. "It was a prerogative," the bishops declared, "which their lord held chief above anything in his government, and in which it was clear that he excelled all other kings." On the other hand, no one in those days imagined Christianity without Christendom, and Christendom without a Pope; and all these bishops understood exactly as Anselm did the favourite papal text, "Thou art Peter, and on this rock I will build my Church." Nobody in those days doubted the divine authority of the Pope: the claim on which the Norman kings laid so much stress had naturally and reasonably arisen from the contest of rival popes, and the doubt who was really the true Pope. No one had held more intimate relations with Rome, or made more use of the Pope's power, than William the Conqueror. But with Anselm, the only question that there could be, who was the Pope, was, as he had from the first declared, no question at all; he, with Normandy, and all Gaul, had recognized Urban as the true Pope. It was part of William's policy of mingled bullying and trickery, the trust placed in evasion and delay by a man who doubted of all men's straightforwardness and disinterestedness, and hoped that with time their selfishness would be his sure ally, that he shut his eyes to what was plain from the first, that the Pope whom Anselm had acknowledged, he would stick to.

But the bishops were in heart, as well as by the forms of the law, the king's men. Some of them had bought their bishoprics, most of them were afraid of William, and were always expecting to have to appease his wrath by heavy gifts of money. They saw, too, that a quarrel of this kind was most dangerous to the already precarious peace of their churches; and they refused to be drawn into it. With compliments on Anselm's wisdom, which ought, they said, to be their guide, they declined to give any other advice than that he should submit himself without conditions to the king's will. They were willing, however, to report his words to the king, and the proceedings were adjourned to the morrow. On the Monday accordingly, they met again, and Anselm repeated his question, to which they gave the same answer. They would advise him only on condition of his submitting himself, without qualification or reserve, to the king's will. It was the answer of cowards, convicted by their own conscience, and knowing that all who heard them knew what was in their conscience. "Having said these words, they were silent," says Eadmer, "and hung down their heads, as if to receive what was coming on them." Then Anselm, his eyes kindling, made his appeal. "Since you," he said, "the shepherds of the Christian people, and you who are called chiefs of the nation, refuse your counsel to me, your chief, except according to the will of one man, I will go to the Chief Shepherd and Prince of all; I will hasten to the *Angel of great counsel*, and receive from Him the counsel which I will follow in this my cause, yea, His cause and that of His Church. He says to the most blessed of the apostles, Peter, '*Thou art Peter, and on this rock will I build my Church,*' &c. . . . And, again, to all the apostles, jointly: '*He that hears you hears me, and he that despises you despises me; and he who touches you touches the apple of mine eye.*' It was primarily to St. Peter, and in him to the other apostles; it is primarily to St. Peter's vicar, and through him to the other bishops who fill the apostles' places, that these words, as we believe, were said; not to any emperor whatsoever, not to any king, to no duke, or count. But wherein we must be subject and minister to earthly princes, the same Angel of great counsel teaches us, saying: '*Render to Cæsar the things that are Cæsar's, and the things that are God's to God.*' These are God's words, these are God's counsels. These I allow and accept, and from them will I not depart. Know ye, therefore, all of you, that in the things that are God's I will render obedience to the Vicar of St. Peter; and in those which belong of right to the earthly dignity of my lord the king, I will render him both faithful counsel and service, to the best of my understanding and power." The chief men of the assembly were not prepared for this bold and direct announcement. Their irritation broke out in angry and confused clamour, "so that it might be thought that they were declaring him guilty of death;" and they peremptorily and angrily refused to report Anselm's words to the king, to whose chamber they retired. Anselm, finding no one whom he could trust to inform William of what had passed, went to him and repeated his words in his presence. William was, of course, very angry. He intended that Anselm should be silenced as well as forced to submission; and he looked to his bishops especially to silence him. It was not easy for them "to find something to say which should at once soothe the king's wrath, and not openly contradict the alleged words of God." Eadmer describes their perplexity, as, broken up into knots of two or three, they discussed the matter; while Anselm, who had returned to the church, sat by himself to wait the result, and at last, wearied by the delay, "leaning his head against the wall, fell into a calm sleep."

At length, late in the day, the bishops with some of the lay nobles came to him from the king. Their language was a mixture of coaxing and menace. "The king," they said, "requires peremptorily an immediate settlement, once for all, of the question which had been opened at Gillingham and adjourned at Anselm's request to the present time. The matter was perfectly plain and needed no argument. The whole realm cried out against him for impairing the honour of their lord's imperial crown; for to take away the customs of the royal dignity was as good as taking away the king's crown; one could not be duly held without the other." Then they appealed to his pride and self-interest. "This Urban could be of no use to him; why not shake off the yoke of subjection to him, and be free, as becomes an Archbishop of Canterbury, to fulfil the commands of our lord the king. Let him like a wise man ask pardon, and fall in with the king's wish; and so they who hated him, and exulted over his troubles, would be put to confusion by the restoration of his high place." Anselm, still declining to withdraw his obedience from Pope Urban, asked, as the day was closing, to put off his reply to the morrow, "so that thinking over it I may answer what God shall please to inspire." They judged that this meant that he was wavering. The leader and spokesman on the king's side was the Bishop of Durham, William de St. Carileph. William—by Eadmer's own account, a ready and clever speaker, for he gives him this credit, while he denies him that of "true wisdom"—had, early in the king's reign, begun by measuring his strength against the king; he had resisted the claim of jurisdiction of the king's court on a bishop; he had tampered with, if he had not joined in, the great conspiracy of the Normans under Bishop Odo of Bayeux and Bishop Geoffry of Coutances; he had been forced to make terms with the king, to leave his bishopric, and spend some years in banishment; and now he was reconciled with the king, and had formed the hope, that if he could get Anselm out of the archbishopric he might be his successor. He had done his best to foment the quarrel between the king and Anselm ; and now, encouraged by Anselm's request for delay, he boldly engaged to William either to make him renounce the Pope, or to force him to resign the see by the surrender of the ring and staff. Either would suit William's policy: Anselm would be discredited and unable to speak and act with authority, if he gave up the Pope ; or the king would be rid of him altogether, and have established his absolute power by the most signal proof of strength. " For what he wished was to take from Anselm all authority for carrying out Christian religion. For he had a misgiving that he was not in complete possession of the royal dignity, as long as any one in all the land was said, even in matters of conscience (*secundum Deum*), to hold anything or to have any power, except through him." The Bishop of Durham, accordingly, returned to Anselm with the king's final summons. Anselm had dared to make the Bishop of Ostia Pope without the king's authority in this his England. " Clothe him again, if you please, with the due dignity of his imperial crown, and then talk of delay. Else, he imprecates the hatred of Almighty God on himself, and we his liegemen join in the imprecation, if he grant even for an hour the delay you ask for till to-morrow. Therefore, answer at once, or you shall on the spot feel the doom which is to avenge your presumption. Think it no matter of jest. To us it is a matter of great pain and anger And no wonder. For that which your Lord and ours has as the chief prerogative of his rule, and in which it is certain that he excels all other kings, you, as far as you can, rob him of, against the faith you have pledged him, and to the great distress and trouble of all his friends." But William de St. Carileph had overshot his mark and mistaken the man with whom he had to deal. This threat of instant summary judgment at the king's will and word might frighten; but if it did not frighten, it would be thrown away on anyone who could appeal to the by no means dormant ideas of law and justice. Anselm listened patiently, and replied, "Whoever would prove that, because I will not renounce the obedience of the venerable bishop of the holy Roman Church, I am violating my faith and my oath to my earthly king, let him present himself, and he shall find me prepared to answer him, as I ought, and where I ought." When the Bishop of Durham and his companions came to see the meaning of Anselm's words, "as I ought and where I ought," they recognized in it a plea to which they had no answer; for it meant that no one could pass judgment on an Archbishop of Canterbury, except the highest judge and authority in Christendom, the Pope himself; and the claim came home too powerfully to the minds of men, both as Christians and as Englishmen, for the king's Norman bishops to think of questioning it. The sympathy of the crowd had been with Anselm; but fear of the king had kept down the expression of it to faint murmurs. But now a soldier stepped out of the throng, and kneeling before the archbishop, said, " Lord and Father, thy children, through me, beseech thee not to let thy heart be troubled by what thou hast heard; but remember how holy Job on the dunghill vanquished the devil, and avenged Adam whom the devil had vanquished in Paradise." The quaint attempt at encouragement cheered Anselm. "He perceived that the feeling of the people was with him. So we were glad, and were more at ease in our minds, being confident, according to the Scripture, that the voice of the people is the voice of God."

But in the court there was great vexation. "What shall I do?" says our reporter Eadmer—literally our reporter, for he was present during the whole session:—"Were I to attempt to describe the threats, reproaches, insults, false and foul language with which the archbishop was assailed, I should be judged an exaggerator." The king was exasperated, "even to the dividing of his spirit,"[1] with the failure of the bishops: "What is this? Did you not promise that you would treat him according to my will, judge him, condemn him?" The Bishop of Durham was thoroughly disconcerted; his words on every point were tame and halting; he seemed to have lost his head. He could only suggest what he had refused to Anselm, delay till the morrow. On the morrow, Tuesday morning, Anselm and his companions were in their accustomed seats, waiting the king's orders. For a long time none came. The council was perplexed. The Bishop of Durham had nothing better to recommend than open violence. As a matter of argument there was nothing to be said; Anselm had the words of God, the authority of the Apostle on his side. But his staff and ring could be taken from him by force,

[1] Heb. iv. 12, Vulg.

and he expelled the kingdom. The Bishop of Durham suggested the last expedient which the bishops could agree in. Such a termination to the quarrel would be at least the king's act, not their own, as it would be if they passed judgment on him or on his plea. An impracticable and dangerous leader would be got rid of by lay violence, and they would not be compromised. But if the bishops acquiesced, the laymen of the council were dissatisfied. They were beginning to think that things were going too far. The same feeling which made the commons see in the archbishop the first of Englishmen, the successor of the great Englishman Dunstan, of the great Italian who had turned Englishman, Lanfranc, made the nobles see in him the first of their own order, the Father of the chiefs of the realm, with whom they could have no rivalry, the mediator and arbiter between them and the crown, and the bulwark against its tyranny Only second to the crown, as part of the honour and dignity of the land, was the archbishopric of Canterbury: an injury to its honour was as serious as an injury to that of the crown. The barons refused to agree with the advice of the bishop. "His words did not please them." "What does please you then," said the king, "if they do not? While I live, equal in my realm I will not endure. And if you knew that he had such strength on his side, why did you let me engage in this legal conflict against him? Go, go, take counsel together; for by God's countenance, if you do not condemn him, I will condemn you." One of the shrewdest of them, Robert Count of Mellent, who was hereafter to be one of Anselm's stoutest enemies, answered, apparently with a sense of amusement at the baffled eagerness of the bishops, and perhaps with something of a sportsman's admiration for the gallantry of the single-handed defence, "About our counsels, I don't know quite what to say. For when we have been arranging them all day long, and have settled, by talking them over among ourselves, how they are to hold together, he goes to sleep, and thinks no harm; and the moment they are opened before him, with one breath of his lips he breaks them as if they were cobwebs." The king turned again to the bishops: "What could they do?" It was out of the question, they said, to judge him; but they agreed in the king's strange suggestion, that though they could not judge him, they could withdraw their obedience from him, and deny him their brotherly friendship. This, then, was agreed upon; and, accompanied by some of the English abbots, they finally announced to the archbishop that they withdrew their obedience from him, as the king also withdrew from him his protection and confidence, and would never more hold him for archbishop and ghostly father. Anselm was to become a kind of outlaw, abandoned by all his brethren, deprived of the king's protection and out of the king's peace, put to shame before the whole realm. His answer was calm and temperate. There must be two to make a quarrel, and he on his part would not quarrel either with them or with the king. He renewed his own promise of fidelity and service to the king; he would still hold himself responsible for the king's spiritual welfare, as far as the king deigned to allow him; and, come what might, he should still retain the authority and name of the Archbishop of Canterbury. William heard his answer with displeasure; he had probably expected submission or resignation. There was still one more thing to do: the ecclesiastical members of the council had formally deserted Anselm, but the laymen had not. The king turned to them: "No man shall be mine," he said, "who chooses to be his;" appealing to the feudal feeling about homage: and he called on his barons to follow the example of the bishops. But the tide had now completely turned. They absolutely refused to lend themselves to a precedent so dangerous to all their liberties. They in their turn appealed to the subtleties of feudal customs. "We never were his men, and we cannot abjure the fealty which we never swore. He is our archbishop. He has to govern Christian religion in this land, and in this respect we, who are Christians, cannot refuse his guidance while we live here, especially as no spot of offence attaches to him to make you act differently as regards him."

The answer altered the whole face of matters. It turned what had seemed the winning side into the beaten and disappointed one. It upset all the king's plans, and the three days' laborious and shifty attempts of the Bishop of Durham and his fellows. The laymen, high and low, refused to go with them; and the defeat was confessed. The king, angry as he was, dared not carry things too far with his unruly barons. The bishops had made their sacrifice of honour and conscience for nothing; nothing was gained by the public display of their subserviency, which it was not even thought worth while to follow up. On all sides they met mocking eyes and scowling looks, and heard themselves spoken of in bywords of reproach: "This or that bishop you might hear branded now by one

P

man, then by another, with some nickname, accompanying bursts of disgust : Judas the traitor, Pilate, Herod, and the like." Nor was this all. The king turned upon them, and, as if suspicious of their straightforwardness, put to them a test one by one ; did they renounce obedience to Anselm unconditionally, or only so far as he claimed it by the authority of the Pope? The answers, as might be expected, were various. Those who gave it boldly and without reserve were treated with marks of favour as the king's faithful friends and liegemen ; "those who qualified it, were driven from his presence, as quibblers and treacherous equivocators, and ordered to await the sentence of his judgment in a distant part of the castle. Thus terrified and covered with confusion upon confusion, they skulked away to a corner of the building. There they soon found the wholesome and familiar counsel on which they were wont to rely : they gave a large sum of money, and they were received back into the king's favour."

Anselm, however, could not treat this public intimation from the king, that he was out of the king's protection, merely as a feint. He at once demanded a safe-conduct for one of the outports, that he might quit the kingdom. But it was not William's game that he should leave, still "seised" of the archbishopric ; there was no way to "disseise" him, and the demand was an unpleasant surprise. The bishops had got the king into the difficulty with their advice, and he had now in his irritation broken up his party among them, by inflicting on them the humiliation of the test question about their sincerity in renouncing Anselm. He consulted with the barons ;

and by their advice, the archbishop was again told to retire to his lodging and come on the morrow for his answer. Early on Wednesday morning he received a message : " Our lord the king desires you to come to him." He went, anxious to know his fate, divided between the hope of escape from his burdens and the fear of remaining in England. " We mounted up, we went and took our seat in our accustomed place, eager to know the final issue of our matter." The message came in the shape of a proposed adjournment of the whole question. Anselm said that it was only an attempt to gain time ; but it was not for him to refuse delay; and a "truce" was agreed upon till the following Whitsuntide ; the king still intimating that the question could only be settled on his present terms.

Anselm accordingly left the court. But the policy of annoyance and ill-usage did not cease. The king's ill-humour vented itself on his friends. Baldwin of Tournai, a monk of Bec, who had been much in Anselm's confidence, was summarily expelled the kingdom. The archbishop's chamberlain was arrested in his very chamber before his eyes. The vexatious system of the king's treasury and law courts was carried on against the monks at Canterbury. "That Church," says Eadmer, "suffered such a storm in all its tenants, that every one agreed that it would be better to be without a pastor at all as they had been, than to have such a pastor as this." The archbishop, according to the ways of the time, spent his time in his various country manors ; Harrow, Hayes, and Mortlake.

# CHAPTER X.

### THE FINAL QUARREL WITH WILLIAM.

> " Whose powers shed round him in the common strife,
> Or mild concerns of ordinary life,
> A constant influence, a peculiar grace;
> But who, if he be called upon to face
> Some awful moment, to which Heaven has joined
> Great issues, good or bad, for human kind,
> Is happy as a Lover; and attired
> With sudden brightness, like a man inspired;
> And, through the heat of conflict, keeps the law
> In calmness made, and sees what he foresaw.
> \*   \*   \*   \*   \*   \*
> Who, with a toward or untoward lot,
> Prosperous or adverse, to his wish or not—
> Plays, in the many games of life, that one
> Where what he most doth value must be won."
>
> WORDSWORTH's *Happy Warrior*

WILLIAM had not the least intention to disown the Pope or to quarrel with Rome; and his first step was an attempt to play off Urban's name and authority on his own side against Anselm. When the question first arose he had sent two of the clerks of the chapel, Gerard, afterwards Archbishop of York, and William of Warelwast, to Rome, to inquire into the state of things between the rival popes; and further, to persuade the Pope, by the means which were usual in those days, and which were supposed even under the reformed papacy of Gregory VII. to have great power at Rome, to send the archiepiscopal pall to the king to be given by him, with the Pope's sanction, to the Archbishop of Canterbury, the name of the archbishop being suppressed. They found Urban in possession of Rome, and acknowledged him; and in answer to the king's request Walter, Bishop of Albano, came to England as papal legate, in company with the two chaplains, shortly before the appointed time at Whitsuntide, bringing with him the pallium. But the greatest secrecy was observed. He passed through Canterbury privately, taking no notice of the archbishop, and proceeded straight to the king. His first object was to secure the formal recognition of Urban in England. Anselm's friends heard with consternation that the Pope's legate had encouraged the king to hope that all his wishes would be granted, and that he had said not a word in Anselm's favour, or done anything on behalf of one whose loyalty to the Pope had cost him so dear. The disappointment was great: "What are we to say? If Rome prefers gold and silver to justice, what help and counsel and comfort may those expect in their troubles who have not wherewithal to pay that they may have right done them in their cause?"

What passed between the king and the Bishop of Albano does not appear. Eadmer says that the legate reported the Pope ready to agree to all the king's wishes, and willing to grant them by special privilege for his lifetime. But the result was that Urban was formally acknowledged as Pope in England. Having recognized Urban, the king then asked for the deposition of Anselm by the Pope's authority. He offered, says Eadmer, a large annual payment to the Roman Church if he could have his wish. But this was too much; and he gave up the project, regretting that he had gained so little by his recognition of Urban, but, as the mistake was past remedy, intending to make the best of it.

At Whitsuntide, Anselm, who had been keeping the festival at his manor of Mortlake, was summoned to the neighbourhood of Windsor, where the king was, and came to Hayes, another of his manors. He was visited the next day by nearly all the bishops, and their errand was once more to prevail on him to make up the quarrel by a payment of money. Anselm was inflexible. He would not do his lord the shame to treat his friendship as a matter of bargain; he asked for it freely, as his archbishop and his subject. If he could not have it on these terms, he asked again for a safe-conduct to quit the realm. "Have you nothing else to say to us?" They then told him of the arrival of the archiepiscopal stole, sent by the Pope to the king. Here it was, to be had without the trouble of the journey. Would he not make some acknowledgment of the benefit to himself? Would he not, for his own credit's sake, offer the king at least what he would have spent on the journey? But he would not hear of it, and bade them leave off. The king saw that his game had been a false one, and threw it up at last frankly. Trouble was abroad, and it was no time to be keeping up a quarrel in which he was baffled, and in which he could not carry the opinion of his subjects with him. Rebellion was threatening in the north: Robert Mowbray, Earl of Northumberland, had refused the king's summons to appear at Windsor; the Welsh marches were always dangerous. William was preparing for a busy and critical summer, and he could not afford to offend his chief men. Without more ado he followed their advice, and freely restored Anselm to his favour. Bygones were to be bygones, and he granted that the archbishop should freely exercise his office as the spiritual father of the realm. They met publicly at Windsor as friends, in the presence of the nobles and the assembled multitude; and while they were conversing, "behold," says Eadmer, "that Roman Walter appears, and pleasantly quotes the verse, '*Behold, how good and joyful a thing it is, brethren, to dwell together in unity.*' And, sitting down, he discoursed somewhat from the Lord's words about peace, praising the revival of it between them, though feeling all the while to his shame that it was not by his exertions that peace had been sown."

It was still hoped that Anselm might flatter the king by receiving the pall from his hands. But he refused: what everyone looked upon as St. Peter's gift it did not belong to the royal dignity to convey to him. His view was the natural one, and he was not pressed. It was arranged that it was to be laid on the altar at Canterbury, and that Anselm was to take it from thence. There accordingly, on the Third Sunday after Trinity, June 10, 1095, it was brought with great ceremony by Bishop Walter in a silver case. Anselm, bare-footed and surrounded by the bishops, took it from the altar. Again, it is said, as at his consecration, the Gospel of the day happened to be the parable of the great supper, with the words about "calling many," and "all with one consent beginning to make excuse." These things then impressed men's minds as significant, and the double coincidence naturally excited much remark. For the time Anselm was left in peace. On his way from Windsor two other bishops who had taken part against him at Rockingham, Osmund of Salisbury and Robert of Hereford, the special friend of St. Wulfstan of Worcester, followed him and asked his forgiveness. They turned, says Eadmer, into a little church by the way, and there he absolved them. His chief antagonist, William de St. Carileph, a foiled and disappointed man, felt the anger of his hard master. His ill-success was harshly visited on him. " He received a summons," says Sir F. Palgrave, " to appear before the *curia Regis*, the 'King's Court,' as a delinquent. Grievously ill, he requested a respite. Rufus rudely and cruelly refused the strictly lawful *essoign, de malo lecti* (the excuse of a sickness which confined him to his bed); one which, according to our ancient jurisprudence, the meanest defendant might claim as a matter of right—swearing the excuse was a sham. The bishop was compelled to follow the court, in which he had recently paraded so proudly; but he sank under the combined effects of vexation and disease, for when he reached Windsor he took again to his bed, from whence he never rose. Anselm diligently and affectionately attended him, received his confession, administered the last sacraments, prayed with him and for him. The bishop's corpse was interred in Durham cloister, before the chapter door. St. Carileph, though urged, refused to allow his decaying body to intrude within St. Cuthbert's towering minster, the noble monument which he had raised." His possessions, like those of other bishops who died in this reign, were seized by Ralph Flambard and his brother Fulbert for the king's use. Three years and a half afterwards Ralph Flambard gained his great bishopric for himself—"the Palatine see" of England.

A year of comparative respite followed. The year 1096 was a busy year for the king. It had begun with the signal vengeance taken by him at Salisbury against the conspirators of the year before, and it was the year of the First Crusade. All Europe was stirred by an impulse which seemed to set not armies but whole populations in motion, and to reverse the long accustomed current of migration, turning it backward to the East. Robert of Normandy, unable to govern, but ready for adventure and fresh conquest, was carried away by the enthusiasm of the time; he had no money, and William saw at last his opportunity arrive. He bought Normandy of his brother for three years. The money was, as usual, to be drawn from England, and the statements of Eadmer and the English chroniclers may well be believed that it was a hard time for England. The lands were racked; the churches spoiled of their treasures—their chalices, and reliquaries, and volumes of the Gospels bound in gold and silver. Anselm only suffered as the rest. He had of course to furnish his contribution, and he judged it but reasonable and fitting that he should do so. But the see had been so impoverished that his own means were insufficient; he had to take two hundred marks of silver from the treasury of the Church of Canterbury; and that it might not be a bad precedent to his successors, he mortgaged to the Church his archiepiscopal manor of Peckham for seven years to repay the debt. It was a good bargain for the monks, and with the Peckham rents they built part of their church. But Eadmer is particular in giving these details, because even while he was writing, there were those who accused Anselm of robbing the Church of Canterbury. Between the king and the monks his money difficulties were not easy to arrange.

But other difficulties were soon to return on him. Wales was as troublesome to William as Ireland was to Elizabeth. He marched through the country, but he failed to subdue it; and he lost many men and horses in the attempt. In 1097 he tried to strike a more serious blow; but little came of it. He came back in ill-humour. Anselm again felt it. He received a letter from the king, complaining of the contingent of soldiers whom the archbishop had sent to the army: "He had nothing but evil thanks to give him for them; they were insufficiently equipped, and not fit for the work required." The king therefore required him to be ready to "do the king right" for their default, according to the judgment of the King's Court, whenever the king chose to summon him. "*We looked for peace,*" said Anselm, when he received the message, "*but no good came; for a time of health, and behold trouble.*" He had, says Eadmer, been biding his time in hope to get the king's ear, and had been restraining the impatience of those who urged him about the state of Christian religion; but now he saw that his opponents were too strong for him. The summons before the King's Court meant at the time a foregone conclusion against the defendant. The king had him now at his mercy, not on a question of religion, but of feudal service. "The king," says Sir F. Palgrave, "was judge in his Court whenever he

pleased. The security of securities, the doctrine that the king had irrevocably delegated his judicial authority to the ermine on the bench, required centuries ere it could be perfected. Let the reader carefully treasure this in his mind, and recollect that when, in Anglo-Norman times, you speak of the 'King's Court,' it is only a phrase for the king's despotism."
" Knowing," says Eadmer, " that all judgments of the King's Court depended on the king's word, and that nothing was considered there but what he willed, Anselm thought it an unbecoming farce to strive as litigants do about a verbal charge, and to submit the truth of his cause to the judgment of a court, of which neither law, nor equity, nor reason were the warrant. He held his peace therefore, and gave no answer to the messenger, looking on this kind of summons as belonging to that class of annoyances which he well remembered; and this only he earnestly prayed, that God would calm them." But he made up his mind that he was powerless to stop the mischief and wrong, for which yet he was looked upon as partly responsible. There was but one course for him. He must seek counsel and support from the head of the Hierarchy and the Church.

At the Whitsun meeting, while people were asking what was to come of this charge, whether Anselm would have to pay a large fine, or to submit to the king and never lift up his head more, he sent a request to the king for permission to go to Rome. The request was a surprise. William refused. " Anselm could have no sin needing such absolution; and as for counsel, that he was more fit to give it to the 'Apostolicus,' the Apostle's Vicar, than the Apostolicus to give it to him." "Perhaps, if not this time, he will grant me leave next time," was Anselm's answer; but nothing more was heard of the charge in the King's Court. Again at a great meeting in August Anselm renewed his request with the like result. In October he came by appointment to the king at Winchester, and again repeated his prayer. The king peremptorily refused, with threats if he persisted in his request, or if he went without leave. The scenes of Rockingham were repeated. Walkelin the Bishop of Winchester took the place which had been filled by William of Durham, and was joined as before by several other bishops. They urged obedience to the king, and the uselessness of going to the Pope. When Anselm urged their duties as bishops of the Church of God, they plainly said, that such high views were very well for a man like Anselm; but they had their friends and relations to think of; they had important business to care for; and they could not afford to "rise to his heights, or despise this world with him." "You have said well," was the answer: "go to your lord, I will hold to my God." But now the barons were against him. It was not according to the customs of the realm that a man of Anselm's dignity should leave it without the king's licence; and they urged strongly that Anselm had sworn to obey these customs. "According to right, and according to God," he immediately rejoined; but the qualification was scouted. The discussion became hot and vehement. Anselm had proceeded straight to the king's presence, when this message about the obligation of his oath was brought to him; and seating himself, according to the custom, at the king's right hand, maintained the necessary limitations of all oaths, and the ties which bound him, as a duty to God, to allegiance to the Head of Christendom. "You, O king," he said, "would not take it easily if one of your rich and powerful vassals hindered one of *his* dependants, who was busy on your service, from doing the duty to which by his fealty he was bound." "A sermon, a sermon!" cried out together the king and Robert Count of Mellent; and this was a signal for a general outcry. Anselm listened, and then went on quietly. "You want me to swear, in order that you may feel safe of me, that I will never more appeal to St. Peter or his Vicar. This is a demand which as a Christian you ought not to make. For to swear this is to forswear St. Peter; and to forswear St. Peter is to forswear Christ, who has made him chief over His Church. When then I deny Christ, then I will readily pay the penalty in your court, for asking for this licence." The Count of Mellent made a scornful reply: "He might present himself to Peter and the Pope; they knew well enough what they were about." "God knows," Anselm answered, "what awaits you; and He will be able to help me, if He wills it, to the threshold of His apostles." The company broke up. A message followed Anselm, to the effect that, if he went himself, he was to carry nothing away with him belonging to the king. "Does he mean my horses, and dress, and furniture, which he may perhaps call his own?" The message was a burst of that mere desire to insult and annoy which William was ashamed of when he had indulged it; and he sent word that Anselm was within ten days to be at the sea, and there the king's officer would meet him, to settle what he might take with him. The parting then had come, perhaps the leavetaking. Anselm's affectionate nature was moved, and he could not restrain a burst of kindly feeling. Nor was William himself unmoved by it. With cheerful and bright countenance he returned to the king: "My lord," he said, "I go. If it could have been with your good-will, it would have better become you, and been more agreeable to all good people. But as things have gone contrary, though on your behalf I am sorry, yet as far as I am concerned, I will bear it with an even mind, and not for this will I give up, by God's mercy, my love for your soul's health And now, not knowing when I shall see you again, I commend you to God; and as a spiritual father to his beloved son, as the Archbishop of Canterbury to the King of England, I would fain before I go, if you refuse it not, give God's blessing and my own." "I refuse not thy blessing," the king answered. He bowed his head, and Anselm lifted his right hand, and made the sign of the cross on him. And so they parted: on Thursday, Oct. 15, 1097.

Anselm returned at once to Canterbury, where, after taking leave of the monks, he took at the altar the pilgrim's staff and scrip, and set forth to Dover. At Dover he was detained a fortnight by the weather, and he found there the king's officer, one of the clerks of the royal chapel, William Warelwast, who lived with him during his detention. When at last the wind became fair and Anselm was embarking, William Warelwast, to the surprise and disgust of the bystanders, came forward, and required all the baggage to be searched. It was meant as a parting indignity; and it came the worse from an ecclesiastic who had been living all the time at Anselm's table. But no treasure was found; and he and his company landed safely at Witsand. William immediately seized the property of the see, and kept it till his death.

And thus began that system of appeals to Rome, and of inviting foreign interference in our home concerns, which grew to such a mischievous and scandalous height; and Anselm was the beginner of it. Yet he began it not only in good faith but with good reason. He had the strongest grounds and the most urgent motives for insisting on it; and his single-handed contest with power in order to maintain it was one of the steps, and though one serving but for the time, not the least noble and impressive of the steps, in the long battle of law against tyranny, of reason against self-will, of faith in right against worldliness and brute-force. It is true that, unanswerable as Anselm's pleas were according to the universal traditions and understandings of the time, the instinct of the lawless king and his subservient prelates was right, even when they knew not how to silence Anselm and their own conscience, and were leagued together, the one to defy all control, the other to uphold injustice as the price of serving their own interests. They were right, though for wrong reasons, in their jealousy of any rival to the crown in England: and experience has amply shown, century after century, that supreme and irresponsible authority has no protection against the most monstrous abuse by being for spiritual ends; and that the power of that great tribunal which Hildebrand imagined and created, to keep the great ones of the earth in order and to maintain the right of the helpless against the mighty, quickly became, in the hands of men, as lawless, as unscrupulous, as infamously selfish, as the worst of those tyrannies of this world which it professed to encounter with the law of God and the authority of Christ. But in Anselm's time all this was yet future, and men must do their work with the instruments and under the conditions of the present. To him the present showed a throne of judgment, different in its origin and authority from all earthly thrones; a common father and guide of Christians whom all acknowledged, and who was clothed with prerogatives which all believed to come from above; a law of high purpose and scope, embodying the greatest principles of justice and purity, and aiming, on the widest scale, at the elevation and improvement of society; an administration of this law, which regarded not persons and was not afraid of the face of man, and told the truth to ambitious emperors and adulterous kings and queens. In England Anselm had stood only for right and liberty; he, the chief witness for religion and righteousness, saw all round him vice rampant, men spoiled of what was their own—justice, decency, honour, trampled under foot. Law was unknown, except to ensnare and oppress. The King's Court was the instrument of one man's selfish and cruel will, and of the devices of a cunning and greedy minister. The natural remedies of wrong were destroyed and corrupted; the king's peace, the king's law, the king's justice, to which men in those days looked for help, could only be thought of in mocking contrast to the reality. Against this energetic reign of misrule and injustice, a resistance as energetic was wanted; and to resist it was felt to be the call and bounden duty of a man in Anselm's place. He resisted, as was the way in those days, man to man, person to person, in outright fashion and plain-spoken words. He resisted lawlessness, wickedness, oppression, corruption. When others acquiesced in the evil state, he refused; and further, he taught a lesson which England has since largely learned, though in a very different way. He taught his generation to appeal from force and arbitrary will to law. It was idle to talk of appealing to law in England; its time had not yet come. But there was a very real and living law in Christendom; a law, as we know now, of very mixed and questionable growth, yet in those days unsuspected, and in its character far more complete, rational, and imposing than any other code which had grown up in that stage of society— equal, impartial, with living and powerful sanctions. On it Anselm cast himself. *We* see, perhaps, in what he did, an appeal against his king, against the constitution of England and the independent rights of the nation, to a foreign power. If we see with the eyes of his own age, we shall see the only appeal practicable then from arbitrary rule to law.

If anyone wishes to see the modern counterpart of this quarrel on a still vaster and more eventful scale, let him read the detailed history of the conflict between the Emperor Napoleon and Pope Pius VII.[1] There, as in this case, on the ultimate rights and grounds of the controversy, sympathies were, in

D'Haussonville, L'Église Romaine et le Premier Empire.

England at least, much divided. All but those who accept the claims of the Roman see, will think that the Pope was fighting for a power based for centuries on usurpation and false teaching, and in its results full of mischief to the world. All but those who think religion the creature and minister of the state, will hold that if Napoleon resisted wrongful claims and upheld the just demands of law and civil government, he did so with cruel contempt for the faith and consciences of men, with the most arbitrary and insolent imposition of his own will. The cause of religious freedom was mixed up with that of the misgovernment of the Roman court; the cause of civil independence was mixed up with that of pitiless despotism. In the conduct of the quarrel, too, though the balance of wrong was immeasurably on one side, the side which suffered such monstrous injury was not free from blame: Pius VII. did many things which, though they were as nothing compared with the wickedness of his oppressor, yet must be read of with regret. But the quarrel was, after all, one between true sense of duty and belief in spiritual truth on the one hand, and brutal irresistible force, professedly contemptuous of truth and duty, on the other. It was a contest between the determination to do right at all hazards, held to under the severest trials with a meek dignity and an unfailing Christian charity; and the resolution to break that spirit, now with the most terrible menaces, now with the most incredible and astounding indignities, now with the coarsest and vulgarest temptations of money or selfish convenience.

# CHAPTER XI.

#### ANSELM ON THE CONTINENT.

> "It is not long since these two eyes beheld
> A mighty prince of most renowned race,
> Whom England high in count of honour held,
> And greatest ones did sue to gain his grace;
> Of greatest ones, he greatest in his place.
> \* \* \* \* \*
> I saw him die, I saw him die, as one
> Of the mean people, and brought forth on bier;
> I saw him die, and no man left to moan
> His doleful fate, that late him loved dear;
> Scarce any left to close his eyelids near;
> Scarce any left upon his lips to lay
> The sacred sod, or requiem to say."
> SPENSER'S *Ruins of Time.*

ANSELM, in the month of November 1097, began his winter journey to Italy, accompanied by two friends, Baldwin of Tournai, his most trusted agent, and Eadmer, who has preserved in his simple and clear manner a curious record of the details of a journey in those days. Their resting-places were generally the monasteries which were to be found at the end of each day's ride. Anselm, of course, was received with honour; but there was, besides, a charm about his personal presence and manner, which Eadmer delights to dwell upon. At St. Omer, he relates, children were brought to Anselm in great numbers for confirmation, and then, as no bishop had confirmed there for a long time, came grown persons. "Men and women, great and small, you might see rushing from their houses, and crowding to our lodging." He spent several days there, and on the last morning, just as they were mounting their horses, a young girl came begging with tears to be confirmed. He would not have refused, but his companions objected to being delayed: there was a long day before them; it was dangerous to be overtaken by the night in unknown roads; there were others, too, waiting about the door who would make the same request. He was overruled, and they started. But as they rode along, the poor girl's wish came back to his thoughts and made him very unhappy. He could not forget it; and while he lived, he said, he should never forgive himself for having sent the child away with a refusal.

He spent Christmas at Cluni, where he had a friend in the abbot, Hugh, the old superior of Prior Hildebrand, the counsellor of Pope Gregory; and he spent the rest of the winter with another Hugh, also one of Gregory's friends, like him a monk of Cluni, the energetic and ambitious Archbishop of Lyons, who had almost added another to the anti-popes of the time, because he was not chosen Pope in Gregory's place. In the spring, Anselm, with his two companions, travelling as simple monks, passed into Italy by the Mont Cenis, which so many years before he had crossed, going northwards to find his calling. Eadmer likes to tell of the perils of robbers which they escaped, and which were increased in their case, partly by the reports of the wealth of an Archbishop of Canterbury, partly by the hostility of the partisans of the emperor and the anti-pope, who held the passes, to all travellers who were on the side of Pope Urban. He tells, too, with a kind of simple amusement, how well they preserved their *incognito* how the monks at different monasteries told them about Anselm's movements, or asked news about him; and how skilfully Baldwin put them off from any suspicion about their unknown guest. He stopped for Passiontide and Easter at the monastery of St. Michael, near Chiusa, the convent on the great hill that seems to shut the valley between Susa and Turin; the spot where the Lombard Desiderius vainly tried to make his stand against Charles, King of the Franks—the *Sagro di San Michele*, one of the burial-places of the kings of the House of Savoy, which still arrests travellers, who can be tempted to turn aside from the hurry of the railway, by a singular mixture of natural beauty with ancient remains of great interest. In due time they arrived at Rome.

At Rome they, like so many others, were to find disenchantment, and to come on those hard resisting realities of difficulty and necessity which cause such abatements and retrenchments in all practical theories. The Pope in Anselm's theory was the divinely constituted and divinely supported father of Christendom, the oracle of truth, the defender of the oppressed, the avenger of wrong, armed with power from Heaven, before which the proud must quail; in the reality, he was a conscientious but wise and cautious old man with long and varied experience of the world, encompassed with trouble and danger, and hardly maintaining a very precarious footing; with the empire and half Italy against him, with an anti-pope keeping St. Angelo in Rome itself, and fully alive to the necessity of prudence and a wary policy. Nothing could exceed the honour and sympathy shown to Anselm. He was lodged in the Lateran with Urban; he was shown to the court as the great champion of its claims in distant and strange England; Eadmer, in his delight and admiration, does not know which to be most pleased with, Anselm's modesty and humility, and the irresistible charm of his unselfishness and sweetness, or the extraordinary respect paid to him. "In assemblies of the nobles, in stations, in processions, he was second only to the Pope himself." The Pope spoke of him as his equal, "the Patriarch, the *Apostolicus* or Pope of a second world." But Urban had many disputes on his hands, and he would not, if he could help it, add another with so reckless and so dangerous a person as William of England. Letters, of course, were written, to remonstrate and require amendment. Letters came back, accusing Anselm of leaving England without the king's leave; and with the letters, what ordinarily accompanied them, gifts of money, not of course for Urban, who was quite above all suspicion, but for the people round him, of whom it is equally taken for granted, by Eadmer as by other writers of the time, that money was of much power with them. William's envoys were roughly and sharply chided; his conduct was declared to be without excuse. Anselm's cause was laid before councils; threats were held out if amendment was not shown by a fixed time. But when a year and a half had passed, Anselm and his company became convinced that the Pope could do nothing for them; he had too much on his hands to take up in earnest another serious quarrel; and it was plain that he was not going beyond words and threats. He tried to make up by the honours which he lavished on Anselm for the little substantial help he was able to give him.

Rome was an unhealthy residence for strangers; and after his first reception, Anselm accepted the invitation of an old Italian scholar of Bec, now abbot of a monastery at Telese, on the Calore, near Benevento, to take up his abode with him. The Pope approved of the arrangement: Abbot John was "the Joseph sent before by God's providence to prepare for his father Jacob." The summer heats were "burning up everything round," and made even Telese a dangerous sojourn for the northern strangers; and the abbot transferred them to a mountain village belonging to the monastery, called Schlavia (Schiavi). Here, amid his wanderings and troubles, Anselm had a summer of respite and refreshment. The little village was perched on a hill-top; there was no one living in it but the labourers and a monk who superintended them: the summer sky was bright, the mountain air was sweet and fresh and healthy, while the plains were fainting with the heat. After his vexed and weary life, the old man's heart leaped up at the charms of nature and repose. *Hic requies mea*, he broke forth, in the words of the Psalm—" Here shall be my rest for ever: here will I dwell, for I have a delight therein." He went back at once to his old habits of life, as when he was a simple monk, and before he had any office; he resumed his old train of work. In the midst of the strife and troubles of his last year in England, he had thought out, and had begun to compose a work which was, like other works of his, to open new views in theology, and permanently to affect the thoughts of men. It was the famous dialogue, *Cur Deus Homo*, in which, seeking the rational ground of the Incarnation, he lays down a profound and original theory of the Atonement, which, whether accepted or impugned, has moulded the character of all Christian doctrine about it since. What he began amid the fears and distresses of uncongenial England, he finished in the light and peaceful summer days of his mountain retreat at Schiavi. As was to be expected, the presence of such a man raised the expectation of miracles. The name of the Archbishop of Canterbury clung for centuries to a well of fresh and health-giving water, the spring of which was said to have gushed out of the rock in answer to his prayers.

But he could not long enjoy retirement. He had to meet the Pope in the camp of the Norman Duke of Apulia, before Capua; and there Eadmer notices again that ever-present charm of face and manner which attracted to him the reverence and interest of the heathen "Saracens" of Duke Roger's army, over whom Anselm's presence exercised such a spell that they always saluted him as he passed by, "raising their hands to heaven, kissing their hands to him, and kneeling down before him;" and many of them would have given themselves to him to be taught and converted by him if they had not been afraid of the Duke's cruel discipline. He earnestly entreated the Pope to relieve him of the archbishopric: his experience of William showed that they never could work together; and travellers from the West brought over new stories of his brutal scorn for all religious belief and feelings. But such a step did not suit the papal policy any more than a declared breach with the king. All kinds of good reasons were addressed to Anselm why he should keep his archbishopric. He was invited to be present at the Council of Bari (October 1098), of which Eadmer gives, after his fashion, a curious account. Anselm was made much of; the famous theologian was called upon to defend the language of the Western creed against the Greeks; and Eadmer tells of the flattering language in which the Pope invited him to address the assembly, of the mingled interest and curiosity of the audience, not quite familiar with his name, but crowding and getting the best seats to hear one whom the Pope so distinguished, and of the admiration which his learning and arguments excited. The Pope proceeded to lay before the council Anselm's dispute with the king, and the sympathy of the council was so roused, that when the Pope asked their opinion, they were of one mind in advising the king's excommunication; and it was hindered only, says Eadmer, by Anselm's intercession. It may, perhaps, be doubtful whether the Pope meant more than a demonstration. From the council at Bari they returned for the winter to Rome. There, also, appeared William Warelwast, with whom Anselm had parted on the beach at Dover, to state the king's case against Anselm. In the public audience the Pope was severe and peremptory. But Warelwast prevailed on the Pope to grant a private interview; he distributed his gifts among those about the Pope; and the result was that nine months' grace was granted to the king to arrange the matter instead of three, from Christmas 1098. "Seeing which things," says Eadmer, "we understood that we vainly looked for counsel or help there, and we resolved to ask leave to return to Lyons." But the Pope could not let Anselm go. A council was to be held about Easter time at the Lateran, and he must wait for it. Meanwhile every honour was paid to him. When the council met, the masters of ceremonies were puzzled where to place him; for no Archbishop of Canterbury had ever attended a council in Rome. The Pope ordered a seat to be set for him in the most honourable place. The council (April, 1099) renewed various decrees of discipline on the subjects which occupied the Church reformers of the time; simony, clerical marriage, and lay investiture. The English ecclesiastics heard the decree of excommunication passed with acclamation against all who gave and all who received the investiture of churches from lay hands, and who, for church honours, became "the men," of temporal lords; that is, against what had been the established and unquestioned usage in England and Normandy to which Anselm himself had conformed. But a remarkable incident startled and impressed the assembly. When the canons were to be read in St. Peter's, the crowd being very great, and there being much noise made by the stream of people going and coming at St. Peter's tomb, the Bishop of Lucca, Reinger by name, a man of tall stature, and loud and ringing voice, was appointed to read them. He began; but when he had got a little way his countenance kindled, and under the influence of strong emotion he stopped. "What are we doing here?" he said, looking round the assembly. "We are loading men with laws, and we dare not resist the cruelties of tyrants. Hither are brought the complaints of the oppressed and the spoiled; from hence, as from the head of all, counsel and help are asked for. And with what result all the world knows and sees. One is sitting among us from the ends of the earth, in modest silence, still and meek. But his silence is a loud cry. The deeper and gentler his humility and patience, the higher it rises before God, the more should it kindle us. This one man, this one man, I say, has come here in his cruel afflictions and wrongs, to ask for the judgment and equity of the apostolic see. And this is the second year; and what help has he found? If you do not all know whom I mean, it is Anselm, Archbishop of England:" and with this he thrice struck his staff violently on the floor, and a burst of breath from his closed teeth and lips showed his indignation. "Brother Reinger," exclaimed the Pope, "enough, enough. Good order shall be taken about this." Reinger, drawing his breath, rejoined, "There is good need. For otherwise the thing will not pass with him who judges justly." And proceeding to read the canons, he finished with a further warning before he sat down. But this burst of feeling led to nothing, and meant nothing. "On the following day," says Eadmer, "we got leave, and we left Rome, having obtained nought of judgment or advice through the Roman Bishop, except what I have said."

Anselm found his way again to Lyons, and lived there, helping his friend the archbishop. In the following July (1099) Urban died. "May God's hatred light on him who cares for it," is said to have been William's remark when he heard it: "and what sort of person is his successor?" "A man in some respects like Anselm," was the answer. "By God's countenance, then, he is no good. But he may keep to himself, for his Popeship shall not this time get over me. I will use my freedom now." Everything seemed to prosper with him, says Eadmer; even the wind, if he wanted to cross to Normandy, served his wishes. "It seemed as if God would try how far he might be touched by having all things to his mind." There was no longer any one to trouble him, duke, king, or pope. Ralph Flambard became Bishop of Durham. William built no churches, but he completed a great memorial of himself, destined to witness more memorable scenes of English justice and English injustice than any other place in the land, the great Hall at Westminster. There in 1100, for the second time, he wore his crown at Pentecost, and gathered his great council. On the second of the following August he perished by an uncertain hand in the New Forest.

Anselm had been all this time in Gaul, spending his time partly at Lyons, partly at places around, Vienne, Cluni, Macon, confirming, preaching, writing. When he confirmed for the Archbishop of Lyons, the people flocked to him to receive the "holy anointing;" whole days were spent in the administration, and his attendants were very weary; but he never lost his bright and cheerful mood, and never would send the people away. "So that," says Eadmer, "there grew up an extraordinary and incredible affection for him among all the people, and his goodness was spoken of far and wide." From such a man the ideas of the day expected miracles; the sick came to him for relief; his attendants were ready to believe that they had good reason for coming; and Eadmer has his confident stories of cures, which he relates as an eye-witness. As Eadmer tells them, they do not read like inventions; they are the genuine impressions, told in good faith, of one whose whole manner of thought made them to him the most likely things in the world. As regards Anselm himself, as far as appears from Eadmer, he believed, like everybody else, that miraculous help might be expected and bestowed; he believed in the probability of such answers to prayer; but he shrunk altogether from the thought of miraculous gifts being entrusted to him or ascribed to him. Two stories illustrate at once the way in which people believed, and the natural behaviour of a good man, humble and true, and trying to think as he ought about himself, who did not disbelieve the possibility or even the frequency of such exercises of God's power and mercy.

"At Vienne," says Eadmer, "when he was taking his repast after having celebrated mass and preached, two knights came before him, in form and voice showing the marks of serious illness, and asking him to deign to give them some crumbs from the bread which he was eating. 'No,' he said, 'I see that you want neither a whole loaf nor crumbs. But if you are pleased to partake, there is plenty of room; sit down, and, with the blessing of God, eat what is set before you.' They had not come for this, they answered. 'I cannot do anything else for you,' he said, for he perceived what they had meant. One of those who were sitting on his right saw that they had come for health, and that Anselm would do nothing which might be set down to a miracle; so, as if tired of their importunity, this person took a fragment from the table and gave it them, and told them to retire, lest they should annoy the archbishop. They accordingly went out with his blessing, and tasted the bread. After dinner they took me aside, and earnestly begged of me to help them to receive the communion of the Lord's body and blood from his hands at mass. I willingly agreed, and told them when and where it might be done. They answered thankfully, and said, 'We will certainly come, if by this medicine which we have received from his table we are not relieved from the deadly quartan fevers and intolerable pains of body from which we suffer. And this shall be a sign between us and you: if we get well, we will not come; we will come if we do not.' And so we separated." They did not come back; and hence Eadmer supposes that they were healed.

On another occasion "he was met, when on his road to Cluni, by an ecclesiastic, whose sister was out of her mind, and who with tears besought him to give her his blessing and lay his right hand on her. 'By the wayside where you will pass she is held by a number of people, who hope that if you, my lord, will lay your hand on her, she by God's mercy will be straightway restored to her mind.' But Anselm passed on without speaking, and as if not hearing. When the priest insisted with many prayers, Anselm sent him away, saying most earnestly, that on no account would he venture on so strange an act. Meanwhile we went on, and beheld her in the midst of the crowd, showing all the signs of raving madness. The people surrounded Anselm, held the reins of his horse, and redoubled their entreaties that he would lay his hand on the miserable woman. He resists, saying that what they ask is against good sense and wisdom. They, after the manner of the common people, urge whatever comes into their heads, hoping to prevail at least by rude pressure. Then, seeing that he could not otherwise escape, he yielded to them in this alone, that he did for her what he never refused to any one ; he lifted up his right hand and signed her with the sign of the holy cross. And then, urging his horse, he hastened away, and pulling the head of his cowl over his face, he kept apart from his companions, and gave vent to his tears at the distress of the unhappy woman. So in sorrow we arrived at Cluni, and she, pushed on by the crowd, went home. Her foot had scarcely touched the threshold when she was restored to health, and the tongues of all broke out in praise of Anselm. When we heard it at Cluni, we were glad, and gave glory and thanks to God for His mercy."

As no history at this time, even if only concerned, so far as this was possible, with secular affairs, was without miracles, it cannot be expected that such a life as Anselm's could be witnessed without expecting them, or told without implying them. They were part of the unquestioned belief and tacit assumptions of everybody who lived round him. Undoubtedly he believed that such things happened. What might be looked for in a good man, with such a belief, is that he would not refuse his prayer or his blessing, but that he would give no encouragement to the ready disposition to ascribe to him special power and favour. And it seems plain that while Eadmer was only too glad to believe miracles of his great master, Anselm was as far as possible from wishing him to do so.

All our authorities speak of presages of different kinds preceding William's death. Such stories are probably the reflection, after the event, of strong feelings before it, surviving in men's memory; but it is remarkable that there should have been such a variety and such a number of stories of the kind. The different writers record their own omens; Eadmer among the rest. One of these stories has a curious little touch of the domestic ways of the time. It was at Lyons: "The feast of St. Peter, which is celebrated on the 1st of August, was at hand; and having said matins, we, who were constantly about Anselm, wished to allow ourselves some sleep. One clerk was lying near the door of the chamber, and, not yet asleep, had his eyes shut to go to sleep. And lo! a young man, in dress and countenance of no mean appearance, stood and called him by his name—'Adam, are you asleep?' 'No,' answered the clerk. The young man said, 'Would you hear news?' 'Gladly.' 'Know then, for certain,' said the other, 'that all the quarrel between Archbishop Anselm and King William is ended and appeased.' At these words the clerk eagerly lifted up his head, and opening his eyes, looked round. But he saw no one."

The news reached Anselm at the Abbey of "God's House" (*Casa Dei, Chaise Dieu*), near Brioude, in the Auvergne country, a little place on the top of a hill, where, though the monastery has disappeared, a remarkable church, but much later than Anselm's time, still remains, with the tombs in it of two Popes, Clement VI. and Gregory XI., two of the French Avignon line, whose family came from the neighbourhood. Within a week after William's death, two monks, one of Canterbury, the other of Bec, were at Chaise Dieu with the tidings. Anselm had not ceased to pray for the king. Eadmer says that he was greatly affected; he was at first thunderstruck and silent; then he burst into "the bitterest weeping." The party returned to Lyons; and messenger after messenger soon arrived from England, from Canterbury, from the king, from the great men of the realm, urging his instant return. The land was in suspense till the archbishop went back to sanction what was done, and business was at a standstill in the uncertainty created by his absence. The new king, Henry, was especially pressing, promising redress of abuses, and willing attention to his counsel. On the 23rd of September Anselm's party landed at Dover; and shortly after he was with the king at Salisbury.

So sudden and unthought-of an end as William's might have thrown England into confusion; but there had been a man on the spot equal to the crisis, and probably long prepared for it. Henry, the youngest of the Conqueror's sons, was hunting in the New Forest when his brother was shot. As soon as he heard of what had happened, he immediately did as William had done before him: he seized the treasure at Winchester, and he laid his claim to the crown before the Witan, the prelates and barons assembled about the king; in this case only a certain number of the great council which gathered to the court three times a year. The king's title had not yet become a matter of pure inheritance: one man's title was better than another's, and birth was an important, for the most part a preponderating, element in it; but birth alone was not a complete and conclusive claim. It had to be formally and distinctly accepted by the representatives of the land; it had to be sealed and hallowed by an almost priestly consecration at the hands of the chief bishop of the Church; and it had to be accompanied by the most solemn promises to the people of justice, mercy, and good laws. "On the Thursday [Aug. 2] William was slain," writes the Peterborough chronicler, "and on the morrow buried; and after he was buried, the Witan, who were then near at hand, chose his brother Henry for king; and he forthwith gave the bishopric of Winchester to William Giffard and then went to London; and on the Sunday following [Aug. 5], before the altar at Westminster, he promised to God and all the people to put down the injustice which was in his brother's time, and to keep the best laws that stood in any king's days before him; and after this, Maurice the Bishop of London hallowed him to be king; and they all in this land submitted to him, and swore oaths and became his men." Informal as the transaction appears, described with the simplicity of a narrative from the Books of Kings, it was the right and legitimate procedure—it was the way in which by the custom and law of England the right of the crown was then given and acquired.

But Henry knew that he would have to fight for it. Robert of Normandy was on his way home; he had never given up his claim, though his father had refused to sanction it; and Robert was sure of a strong party among the Normans in England. At any rate, Henry might expect as a matter of course to have his strength tried. His first steps were to win the feelings of the country on his side by reversing the misrule of the late reign. He imprisoned Ralph Flambard, now Bishop of Durham, in the Tower. He at once recalled Anselm. Far from scrupulous himself, he yet disliked the coarse profligacy and riot which had reigned in William's court, and at once put them down. Before the end of the year he tried to bind himself by another tie to Englishmen, by marrying [Nov. 11] the English maiden, Edith, the daughter of Malcolm King of Scotland, and the noble and saintly Margaret, one of the last remaining children of the old English line of kings, "through whom the blood and the right of the Imperial House of Wessex have passed to the Angevin, the Scottish, and the German sovereigns of England."[1]

Some of Anselm's first dealings with Henry were with reference to this marriage. He did for Henry, what Lanfranc had done for Henry's father; he protected a marriage fair and honourable in all ways, and far more deserving of respect than most of the great marriages of those days, from the prejudices and narrow rigour of his own order and his own party. And he did this more bravely and with less of compromise than Lanfranc; he boldly and outright threw aside objections, which to many of the strict people of the time must have seemed formidable. Edith, in the troubled times which had ended in her father's death by Norman treachery, and her mother's death in the same week from a broken heart [Nov. 13, 19, 1093], had been sent to England, to be under the care of her aunt Christina, Abbess of Romsey. "She was very beautiful. She inherited her mother's

[1] Freeman, ii. 370.

talent, her mother's warm affections, sweetness, patience, piety, and had profited by all the cultivation, both intellectual and moral, that Margaret had bestowed."[1] Such a lady was likely to have suitors. But she was said by her aunt Christina to have made her profession as a nun; and while William the Red lived she continued at Romsey, wearing the nun's dress. When Henry became king, his thoughts turned to Edith; it is said that he had before been a suitor for her hand; and such a marriage would obviously be a politic one. One difficulty was soon disposed of in those days; the Welsh lady with whom he had been living, after the fashion of the house of Rollo, though she was not his wife, and who had borne him several children, was dismissed and married to one of his military chieftains, Gerald of Windsor, whose lands were in Pembrokeshire. The other difficulty was more serious. It was commonly believed that Edith had taken the vows as a nun. She denied it, and accounted intelligibly enough for wearing the nun's dress and countenancing the belief that she had taken the veil, in days like those of William the Red. Her aunt had forced her to wear it to save her from Norman brutality, and had also wished to make her a nun in good earnest. But the niece had resisted, in spite of blows and hard words; when she dared, she would tear off her nun's headgear, throwing it on the ground and stamping upon it.

If her ecclesiastical judge had been a formalist or a pedant, she might have found it hard to make him believe her story. But Anselm, when she appealed to him as the highest Church authority, put

[1] Palgrave, iv. 366.

aside the ecclesiastical prejudices which might have told with many against her, and ordered a full and impartial investigation. She offered to submit her account of the matter to the judgment of the whole Church of the English. An assembly of great persons, religious and secular, was held at Lambeth, then a manor belonging to Rochester. Commissioners were sent to the monastery where Edith had been brought up. Anselm opened the matter, but abstained from taking any side, and left it to the justice of this great jury to decide on the facts. For the principle of the case, there was a precedent fortified by Lanfranc's great authority. He had on grounds of equity released from actual vows women who had taken them from fear of the violence which followed on the Conquest. The assembly gave their verdict for her. With this judgment, and with her solemn and circumstantial account of her repugnance to take vows, which Anselm himself must have thought as high and noble as they were inviolable, he was satisfied. He pronounced her free; he frankly accepted her story; and he refused the confirmation which she offered of any of the further proofs or ordeals which were in use at the time. Before a great gathering of the nobility, and the "lesser people" crowding the doors of the church and surging all round it, to witness the marriage and benediction of the new queen, Anselm stood up and declared the manner and result of the inquiry; and then, according to the custom still in use, called on anyone who doubted, or who thought that by the Christian law the marriage was unlawful, to stand forth and speak his mind. Such a challenge in these days, as we have seen in the case of the

Conqueror's funeral, was not simply formal; but a shout of assent was the answer.

This judgment, larger and more generous than would have been given by many good men of his day, gave to Henry a queen who was worthy of her place, whose influence was throughout for gentleness and right, and who, under her changed Norman name, adopted perhaps from Henry's mother, became dear to Englishmen as " Good Queen Maude." But there were many people, Eadmer says, relating the matter as having been present and as having seen and heard everything, who blamed Anselm for his departure from the hard and severe rules by which such cases were commonly disposed of; rules which were often made merely to create an occasion for a dispensation or a privilege, granted not to simple equity but to a heavy compensation.

# CHAPTER XII.

ANSELM AND HENRY I.

" We would every deed
Perform at once as grandly as it shows
After long ages, when from land to land
The poet's swelling song hath rolled it on.
It sounds so lovely what our fathers did,
When in the silent evening shade reclined,
We drink it in with music's melting tones.
And what we do, is, as it was to them,
Toilsome and incomplete."
GOETHE'S *Iphigenia* (ii. 1), translated by
MISS SWANWICK.

ANSELM came back to England with good hope to do something for the great purpose for which he now lived—the purification and elevation of life, first in the clergy; then in the monasteries, which were the pattern schools and models of religion and devotion; and then in the lay society, with which, monk as he was, he had such strong sympathy, and which he looked upon as specially his charge and flock as being the first spiritual officer of the English Church. The new king had solemnly promised to put an end to the odious wrong and the insolent tyranny of the last reign. "The holy Church of God I make free, so that I will neither sell it nor let it to farm; nor on the death of archbishop, or bishop, or abbot, will I take anything from the domain of the Church, or from its men, till the successor comes into possession;"—this had been the first article of the kingly promise given at Westminster, when the Bishop of London, in Anselm's absence, had consecrated and crowned him king.

Henry's position, too, was still insecure. Robert was back in Normandy with a newly-married wife, fresh from the glory of the Crusade, and fully intending to dispute the claims of the younger brother, whom both he and William had been accustomed to despise and to make use of, and whom he had joined with William in excluding from the succession. The English feeling was strong for Henry: he was not without friends among the Norman barons; but as a body the Normans were not to be trusted till they had learned to know the strength of their master. They had accepted Henry in Robert's absence, many of them with a secret preference for Robert, a king who would let them have their own way, and a secret dislike for Henry, a king who perhaps might not; and with a reserve which fear only, or the sense of their own interest, could at last bring to an issue. Henry had made to them, as well as to the Church, large promises. They were not content with general engagements against bad customs and unjust exactions; a number of the alleged usurpations by the crown on the rights of landowners, of arbitrary exactions and acts of power, of abuses in the administration of justice, were specified and definitely condemned; and a great charter, of which copies were sent to the shires of the kingdom and laid up in the treasuries of cathedrals and abbeys, attested the liberties which had been granted to his barons and all his faithful people by King Henry, "by God's appointment elected by the clergy and people, by God's mercy and the common counsel and assent of the barons of the realm of England, crowned king thereof." Henry had much on his side in the hopes which he inspired, in the acceptance of the nation, in his own consciousness of ability and strength. But he could not afford yet to overlook anything which could make him more secure; and a good understanding with a man of Anselm's high place, reputation, and popularity, was very important to him.

But there were difficulties in the position of each of them which were not long in showing themselves. Henry, whom the world hardly knew yet, who had since his father's death been buffeted by fortune, and had gone through the experiences of a princely exile while patiently biding his time till his father's dying words of prophecy should be fulfilled; who had alternately made himself useful to both his brothers, and had received scant recompense from them—combined with an outward self-command and easiness of manner, strongly contrasting with his father's hardness and his brothers' boisterous and overbearing roughness, an iron strength of will, not less tenacious and formidable than theirs, though disguised for a time under softer manners and an apparently more pliant temper. There were two points in which it at once disclosed itself. Amid all his concessions he peremptorily refused any relaxation of the hateful and merciless forest laws; to the mighty hunters of William's family the crown was not worth having, without the cruel privileges of the chase. There was yet another matter on which he was resolved to yield nothing. The ecclesiastical "customs" which had been in force in his father's time he would maintain. Bishops and abbots should not only be appointed by him, but they should, like his barons, become "his men;" they should receive the investiture of their offices from him; the pastoral staff which was the token of their spiritual authority they should take from his hand. "I will have all the crosiers in England in my hand," was a saying ascribed to the Conqueror; and, in spite of the canons then beginning to be passed from time to time at Rome, Lanfranc had not contested the point, and Anselm himself had, as a matter of course, complied with the custom when he received the archbishopric from William Rufus. There were obvious reasons why Henry should maintain his claim. To resign it would have been to seem to show himself weaker at the critical beginning of his reign than his father and brother. There was no strong feeling against the custom among the English or Norman clergy. It gave him a special and personal hold on the service and obedience of the Church, entirely analogous to that which he had over the allegiance of his barons and tenants. It was a good deal more than the right of nomination and patronage. That was much; but it was much more that bishops, when appointed, should not only acknowledge his authority as faithful subjects, but should be bound to him by the special ties, first, of having become "his men," and next of holding, not their temporal possessions only but their office itself, by a significant form which made it seem simply a derivation from his authority. These customs had been accepted as a matter of course, without complaint, without protest, without remark, by the religious men of the Conqueror's age. That they had not only given rise to intolerable abuse and mischief in his brother's time, but that they had deeply corrupted the spirit of churchmen, and made them look upon their office as a thing that might be bought and sold, and then used with courtly subservience or cynical selfishness, was hardly a consideration which could be expected to weigh with Henry, or to keep him from stiffly asserting his claims. For a man of Henry's temper, bent as strongly as his father or his brother on beating down or eluding every check on his will and his power, the spectacle of the way in which, in the late reign, the Church had been humbled, degraded, and reduced to helplessness, would be distasteful only from the frantic extravagance which had defeated its own ends.

It was natural for the king to insist on these cherished customs of homage and investiture. He thought that they signified a great deal, and so they did; but to Anselm also they signified a great deal. He had made no difficulty, as we have seen, in conforming to them at his own election; but much had happened since then. He had been the witness and the victim of the system which placed the duty and conscience of Christian bishops under the heel of feudal royalty, and gave to insolent oppression the right of appealing mockingly to their own oaths of fealty and acts of submission as the bonds of their unconditional and uncomplaining submission. A reign like that of the Red King was a lesson not to be soon forgotten: the "customs" which had seemed so natural and endurable under the father, had received a new meaning and a new sting under the policy of the son. Further, Anselm was in a new position compared with that of Lanfranc, and with his own at his election. William's violence had driven him abroad; and there he had been compelled to become cognizant, in a far more distinct way than before, of the legislation by which Church rulers and Church councils on the Continent were attempting to meet the rival claims of the feudal lords. No one then doubted the authority of that great office which they believed to be held in succession from the Prince of the Apostles. They might doubt between the claims of this or that pope or anti-pope; they might question the wisdom of the pope's decisions, or disobey his orders, or defy his excommunications, or bribe his advisers, or imprison his person; but the general belief in his authority was no more impaired by such things than resistance and disobedience affected the general persuasion of the authority of kings. The see of St Peter was the acknowledged constitutional centre of spiritual law in the West to all that "diversity of nations who were united in the confession of the name of Christ;" it was looked upon as the guide and regulator of teaching, the tribunal and court from which issued the oracles of right and discipline, the judgment-seat to which an appeal was open to all, and which gave sentence on wrong and vice without fear or favour, without respect of persons, even the highest and the mightiest. The ideal was imperfectly realized; it was marred by the extravagance of assertion, the imperiousness of temper, the violence of means with which these claims were urged; it was spoiled by the inextricable mixture of by-ends with grand and noble purposes, of unscrupulous cunning and crafty policy with intense and self-sacrificing conviction; it was more fatally degraded and discredited by the selfish and faithless temporizing, and the shameless greediness, which grew into proverbs wherever the name of Rome was mentioned. And every succeeding century these things grew worse; the ideal became more and more a shadow, the reality became more and more a corrupt and intolerable mockery. But if ever there was a time when the popes honestly endeavoured to carry out the idea of their office, it was just at this period of the Middle Ages. They attempted to erect an independent throne of truth and justice above the passions and the force which reigned in the world around. It is the grandest and most magnificent failure in human history. But it had not then been proved to be a failure; and those whose souls believed in truth and thirsted for purity, righteousness, and peace, amid the wrong and confusion of their time, turned to it with hope and loyalty. Anselm probably had troubled himself little with distant Rome and its doings while busy in the cloister of Bec with teaching and meditation. The hopelessness of all justice at home drove him on what offered itself, and was looked on by all, as the refuge for the injured and helpless. And while there he had of necessity become acquainted for himself with the stringency and earnestness with which the highest Church authority had condemned the customs of homage and lay investiture. It was doubtful whether he had not himself come under the penalties pronounced against them. He had been present at solemn councils where the prohibitions against them were reiterated in the plainest and most peremptory manner. After what he had seen and heard at Rome, it would be impossible for him henceforward to appear to sanction usages in which he himself had once seen no harm.

Henry appears to have brought on the question in an extreme and unusual form, at his first meeting with Anselm at Salisbury. He demanded from Anselm a renewal of homage, and required that he should receive the archbishopric afresh by a new act of investiture. "Lofty as the pretensions of the crown had been," says Sir F. Palgrave, "this demand was entirely unprecedented, at least so far as we can collect from any existing historical evidence. It imported that, on the death of the Sovereign, the archbishop's commission expired—that his office was subordinate and derivative, and the dignity therefore reverted to the crown." The principle of a fresh grant of lands and privileges at the demise of the lord was not unknown in civil matters; but "we have no trace that this principle was ever extended to the Church." Henry appears to have meant by this demand, which went beyond what had been claimed by his predecessors, to put the meaning of these forms beyond question, and to settle a point raised and left uncertain by the disputes; perhaps he intended it as an answer beforehand, and a forward step in meeting, what he must probably have known, would now be the demands of the Church for the abolition of "the customs." "Cherishing the *consuetudines paternæ*," the hereditary "usages," says Sir F. Palgrave, "and pledging himself in his own heart and mind not to abate a jot of his supremacy over the clergy, he would exercise his authority in Church affairs somewhat more decently than his father, and a great deal more than his brother; but that was all."

Anselm, when the demand was made, at once stated his position. He had no choice. He had heard with his own ears the canons of the Church and the solemn decisions and sanctions of a great council. "If his lord the king," he said, "was willing to accept these laws, they could work together. If not, there was no use in his remaining in England; for he could not hold communion with those who broke these laws. He had not come back to England to live there on condition of disobedience to his spiritual head. And he begged a plain decision, that he might take his course." Both parties behaved with dignity and temper, fitting the gravity of the question. "The king was much disturbed; for it was a grave matter to lose the investitures of churches and the homages of prelates; it was a grave matter, too, to let Anselm take his departure, while he himself was not yet fully confirmed in the kingdom. For on one side it seemed to him to be losing, as it were, half of his kingdom; on the other, he feared lest Anselm should make his brother Robert, who would most easily be brought into subjection to the apostolic see, King of England." It was agreed that the matter should be referred to the Pope, things remaining unchanged till an answer could come back from Rome. Anselm knew enough of the temper of Rome to be sure that the appeal which Henry made for a direct exemption from the general law was hopeless ; but all along in this matter of investiture his line was simple obedience to authorities and rules which, even in the ideas and belief of his antagonists, had a rightful and paramount claim to it. There is no appearance that personally he felt very strongly about the matter of the dispute; it was with him purely a question of obeying, what to him and to his age represented the law of God against the will and power of man. But Henry's proposal, if merely for the purpose of gaining time, was not an unreasonable one, and the Archbishop wished to avoid anything that might seem to endanger the new order, or to give ground to the suspicions or the hopes of those who looked on the dispute as it might affect the interests of Robert. In the meanwhile, the king and the archbishop remained good friends; Anselm's good sense and justice gave the king his English bride; and at Martinmas (Oct. 11, 1100), he gave his benediction to Edith-Matilda as wife and queen.

It was not the only service which Henry owed him. The critical first year of his reign was yet to be passed. Ralph Flambard, Bishop of Durham, had escaped from the Tower, and was in Normandy stirring up Robert against the new King of England, as Odo Bishop of Bayeux had passed from his prison to stir up Robert against William the Red. Flambard's familiar acquaintance with England was dangerous; he knew who was doubtful, and who could be corrupted, and how to corrupt them. He gained over the sailors who were to defend the Channel. Under his guidance, Robert landed at Portsmouth. At the first news of the approaching invasion, Henry, suspecting his nobles and suspected by them, had endeavoured to bind them to him by a new and distinct compact. "The whole nobility of the realm, with a multitude of the people, when they met to receive the engagement of the king's faith, made Anselm their arbiter between themselves and the king, that to him, in their stead, the king, holding his hand in Anselm's hand, should promise to govern the whole kingdom in all things, as long as he lived, by just and holy laws." But when it was known that Robert was actually in England, the Norman chiefs at once, forgetful of their plighted troth, prepared to desert the king. The English and the common soldiers were true; but the king's camp was full of the fears, mistrust, disloyal balancings of the Norman lords. Anselm knowing most about their suspicions and disaffection, was afraid to speak of all he knew, for fear of driving them at once to Robert's side. But he was the only man the king could trust. He threw his influence on Henry's side. He brought the Norman chiefs, one by one, to the king, that seeing one another face to face they might be reassured by mutual explanations and intercourse. Henry made him fresh promises. Anselm made a public appeal to the chiefs, in the presence of the army, not to shame themselves by breaking their faith and betraying their king. The danger was weathered. A battle was avoided at a critical time; Henry submitted for the present to hard conditions, and Robert, finding the Norman lords less forward than he expected, and fearing Anselm's excommunication against him, as an unjust invader, made peace. Henry was to have his revenge in a different fashion at Tinchebrai; but at that time, says Eadmer, if Anselm's fidelity and exertions had not turned the scale, King Henry would have lost his possession of the realm of England.

The answer from Rome had been long in coming, but it came at last. Henry had asked, so the Pope put it, that, as a special favour in return for the reversal of his brother's policy and his good-will to the Church, he might be privileged by the Roman Church to make bishops and abbots by the delivery of the pastoral staff. It was not the exact account: Henry never wavered about his claim; and the indulgence he professed to ask for was, not that he might keep the usages, but that Anselm might comply with them. To this Pope Paschal had answered as might have been expected. He was willing to grant many favours and indulgences, but not this. His long letter contained the current arguments and usual texts and quotations, common since the time of Gregory VII.; but through its false analogies and forced parallels, and the extravagant and conventional exaggerations of its rhetoric, a true and reasonable feeling is apparent of the shame and mischief of allowing great Church offices to be disposed of by the kings and princes of the time, without an effort to assert their meaning and sacredness, and to force the world to acknowledge their paramount spiritual and religious character. A breach now seemed inevitable. Anselm was called to the court, and required, as in the first instance, to give way. His answer was the same: he threw himself on the decrees of the Roman Council at which he had been present. "What is that to me?" said the king: "I will not lose the customs of my predecessors, nor suffer in my realm a man who is not mine." The bishops and nobles this time fully took part with the king; as before, says Eadmer, there was going to and fro between the king and the archbishop, all striving to comply with the king's will and earnestly insisting that he should not be subject to the obedience of the Roman Pontiff. The dispute was inflamed, Eadmer says, by the influence of Duke Robert and his friends, who remembered what Anselm had done against them; but Henry wanted no urging, and fully knew his own mind. But it was not yet convenient to come to an open quarrel. England was not yet fairly in hand. On the troublesome Welsh border, the worst and most hateful of the bad house of Talvas and Mabel of Belesme, the restless and pitiless Robert, who seemed bent on fulfilling his grandfather's curse on William the Bastard by urging on his children to destroy one another, had succeeded his brother Hugh, the only one of Mabel's children of whom any good is told, in the great earldom of Shrewsbury and the guardianship of the Welsh marchland. He was lord, too, at the other end of England, of Arundel on the Sussex shore. He had done homage to Henry; he had deserted to Robert; and the year following the treaty (1102) he was in full revolt, letting the Welsh loose upon the English shires, and holding the castles which he had fortified and prepared, in Sussex, in Yorkshire, and on the Severn, as centres of rebellion. Henry met him vigorously, and crushed him; and Robert of Belesme was driven from England, once again to try his strength against his mightier foe, to fail, and at last to end his days in one of Henry's prisons But while he had

Robert of Belesme on his hands, Henry probably thought it best to temporize with Anselm. At any rate, he again made conciliatory advances to the archbishop, and proposed a second embassy to Rome of more distinguished persons: Gerard, now Archbishop of York, one of William the Red's chaplains and envoys to Rome, and two bishops, together with two of Anselm's most trusted friends, Baldwin, his late companion, and another. Men of such weight and knowledge of affairs could explain, it was said, to the Pope the difficulties of the case and the critical state of matters better than could be done by letter or by agents of less dignity and consequence. Accordingly they went; in their public audiences they found the Pope inflexible, and indignant that he should be pressed to tear up the deliberate ordinances of the holy Fathers and of his predecessors for the threat of one man. He would not do so, he said, to save his head. Letters were written in the same firm tone as before to the king and to Anselm, and with these the envoys returned home.

A curious transaction followed. On the return of the envoys, an assembly of the great men was summoned in London, and Anselm was again required by messengers from the king to submit to the "usages." But the Pope's letter to the king was not made public. Anselm showed to every one who chose to see it the letter which he had himself received, and asked that the letter to the king should be made known. But Henry refused; he put aside the Pope's reply as irrelevant, and, throwing himself on his own rights, required unconditional submission. Meanwhile, the Pope's letter to the king got abroad. Then occurred a scene, which is like nothing so much as some of the passages in Napoleon's negotiations through the bishops of his party with Pius VII. The Archbishop of York and his brethren, the bishops of Chester and Thetford, announced what they declared on the faith of bishops to be the real result of their embassy. The Pope, they said, in a private interview, had charged them with a verbal message to the king, that so long as he acted as a good king and appointed religious prelates, the Pope would not enforce the decrees against investiture. And the reason, they said, why he could not give this privilege in writing was lest, if it became public, other princes might use it to the prejudice of the Roman see. They also, equally on their faith and honour as bishops, conveyed, in the Pope's name, his commands to Anselm to give them full credit, and follow their counsel. If he refused, the king might act as he pleased on the Pope's authority, in spite of Anselm, and might, if Anselm still insisted on the Pope's letter, banish him from the kingdom. This strange story took everyone by surprise, and called forth immediate remonstrance from Anselm's representatives. They had heard nothing of the message, which was utterly inconsistent with everything which had passed in public between them and the Pope. When the bishops insisted that the Pope's language was one thing in public, and another to themselves in a private interview, Baldwin indignantly charged them with breaking their canonical oaths and making the apostolic see infamous. But they held to their story, and there was a strong division of opinion and hot altercation in the excited assembly. When one side insisted on the authority of the actual document, sealed with the Pope's signet, the rejoinder was fierce and insolent. The word of these bishops ought to weigh more than parchments,—" sheepskins, with a lump of lead at the bottom," backed by the testimony of "paltry monks, who, when they renounced the world, lost all weight as evidence in secular business." "But this is no secular business," said Baldwin. "We know you," was the reply, "to be a man of sense and vigour; but difference of rank itself requires us to set more by the testimony of an archbishop and two bishops than by yours." "But what of the testimony of the letters?" he asked. He was answered with a sneer: "When we refuse to receive the testimony of monks against bishops, how could we receive that of sheepskins?" "Woe! woe!" burst forth from the shocked and excited monks, "are not the Gospels written on sheepskins?"

Of course in such a dead lock, there was nothing for it but to send another deputation to Rome; and in the meanwhile a compromise was agreed to. The king was to act as if the bishops had truly reported the Pope's intentions; he was to be at liberty to invest fresh prelates, and Anselm, till the real fact was known, was not to refuse communion with them. Anselm, on the other hand, until things were cleared up, was not to be required to consecrate them. He felt keenly, as was natural, the embarrassment of his position. He wrote to the Pope, stating what had happened, and begging to know for certain what the Pope meant him to do. If the Pope thought proper to take off generally in England the excommunication pronounced against lay investiture, or to make special exceptions, let him only say so distinctly. Anselm felt all through that the matter was one of positive law, and that he was but an officer bound to carry out, at all personal inconvenience, the acknowledged law of the Church, and the commands of his lawful superior. He only entreated for clear instructions. "I am not afraid," he wrote, "of banishment, or poverty, or torments, or death; for all these, God strengthening me, my heart is ready in obedience to the apostolic see, and for the liberty of my mother the Church; all I ask is certainty, that I may know without doubt what course I ought to hold by your authority."

The king gained time. He did not wish to quarrel if he could help it; and probably thought that he had more chance at Rome than with Anselm. He proceeded at once to invest two of his clerks with bishoprics. He gave Salisbury to his chancellor Roger, originally a poor priest of Caen, who had followed him in his adverse fortunes, and had first pleased Henry by the speed with which he got through his mass; and who rose to be one of the greatest and richest of the king's servants. He gave Hereford to another Roger, the superintendent or clerk of his larder. It is hardly wonderful, with such appointments, made as a matter of course, from men broken in to the ways of feudal courts, and accustomed to make themselves useful in them, ecclesiastics in nothing but their qualifications as scribes, accountants, and clever men of business, that bishoprics were indifferently filled; and that those who wished to see them filled as they ought to be, thought nothing too much to do and to suffer, in order to break down the prescriptive system, which made these appointments seem natural and fit.

Anselm also gained what he had from the first been asking for. A council in those days was the ordinary and approved remedy for disorders in the Church and society; as later a parliament was for disorders in the State and Church also. A great council was held, with the king's consent, about Michaelmas 1102, at Westminster, of the bishops and abbots of the whole realm. "In this council," it is said, in the record of it drawn up by Anselm, "were present, by the request made by Anselm the archbishop to the king, the chief men of the realm, so that whatever was decreed by the authority of the said council might be kept safe by the harmonious care and solicitude of each order. For so it was necessary, seeing that for many years, the observance of synods having been intermitted, the thorns of vice had grown up, and the earnestness of Christian religion had grown too cold in England." The subjects of its decrees and orders were many; but in general it may be said to have had in view two things: to draw tighter the strings of discipline among the clergy, and to arrest the tendency always at work among them to forget their calling in the liberty and the business of ordinary life; and, next, to strike hard at some special forms of gross and monstrous depravity with which society was at this time infested, and which seem to have broken out and become fashionable in the younger generation since the Conqueror's death. Abbots who bought their offices, and clergy who would not put away their wives, were visited equally with the severity of the council. Among the canons is one against the "wicked trade used hitherto in England, by which men are sold like brute animals." But to enact was one thing, to enforce another.

The Council of London, Eadmer says, soon made many transgressors of its rules among all sorts of men. Anselm had proposed to publish weekly its excommunication against the more heinous sins. But he found it expedient to alter this. All that immediately came of the council was the proof that the Church felt that it ought not to look on sin with indifference. But most of the bishops were too deeply tainted with the worldliness which their canons denounced to give any hearty support to Anselm in his efforts to correct it. Yet these efforts were not in vain., His earnest spirit, his high ideal, and his single-minded zeal against what was wrong were beginning to raise the tone of the religious society round him, though but gradually and partially. A proof of this was shortly after given in a quarter where it was least to be expected. One of Henry's first acts had been to nominate William Giffard to the bishopric of Winchester. His name suggests that he belonged to the family of the Giffards, Earls of Buckingham and Counts of Longueville in Normandy, a house descended from a sister of the famous Duchess Gunnor, the wife of the first Duke Richard. He had long belonged to the king's chapel : he had served the Conqueror ; he is called chancellor under the Red King ; he was an ecclesiastic deep in the secular business of the court, and much trusted by it. A change of ideas must have been setting in when William Giffard, Henry's first choice for a bishopric, positively declined to receive investiture by the pastoral staff from the king's hands. The appointment appears to have been a popular one ; it is said that the clergy and people of Winchester pressed to have him ; that he was "elected" by them; and finally, by the king's consent or connivance, he had publicly received the pastoral staff and the charge of the bishopric from Anselm's hands. The king now called on Anselm to consecrate him, and with him the two new bishops of Salisbury and Hereford. The "king's larderer" had died shortly after his nomination, having vainly made the strange request that Anselm would give a commission to the bishops of London and Rochester to consecrate him bishop on his death-bed; and in his place had been named Reinhelm, another clerk of the royal chapel, who was chancellor to the queen. This demand was a departure from the terms, on which both parties had agreed to wait for the issue of a reference to Rome. Anselm looked on it as an attempt to steal a march on him, and, says Eadmer, was somewhat moved by it "from his tranquillity of mind." He was willing to consecrate William Giffard, but refused in the most solemn way, "with the sanction of an oath," to consecrate the other two. On this refusal the king ordered Gerard, the Archbishop of York, to consecrate. Gerard was ready enough; he was a courtier, an old antagonist of Anselm's, and only too glad to mortify the pride of the rival see of Canterbury. But the tide was turning. The strong feeling for the honour of Canterbury may have had something to do with it. To every one's surprise, the new bishop-elect of Hereford brought back to the king the ring and staff with which he had received investiture, regretting that he had ever taken them, and feeling sure that to receive consecration from Gerard's hands would be to receive a curse instead of a blessing. The king was very wroth, and drove him from the court. The consecration of the other two was appointed to take place in London. All was ready, the church was full, the bishops were assembled to ask the solemn preliminary questions, when William Giffard's conscience smote him, and interrupting the service, he declared that he would rather be spoiled of all his goods than receive consecration in such a fashion. Gerard, trying to mortify Anselm, had brought unexpected humiliation on himself. The service was broken off, and the bishops in confusion and anger retired to report the matter to the king. "Then the shout of the whole multitude who had come together to see the issue rung out; with one voice their cry was, that William was a friend of the right, that the bishops were no bishops, but perverters of justice." William Giffard was summoned to the presence of the king, to hear the complaints of the bishops and the threats of the court. "There he stood," says Eadmer, "but he could not be drawn aside from the right; so he was despoiled of all that he had and banished from the realm." Anselm's expostulations were of course useless.

In due time the Pope's answer to the reference arrived. As was to be expected, he indignantly disavowed the verbal message attributed to him by Gerard of York and his companions: he reiterated the prohibitions against lay investiture, and excommunicated the bishops as liars, and false to their trust. That they should have lied outright, with the certainty of being found out, seems more incredible than that they should have blundered. Pope Paschal was "no Gregory," as one of Anselm's correspondents said; he was very desirous to keep well with Henry in his own critical position; and in his first letter to Anselm after his own election he lays great stress on getting the revenue which the Roman Church derived from England, and which, he said, it sorely needed. It is possible that he may have held out some vague hopes or hinted some ambiguous civilities, which Gerard misunderstood or made too much of. But, on the other hand, the bishops' story was a very circumstantial one, and nothing in Paschal's character warrants us in thinking that he was willing to give way privately on a point on which he was so stiff publicly. And the writers who mention the story, Eadmer and William of Malmsbury, take for granted, in accordance with Paschal's account of the matter, that the whole thing was a trick, not of the Pope to make things pleasant, but of unscrupulous court bishops to gain time.

But no one yet knew what the Pope's letter, which was directed to Anselm, contained. The king would not hear of having it read to him, or its contents reported to him; he probably knew what it contained. Anselm would not break the seal, lest, if the king should ask to see it and found it unsealed, he should talk of forgery and interpolations. Anselm feared also lest its contents might at once force him to extreme measures with some of the bishops; and it was not opened till Anselm was out of England. But in the middle of Lent (1103) Henry, on some pretence, suddenly appeared at Canterbury. The reason soon appeared. His patience, he let Anselm understand, was exhausted, and he must have his own, as his predecessors had had, without evasion and without delay. "What had he to do with the Pope about what was his own? Let all who loved him know for certain that whoever denied him his father's usages was his enemy." "I neither am taking, nor wish to take from him anything that is his," was the answer; "but to save my life, unless the same see which laid on the prohibition takes it off, I may not consent to him about the matters which I heard with my own ears decreed in the Roman Synod." The king was known to be exasperated and disposed for extreme measures; people began to talk of personal violence. Things looked dangerous. "I have seen," says Eadmer, "the very chief men, on whose advice the king relied, in tears at the prospect of the mischief to come." Prayers were made that evil might be averted. But, in the midst of the excitement, Henry's tone at once changed. "Would the archbishop go himself to Rome, and try what he could do with the Pope, lest the king by losing the rights of his predecessors should be disgraced." Anselm answered that if the chief men of the realm thought it right for him to go, weak as he was, he was ready according as God should give him strength; but that if he should reach the successor of the apostles, he could do nothing to the prejudice of the liberty of the Church or his own honour; he could but bear witness to facts. The reply was that nothing more was wanted; the king's envoy would be there also, to state the case for his master.

This was arranged at the Easter court at Winchester (1103). Anselm returned to Canterbury, and four days after set out on his journey to Rome. In contrast with his first departure, Eadmer says that he departed "in the king's peace, invested with all that belonged to him." Correspondence was kept up in measured but not unfriendly terms. Anselm landed at Witsand, and proceeded by Boulogne to Bec and Chartres. He had friends everywhere: the Countess Ida, the mother of two kings of Jerusalem, at Boulogne; the Countess Adela, the Conqueror's daughter, at Chartres; and at Chartres he was also welcomed by the famous Bishop Ivo, one of the most learned and moderate canonists of the time, Anselm's fellow-pupil under Lanfranc at Bec, who was not at first, though he became so afterwards, of Anselm's mind on the great question of the day. The season was an unusually hot one; every one said it was madness to attempt a summer journey to Italy; and Anselm was persuaded to delay. He spent the time at his old home at Bec. Such delay probably suited the king. Partly because he had rather that Anselm, now that he was out of England, should not tell his own story at Rome, partly perhaps from a real feeling of kindness which seems to have been between the two men in spite of their differences, he became anxious for "his archbishop's" health, and wrote, urging him to spare himself the fatigue of the journey, and do his business by envoys. But Anselm had already set out at the end of August, and his answer is dated from the valley of Maurienne, at the foot of Mont Cenis. At Rome he found his old acquaintance, the searcher of his baggage at Dover, his opponent at Rome in the days of Pope Urban, William Warelwast, who had probably made more journeys to Rome in the king's service than any other of the clerks of the chapel. In due time the subject was brought before the Pope and the Roman court. William Warelwast was an able and bold advocate of the king's rights. He asked that the Pope would sanction and legalize for

King Henry the old customs of William the Conqueror. He urged the humiliation of depriving him of well-established usages; and he dilated on the munificence of the English kings, and on what the Romans would lose by offending them. His words, and it may be something more, brought over a good many of his Roman hearers. "The wishes," it was said, "of so great a man as the King of England were on no account to be overlooked." Anselm was silent. "He would not," says Eadmer, "give his advice that mortal man should be made the door of the Church;" but all along his part was not to press his own view, but to take the law from the supreme judge. Paschal also had only listened. Warelwast thought he had made an impression, and might venture to clench it. "Know all men present," he added with vehemence, "that not to save his kingdom will King Henry lose the investitures of the churches." "Nor, before God, to save his head, will Pope Paschal let him have them," was the immediate retort. William was taken aback, and the feeling of the assembly veered round. The advice was given by the Pope's counsellors that Henry should be indulged in some matters of custom, which might put him in good humour, and not give cause to other princes to take offence: that he himself should be personally exempted from excommunication; but that the prohibition of investiture must be maintained, and all those who had infringed it regarded as excommunicate. A letter, such as commonly came from the milder popes at this time, of compliment, remonstrance, and devotional appeal, firm, but leaving the door open for further negotiation, was sent to the king. With arguments from

Scripture texts, like "I am the door," assurances that the customs claimed were really of no value, and with large promises of consideration for the king's wishes, were mingled congratulations on the birth of his son, "whom," adds the Pope, "we hear that you have named by the name of your famous father, William." To Anselm the Pope gave his blessing, and the confirmation of the Primacy of Canterbury. There was nothing more to do at Rome, and Anselm prepared to return to England.

He was escorted through the Apennines by the great Countess Matilda. On the road they were joined by William Warelwast, who had remained behind at Rome in the hope of doing something more in Anselm's absence; but he found the attempt useless. He travelled in Anselm's company over the Alps; but he was in a hurry to get home, and turned off before they reached Lyons, where Anselm was to spend Christmas. Before he went he delivered to Anselm a message from the king: it was his last word; but it was accompanied with assurances of the king's love and good-will to the archbishop. "I had hoped," he said, "that our business at Rome would have had another issue, and I therefore deferred till now to communicate what my lord bid me say to you But now I must tell you. He says that if you return, to be to him what your predecessors have been to his, he desires and will gladly welcome your coming." "Have you nothing more to say?" Anselm asked. "I speak to a man of understanding," was the only answer. "I understand," said Anselm. There was no difficulty in understanding, though he wrote to Henry to ask if Warelwast had rightly delivered his message. Warelwast went forward on his journey, and Anselm a second time took up his abode at Lyons with his friend Archbishop Hugh.

The matter was left exactly as Henry wished it. The Pope had no intention of quarrelling with the king. He saved matters with Henry by exempting him personally from the Church laws, and with his own conscience by enforcing it against everybody else. Paschal had serious difficulties on his hands at home; and this seemed to be the most hopeful way of arranging the English question. He compromised and surrendered nothing; but he kept up negotiations and interchange of friendly messages with Henry. Henry also had not given way; and he personally was saved harmless. Anselm's hands were for the present tied, and he could not speak or influence others by his presence in England. But not even with him was Henry inclined to deal as the Red King had done. On Warelwast's return, the revenues of the archbishopric were seized for the king's use. But he appointed, as receivers, two of the archbishop's own "men," with the "kindly forethought," says Eadmer, "that as they were bound by fealty and oaths to Anselm, they would exercise their office less vexatiously to the tenants"—an intention which Eadmer intimates was imperfectly fulfilled. The correspondence between the king and the archbishop did not cease, and it was kept up in words of good-will and grave courtesy. "You tell me," writes the king, "that you cannot come to me nor be with me, as Lanfranc your predecessor was with my father. I am very sorry that you will not do so. If you would, I would gladly receive you; and all the instances of honour, dignity, and friendship which my father showed to him

T

I would show to you. But our lord the Pope has sent to me his requests and admonitions on certain points. Wherefore I wish to send ambassadors to Rome, and by the counsel of God and my barons answer our lord the Pope about them, and ask for that which I ought to ask for. When I have received his answer, I will write to you as God may put it into my mind. Meanwhile I am willing that you should have what is convenient from the profits of the Church of Canterbury; though I do this unwillingly; for there is no man living whom I would rather have in my kingdom with me than you, if there was nothing with you against it." The queen, who was ever full of love and reverence for Anselm, and with whom he kept up a constant correspondence, assured him that her husband's mind towards him was much more softened than many people thought, and that her influence should not be wanting to produce agreement and harmony between them. But there was no sign of relenting, or of any intention to alter or give up the usages. Hard things were said of Anselm. The king declared that he alone thwarted him,—implying that the Pope would have been more favourable, but for Anselm. Anselm's answer, that he could not do, under altered circumstances, what Lanfranc had done, gave a natural and obvious handle for invidious reflections; his steady friend Queen Matilda writes regretfully that his intemperate words had disturbed the evenmindedness of the king and the nobles. "I have said nothing," he writes in reply, "against the king's father and Archbishop Lanfranc, men of great and religious name, when I said that neither in my baptism nor in my ordination had I pledged myself to their laws and customs, and when I declared that I would not deny the law of God. As to what is now demanded of me, on the ground that they did it, I, on account of what with my own ears I heard at Rome, cannot do it without the heaviest offence. But that ill-natured meaning which has been put on my words, according to which I have spoken foolishly, I do not suppose to be so taken either by the king or by you; for the king, as I understand, received my letter in the first instance kindly; but afterwards some one or other, I know not who, spitefully gave it an ill meaning and stirred him up against me."

The precedent of Lanfranc was a point on which Anselm felt himself specially open to misinterpretation. "Some mischievous busybody or other,"—he writes to his "old and ever new friend, Gundulf, bishop of Rochester," the only one of the bishops who had stuck by him throughout,—" has interpreted my letter to the king out of the evil of his own heart; as if I boasted that I always have kept God's law and slandered the king's father and Archbishop Lanfranc, as if they had lived out of God's law. But they who say this have too small or too evil a mind. In their time, the king's father and Archbishop Lanfranc, great and religious men as they were, did some things which I at this time cannot do according to God's will, or without the condemnation of my own soul."

Anselm's position was a hard one. About the "usages" themselves, he never had the strong feelings of Gregory VII., which were kept up at Rome. Intellectually and morally, his was not a mind to lay great stress on matters of this kind; in temper he was too considerate and ready to allow for others, in his ways of thinking he was too intent on wider and loftier views, to see such a question as this with the keen and accurate instinct of a statesman. His own conduct shows that there was nothing in homage or investiture, taken by themselves, to shock him; at first he looked on them as a matter of course. Since then, he had learned that a meaning could be put on them; he had felt what an engine they could be made for hindering a bishop in his duty, and for making him think unworthily of his office. But this of itself was not the reason why he so unflinchingly set himself against the "customs" which Henry truly said were those of Lanfranc and the Conqueror. There is very little of the current argument against them in his own writings. His attitude throughout was that of simple obedience to the law and to its lawful expounder, and his own spiritual superior, though he himself had come to see only too good reason for the law. He had heard the law promulgated. He had heard its authorized interpreter enforce the universal application of it. When there could be no longer any doubt about this, there was nothing left for him but to obey. And to obey was all that he pretended to do. It was the Pope's business to speak in the matter; that was not disputed even in England: what the king wanted, was for the Pope to do, as Popes were too much accustomed to do, to grant some personal privilege or exemption from the general law. And Henry wanted Anselm to believe that, sooner or later, he should persuade the Pope into giving it, and to go on in the meanwhile as if it had been given. This was what Anselm would not do, and for which he was in exile. But let the Pope speak, let him decide in what way he would, let him modify the law entrusted to his administration, let him make what terms seemed to him expedient, and Anselm would be only too glad to go back to the more congenial work of trying to raise up religion and morality in England. What his opinion really was as to what was expedient or right for the Pope to arrange, hardly appears; he would, no doubt, have been glad, when the question about investiture was once opened, to get rid of a mischievous and unbecoming practice; he thought that it was not a matter for trifling; and he thought that on both sides there was too much of an intention to gain time, and to leave things in suspense; but to the decision, when it came, and whatever it was, he was ready to bow. But the decision was just the thing which it seemed hopeless to look for. Embassies came and went; each embassy just avoided bringing things to extremities, and invited another. "The decision of the whole matter," as Anselm wrote to the Pope, "lies with you." Let Paschal dispense with the law; let him take off the excommunication, and Anselm was ready to communicate with those whom the Pope dispensed with, to do homage, to allow investiture, if the Pope thought he could make exceptions to the canons. "You tell me," he says in one of his letters to England, with unwonted sharpness, "that they say that it is I who forbid the king to grant investitures. Tell them that they lie. It is not I who forbid the king; but having heard the Vicar of the Apostles in a great council excommunicate all who gave or received investiture, I have no mind to hold communion with excommunicates, or to become excommunicate myself." And his language on this point never varied.

But, as was not unnatural, the blame of everything was thrown on him. Not unnaturally — for he was the one man who saw his duty and his line perfectly clear, and whom nothing could move from them. He was ready to do whatever the Pope bade him—to resist, to comply, to compromise; only his chief must give his orders. And people felt that it was his unflinching constancy and single-minded purpose which prevented the authorities at Rome, for very shame, from conniving, in the case of distant and rich England, at a breach of their own recent and solemn laws. William Warelwast would have had much more chance of arranging matters at Rome, if he had not had to encounter there, not Anselm's words, but his silence and his readiness to accept the "usages," if only the Pope would take the responsibility of commanding him to accept them. And so everybody, friends and foes, turned on him. The queen wrote, beseeching him somehow or other to find a way out of the difficulty. The monks of Canterbury charged on him the vexations which they suffered in his absence; whatever happened amiss in the church was laid at his door. He was depriving the king of his rights. He was letting the king's wicked clerks invade the Church. He was obstinate and impracticable. He was taking his ease and evading the duty and danger of his post. He was led away by "his iron will;" he was a coward, and "had fled from his flock and left them to be torn to pieces, at the word of one William." "He was busying himself about other men's matters, and neglecting his own work." His letters at this time, differing in their nervous and direct conciseness from the sermon-like fashion of letter-writing—which is his ordinary style, as it was the style of his age—show that he felt keenly, and had to command himself, in noticing and answering the peevish and ill-natured complaints, the gossip, the suspicions, the misinterpretations, the impatient and unreasonable entreaties, which came to him from England.

Anselm waited a year and a half at Lyons, while the king was negotiating at Rome. In March 1105 he received a letter from Paschal, saying that he had excommunicated the counsellors who instigated the king to insist on investiture, and especially Robert Count of Mellent, the shrewdest and most ambitious of them; but that he was waiting for another embassy from England before he settled anything about the king. "Then Anselm understood that it was useless for him to wait at Lyons for help from Rome; for all that he had got in answer to letters and messages was some sort of consolatory promises, bidding him expect something, from one fixed time to another." He had also written more than once to Henry asking for restitution of the property of the see, which without any form of judgment had been seized for the king's use; and had received no answers but polite excuses for delay. He at length resolved to do something himself to bring matters to an issue.

He left Lyons and came northwards. On his road he heard that the Countess Adela of Blois and Chartres, Henry's sister, who had of old treated him with great kindness and had taken him for her spiritual guide, was dangerously ill at Blois. A visit under such circumstances was looked upon in those days as an indispensable duty of friendship and religion; Anselm turned out of his road and went to Blois. She recovered; and then Anselm "did not conceal from her, that for the injury which for two years Henry had done to God and to himself, he was come to excommunicate him."

The countess was alarmed and distressed; and set herself in earnest to avert the blow. Excommunications were the usual, and according to the ideas of the time the lawful, weapons, in contests of this kind about the wrongful seizure of property; and they were not uncommon, even against kings and princes. But an excommunication from a man of Anselm's character, who had suffered so much and so long, was felt to be a more serious thing than ordinary. It was particularly inconvenient to Henry just at this time, when he was preparing for his decisive struggle with his brother Robert for the possession of Normandy. The report spread, and Henry was alarmed. "In many places in England, France, and Normandy, it was noised abroad that the king himself was on the point of being excommunicated by Anselm; and thereupon many mischiefs began to be hatched against a Power not over much loved, which it was thought might be more effectually carried out against one excommunicated by a man like Anselm." But Henry was too prudent to allow things to come to extremities. The Countess Adela carried Anselm with her to Chartres, and through her mediation an interview was arranged between the king and the archbishop. He and the Countess met Henry (July 22, 1105) at the Castle of L'Aigle on the Rille. "They found the king overjoyed at Anselm's coming, and not a little softened from his old harshness." The reconciliation seemed hearty and frank. Anselm was put in possession of the revenues of his see, and restored to the king's friendship. Henry was as gracious as he could be; whenever anything had to be discussed, he would always go himself to visit Anselm, instead of sending for him. Efforts were made that Anselm should at once return to England. But Henry insisted on the old conditions—recognition of the right of investiture. And on this point a reference to Rome was necessary.

Things were only half settled; and Henry made the most of the opportunity in a characteristic way. He was at this time in pressing need of money for his war in Normandy; and the Church of course did not escape "in the manifold contributions, which never ceased," says the English chronicler, "before the king went over to Normandy, and while he was there, and after he came back again." Henry had some skill in inventing, on such emergencies, new *forisfacta*—matters for fines and forfeiture— questions for the *Curia Regis* to settle between him and his lieges. On this occasion he was seized with a zeal for Church discipline. Many of the parochial clergy were living in disobedience to the canons of the late synod of Westminster, which had forbidden clerical marriage; "this sin the king could not endure to see unpunished." So to bring the offenders to their duty, he, of his own mere motion, proceeded to mulct them heavily. The tax, however, proved, unfortunately, not so productive as he had anticipated; and therefore, changing his mind, he imposed the assessment on the whole body of the parochial clergy, innocent as well as guilty, throughout the kingdom. Anselm expostulated; the offending clergy ought to be punished, he said, not by the officers of the Exchequer, but by their bishops. Henry, in his reply, is much surprised at the archbishop's objections; he thought that he was only doing his work for him, labouring in his cause; but he would see to it: "however," he said, "whatever else had happened, the archbishop's people had been left in peace." But as to the mass of the clergy, seizures, imprisonment, and every kind of annoyance, had enforced the tax-gatherer's demands. Two hundred priests went barefoot in procession, in alb and stole, to the king's palace, "with one voice imploring him to have mercy upon them;" but they were driven from his presence; "the king, perhaps, was busy." They then, "clothed with confusion upon confusion," besought the intercession and good offices of the queen: she was moved to tears at their story; but she was afraid to interfere in their behalf. What is a still greater proof of Henry's tyranny is that the court party among the clergy, among them the excommunicated bishops, began to turn their eyes towards Anselm. Gerard of York found himself in trouble, and wrote with apologies and prayers for help to the man whom he had done his best to ruin. A letter was further sent, signed by several of the bishops, entreating Anselm to return, as the only means of remedying the misery of the English Church. "We have waited for peace, but it has departed far from us.

Laymen had broken in, even unto the altar. Thy children," they continue, " will fight with thee the battle of the Lord ; and if thou shalt be gathered to thy fathers before us, we will receive of thy hand the heritage of thy labours. Delay then, no longer; thou hast now no excuse before God. We are ready, not only to follow thee, but to go before thee, if thou command us; for *now* we are seeking in this cause, not what is ours, but what is the Lord's." Among the names attached to this letter are those of Anselm's old opponents, Gerard of York, Herbert of Norwich, and Robert of Chester.

At length, after more delays, more embassies, more intrigues, and bargainings at Rome, the end of this dreary contest came for Anselm ; and except that haggling is part of a bargain, it is not easy to see why it might not have come before. In April 1106, fresh instructions came from the Pope. It released, or gave Anselm authority to release, all who had come under excommunication for breaking the canons about homage and investiture ; thus enabling Anselm to return to England and take part with the offending bishops; but it laid down no rule for the future. Henry was now very anxious to get Anselm to England; but he was detained at Jumiéges and Bec by repeated attacks of alarming illness. The king's letters and messages expressed the warmest interest in him. " All that the king had in Normandy was at his disposal." Henry at length crossed over to Normandy ; he had a great enterprise on hand ; and he found time to visit Anselm at Bec. Various matters were arranged to put a stop to the arbitrary exactions which had grown up under the Red King; and at length Anselm returned once more to England, where he was received with joyful welcome. "My lord the king," Anselm writes in one of his letters, "has commended to me his kingdom and all that belongs to him, that my will might be done in all that is his: in which he has shown the kindness of his good-will towards me, and his affection for me." The queen met him, and prepared his lodgings at the places where he halted ; and, as always, was foremost in her affection and honour for him. Shortly, he received from the king the account of his final victory over his brother Robert, in the decisive battle fought, "on a day named and fixed," at Tinchebrai (Sept. 28, 1106). Henry's enemies were now crushed and in his power; not only his brother, but the more formidable Norman lords, William of Mortagne and the implacable Robert of Belesme. Ralph Flambard recognized the winning side and made his peace with Henry. Henry had regained the realm over which his father had ruled ; and the Norman and English lords soon felt that they had found their master.

But the final arrangement of the dispute with the Church had yet to come. It was not long delayed. It might have been expected that the conqueror of Normandy would have been tempted, if not to extreme terms, at least to his old game of delay and intrigue. But Anselm seems to have won his respect; and Henry was ready for concessions and a fair treaty. " On the 1st of August " (1107), says Eadmer—it would have been at Whitsuntide but for Anselm's illness—" an assembly of bishops, abbots, and chief men of the realm was held in London, in the king's palace ; and for three days continuously the matter of the investitures of churches was fully discussed between the king and the bishops, Anselm being absent; some of them urging that the king should perform them after the custom of his father and brother, and not according to the command of the Pope. For the Pope, standing firm in the decision which had been promulgated thereupon, had allowed the homage which Pope Urban had forbidden equally with investitures; and by this had made the king inclinable to him on the point of investitures. Then, in the presence of Anselm, the multitude standing by, the king granted and decreed that from that time forth for ever no one should be invested in England with bishopric or abbey by staff and ring, either by the king or by any lay hand; Anselm also allowing that no one elected to a prelacy should be refused consecration on account of homage done to the king. This, then, having been settled, fathers were appointed by the king, by the counsel of Anselm and the chief men of the realm, without any investiture of the pastoral staff and ring, in nearly all the churches in England which had long been widowed of their pastors." On the 11th of the same month, at Canterbury, they were consecrated. Among them were William Giffard and Reinhelm, whose unexpected scruples and resolute foregoing of high place first opened Henry's eyes to the reaction which was beginning, even among the clerks of the chapel; among them, too, was William Warelwast, appointed to Exeter, who, after all his hard work at Rome, had ended by becoming Anselm's friend. Among the consecrating bishops was not only Gerard of York, but the Bishop of Durham, Ralph Flambard.

# CHAPTER XIII.

ANSELM'S LAST DAYS.

> " Still glides the Stream, and shall not cease to glide ;
> The Form remains, the Function never dies ;
> While we, the brave, the mighty, and the wise,
> We men, who in our morn of youth defied
> The elements, must vanish ;—be it so !
> Enough, if something from our hands have power
> To live, and act, and serve the future hour ;
> And if, as towards the silent tomb we go,
> Through love, through hope, and faith's transcendent dower,
> We feel that we are greater than we know."—WORDSWORTH.

ANSELM had won a great victory. What was gained by it?

Of the victory itself there can be no doubt. The power which contested it was too mighty and energetic ; the opposition too formidable and resolute ; the object fought for too much prized by those who had to yield it, and too obstinately defended ; the prescription assailed was of too long date, too continuous, and too natural, for it to be a light matter that the issue of the dispute broke through the cherished usages of the Norman kings. That the arrangement was a peaceful compromise, and that the king kept half what he contended for, in his view perhaps the most important half, did not make it less a victory, that any part of what was so valued should be torn from such a grasp by the single-minded constancy of an old man at a distance, whose main weapon was his conviction of the justice of his cause, and his unflinching and undeviating steadiness. To have made so marked a change publicly and deliberately in the relations of bishops to great kings, whose rule was not so much by law as by the loose claims and measures of feudal usages, and to have induced one of the sons of the Conqueror, and, among them, to have induced Henry, the shrewdest, ablest, hardest of them all, to forego part of the customs which he valued at the worth of half his kingdom, was an achievement of which, whatever came of it, no one could mistake the magnitude. It was accomplished, too, with a remarkable absence of those violent measures which were the common weapons on all sides in those days, and which were so freely used in other scenes of this same contest on the continent of Europe. That which determined it as much as anything was Anselm's personal character; the boundless reverence and, still more, the intense love and sympathy called out on all sides, by the union in it of the deepest human tenderness with grave and calm self-command, with unpretending courage, and with that unconscious and child-like meekness, so remarkable in him, with which he bore those great and singular gifts of intellect, in which by this time he was known to be without a living equal in Christendom. Henry, with all his deep and heavy faults, had eyes for this. He knew that in Anselm he had at Canterbury the greatest Christian bishop, the greatest religious example of his age. He felt towards the archbishop, as the great persons about him and his subjects felt—with more admiration, perhaps, of the head, with not so much sympathy probably of the heart, as there was, at least, among the people; much disliking, much resenting, much fearing many of Anselm's ways and purposes, but unable to resist the spell and charm of his nobleness, his force of soul, his unselfish truthfulness. Only Henry, probably, saw it more clearly than the clerks of his chapel, or cunning men of the world like Count Robert of Mellent. He saw that it was, even politically, a mistake to persist even for the sake of "the usages" in forcing a man like Anselm, whom he might gain for a friend, to range himself against him. Slowly and reluctantly, but not insincerely at last, he made up his mind to come to terms; and when he had done so, then with the frankness of a really powerful mind, he let his admiration for his antagonist have its way. No honour, no confidence was too much for Anselm. Further, when the question was to be settled, Henry settled it openly and fairly; in the way which was the lawful way of witnessing and establishing important constitutional matters; in a great council of the realm, where it was debated, decided, and then proclaimed before the people, gathered to hear the proceedings of their chiefs, and to sanction these proceedings by their presence.

This was the victory; but what was gained by it? It was of course, directly and outwardly, the victory of a cause which has never been popular in England; it renewed and strengthened the ties which connected England with that great centre of Christendom, where justice and corruption, high aims and the vilest rapacity and fraud, undeniable majesty and undeniable hollowness, were then, as they have ever been, so strangely and inextricably combined. Anselm's victory, with its circumstances, was one of the steps, and a very important one, which made Rome more powerful in England: even with the profound and undoubting beliefs of the eleventh and twelfth centuries, that did not recommend it to the sympathy of Englishmen; it is not likely to do so now. But those who judge of events not merely by the light of what has happened since, and of what, perhaps, have been their direct consequences, but by the conditions of the times when they happened, ought to ask themselves before they regret such a victory as an evil, what would have come to pass if, in days like those of William the Red and his brother, with the king's clerical family as a nursery for bishops, and with clerks like Ralph Flambard or Gerard of York, or even William Warelwast, for rulers of the Church, the king and his party had triumphed, and the claims founded on the "usages" to the submission of the Church and the unreserved obedience of the bishops had prevailed without check or counterpoise? Would a feudalized clergy, isolated and subservient, have done better for religion, for justice, for liberty, for resistance to arbitary will, for law, for progress, than a clergy connected with the rest of Christendom; sharing for good, and also, no doubt, for evil, in its general movement and fortunes, and bound by strong and real ties not only to England, but to what was then, after all, the school and focus of religious activity and effort, as well as the seat of an encroaching and usurping centralization, the Roman Church. Men must do what they can in their own day against what are the evils and dangers of their own day; they must use against them the helps and remedies which their own day gives. There was in those times no question of what we now put all our trust in, the power of law; the growth of our long histories and hard experiences, and of the prolonged thought of the greatest intellects of many generations. The power which presented itself to men in those days as the help of right against might, the refuge and protector of the weak against the strong, the place where reason might make its appeal against will and custom, where liberty was welcomed and honoured, where it was a familiar and stirring household word, was not the law and its judgment-seats, but the Church, with its authority, concentrated and represented in the Pope. That belief was just as much a genuine and natural growth of the age, as the belief which had also grown up about kings as embodying the power of the nation; that it was abused by tyranny or weakness was no more felt to be an argument against one than against the other. The question which men like Anselm asked themselves was, how best they could restrain wrong, and counteract what were the plainly evil and dangerous tendencies round them. He did so by throwing himself on the spiritual power behind him, which all in his times acknowledged greater than any power of this world. What else could any man in his struggle against tyranny and vice have done? What better, what more natural course could any man have taken, earnest in his belief of the paramount superiority of spiritual things over material, and of reason over force; earnest in his longing for reformation and improvement? The central power of the Pope, which Anselm strengthened, grew rapidly with the growth and advance of the times: it grew to be abused; it usurped on the powers to which it was the counterpoise; it threatened, as they had threatened, to absorb all rights of sovereignty, all national and personal claims to independence and freedom; it had, in its turn, to be resisted, restrained, at last in England expelled. It went through the usual course of successful power in human hands. But this is no reason why at the time it should not have been the best, perhaps, even the only defence of the greatest interests of mankind against the immediate pressure of the tyrannies and selfishness of the time. If anything else could then have taken its place in those days, the history of Europe has not disclosed it.

It may be thought, on the other hand, that the actual point which Anselm gained was not worth the gaining; that while he gained too much in one way, as regards the influence of the Pope, he was cheated out of the substance of what he had been fighting for in regard to checks on the king in the appointment of bishops. But this was not the view at the time. Then the feeling was that two things had been done. By the surrender of the significant ceremony of delivering the bishopric by the emblematic staff and ring, it was emphatically put on record that the spiritual powers of the bishop were not the king's to give; the prescription of feudalism was broken; a correction was visibly given to the confused but dangerous notions in which that generation had been brought up. In the second place, the king was strongly and solemnly reminded that he owed an account for the persons whom he appointed bishops; they were not merely his creatures; they were not merely elevated and promoted on the terms on which he made a knight or a baron; the office was not his, in the sense that he could sell it. There was a body of opinion to which he owed deference in such appointments; there was an authority with which he must reckon, and which had a right to be satisfied. Whatever the final arrangements were, or if there were any, about the right of appointing and electing prelates (and there is a good deal of variation in the language in which these transactions are described), there can be no doubt that in the case of important dignities, like those of bishops and the great abbots, the king would in the long-run find a way to get them, or the greater part of them, into his patronage. But it was a distinct step that the attention of the public, both ecclesiastical and civil, should be directed to these appointments; that the king should be reminded, even if he went against the warning, as Henry doubtless in many cases did, that there were rules and fitnesses and other claims than his own to be thought of in giving bishoprics. Anselm's struggle raised the general feeling about the calling and the duties of a bishop It was a fit work for the first bishop and pastor of England, of one who sat in the first Christian see of the West; it was worth struggling for; and it was a victory worth having, to have in any degree succeeded in it.

And if nothing else had been gained, or if, when he was gone, the tide of new things—new disputes, new failures, new abuses and corruptions—flowed over his work, breaking it up and making it useless or harmful, this at least was gained, which was more lasting— the example of a man in the highest places of the world who, when a great principle seemed entrusted to him, was true to it, and accepted all tasks, all disappointments, all humiliations in its service. The liberty of God's Church, obedience to its law and its divinely appointed chief, this was the cause for which Anselm believed himself called to do his best. And he was not afraid. He was not afraid of the face of the great, of the disapprobation of his fellows. It was then an age of much more plain speaking than ours, when intercourse between kings and other men was more free, when expression was more homely, and went with less ceremony to the point. But when Anselm dared to tell what he believed to be the truth in the king's court, it was more than the bluffness of a rude code of manners; he accepted a call which seemed divine, with its consequences; the call of undoubted truth and plain duty. That for which he contended was to him the cause of purity, honesty, justice; it involved the hopes of the weak and despised, in the everyday sufferings, as unceasing then as in the days of which the Psalms tell, of the poor and needy at the hands of the proud and the mighty. "There might be much to say against his course; the 'usages' were but forms and trifles, or they were an important right of the crown, and to assail them was usurpation and disloyalty, or it was a mere dream to hope to abolish them, or they were not worth the disturbance which they caused, or there were worse things to be remedied; difficulties there were no doubt; still, for all this, he felt that this was the fight of the day, and he held on unmoved. Through what was romantic and what was unromantic in his fortunes—whether the contest showed in its high or low form—as a struggle in 'heavenly places' against evil before saints and angels, with the unfading crown in view, or as a game against cowardly selfishness and the intrigue of courts; cheered by the sympathies of Christendom, by the love and reverence of the crowds which sought his blessing; or brought down from his height of feeling by commonplace disagreeables, the inconveniences of life—dust, heat, and wet, bad roads and imperialist robbers, debts and fevers, low insults and troublesome friends,—through it all his faith failed not; it was ever the same precious and ennobling cause, bringing consolation in trouble, giving dignity to what was vexatious and humiliating. It was her own fault if the Church gained little by the compromise, and by so rare a lesson. In one sense, indeed, what is gained by any great religious movement? What are all reforms, restorations, victories of truth, but protests of a minority; efforts, clogged and incomplete, of the good and brave, just enough in their own day to stop instant ruin—the appointed means to save what is to be saved, but in themselves failures? Good men work and suffer, and bad men enjoy their labours and spoil them; a step is made in advance—evil rolled back and kept in check for a while only to return, perhaps, the stronger. But thus, and thus only, is truth passed on, and the world preserved from utter corruption. Doubtless bad men still continued powerful in the English Church. Henry tyrannized, evil was done, and the bishops kept silence ; low aims and corruption may have still polluted the very seats of justice; gold may have been as powerful with cardinals as with King Henry and his chancellors. Anselm may have over-rated his success. Yet success and victory it was—a vantage-ground for all true men who would follow him; and if his work was undone by others, he at least had done his task manfully. And he had left his Church another saintly name, and the memory of his good confession, enshrining as it were her cause, to await the day when some other champion should again take up the quarrel —thus from age to age to be maintained, till He shall come, to whom alone it is reserved 'to still' for ever the enemy and the avenger, and to 'root out all wicked doers from the city of the Lord.'"

There is little more to be said of Anselm. Henry was loyal to his agreement. He entirely gave up the investiture of churches, so Anselm wrote to the Pope, even against the resistance of many; and in filling up vacancies he followed not his own fancy, but took the advice of religious men. His adviser in this was Robert Count of Mellent, who had opposed Anselm so keenly; he was the man to whom the king most listened, and he had come round to Anselm's side. The policy of the late reign was entirely changed; "but," says Eadmer, "the count did not love the English, and would not let any Englishmen be promoted to Church dignities." Henry, now that he was safe on his throne, attended to the representations made to him by Anselm and the chief men of the realm, as to the evils which especially pressed upon the poor. Two are mentioned by Eadmer. The Norman kings were ever moving about through their kingdom; and the waste and plunder which accompanied the passage of their numerous attendants through the country had come to be, in the lawless days of the Red King, like the desolation of hostile armies. "No discipline," says Eadmer, "restrained them; they spoiled, they wasted, they destroyed. What they found in the houses which they invaded and could not consume, they took to market to sell for themselves, or they burnt it; or if it was drink, after washing their horses' feet in it, they poured it abroad. Their cruelties to the fathers of families, their insults to their wives and daughters, it shames me to remember. And so, whenever the king's coming was known beforehand, they fled from their houses, and to save themselves and what was theirs, as far as they could, hid themselves in the woods or wherever they thought they would be safest." This marauding of the servants and followers of the court, Henry attempted to check by stern penalties. He was equally severe and inexorable in punishing another crime from which the poor suffered—the coining of false money; and his efforts were not without effect, says Eadmer, in relieving the miseries of the land during all his reign.

Anselm's life was drawing to its close. The re-enactment, and confirmation by the authority of the great Whitsuntide Assembly, of the canons of the Synod of London against clerical marriage, and a dispute with two of the Northern bishops, his old friend Ralph Flambard, and the archbishop-elect of York, who, apparently reckoning on Anselm's age and bad health, was scheming to evade the odious obligation of acknowledging the paramount claims of the see of Canterbury, were all that marked the last year of his life. A little more than a year before his own death, he had to bury his old and faithful friend,—a friend first in the cloister of Bec, and then in the troubled days of his English primacy, the great builder, Gundulf, Bishop of Rochester. Anselm's last days shall be told in the words of one who had the best right to record the end of him whom he had loved so simply and so loyally—his attendant Eadmer.

"During these events (of the last two years of his life) he wrote a treatise 'Concerning the Agreement of Foreknowledge, Predestination, and the Grace of God, with Free Will,' in which, contrary to his wont, he found difficulty in composition; for after his illness at Bury St. Edmund's, as long as he was spared to this life, he was weaker than before; so that, when he was moving from place to place, he was from that time carried in a litter, instead of riding on horseback. He was tried, also, by frequent and sharp sicknesses, so that we scarce dared promise him life. He, however, never left off his old way of living, but was always engaged in godly meditations, or holy exhortations, or other good work.

"In the third year after King Henry had recalled him from his second banishment, every kind of food by which nature is sustained became loathsome to him. He used to eat, however, putting force on himself, knowing that he could not live without food; and in this way he somehow or another dragged on life through half a year, gradually failing day by day in body, though in vigour of mind he was still the same as he used to be. So being strong in spirit, though but very feeble in the flesh, he could not go to his oratory on foot; but from his strong desire to attend the consecration of the Lord's body, which he venerated with a special feeling of devotion, he caused himself to be carried thither every day in a chair. We who attended on him tried to prevail on him to desist, because it fatigued him so much; but we succeeded, and that with difficulty, only four days before he died.

"From that time he took to his bed, and, with gasping breath, continued to exhort all who had the privilege of drawing near him to live to God, each in his own order. Palm Sunday had dawned, and we, as usual, were sitting round him; one of us said to him, 'Lord Father, we are given to understand that you are going to leave the world for your Lord's Easter court.' He answered, 'If His will be so, I shall gladly obey His will. But if He willed rather that I should yet remain amongst you, at least till I have solved a question which I am turning in my mind, about the origin of the soul, I should receive it thankfully, for I know not whether anyone will finish it after I am gone. Indeed, I hope, that if I could take food, I might yet get well. For I feel no pain anywhere; only, from weakness of my stomach, which cannot take food, I am failing altogether.'

"On the following Tuesday, towards evening, he was no longer able to speak intelligibly. Ralph Bishop of Rochester asked him to bestow his absolution and blessing on us who were present, and on his other children, and also on the king and queen with their children, and the people of the land who had kept themselves under God in his obedience. He raised his right hand, as if he was suffering nothing, and made the sign of the Holy Cross; and then dropped his head and sank down. The congregation of the brethren were already chanting matins in the great church, when one of those who watched about our Father took the book of the Gospels and read before him the history of the Passion, which was to be read that day at the mass. But when he came to our Lord's words, 'Ye are they which have continued with me in my temptations, and I appoint unto you a kingdom, as my Father hath appointed unto me, that ye may eat and drink at my table,' he began to draw his breath more slowly. We saw that he was just going, so he was removed from his bed, and laid upon sackcloth and ashes. And thus, the whole family of his children being collected round him, he gave up his last breath into the hands of his Creator, and slept in peace.

"He passed away, as morning was breaking, on the Wednesday before the day of our Lord's Supper, the 21st of April, in the year of our Lord's Incarnation 1109—the sixteenth of his pontificate and the seventy-sixth of his life."

The story of his departure, told so simply and naturally, has its fringe of wonder and legend. The balsam with which his body was embalmed seemed inexhaustible; the stone coffin, which seemed too small, wonderfully enlarged itself. The eye of admiration and affection was ever on the look-out for strange accompaniments of memorable events, and readily saw them; it was more true and more to be depended on in seeing into heart and character than into the outward facts of nature round it.

Those who remember Walton's account of the death-bed of Richard Hooker will notice more than one point of likeness between the narrative of the twelfth century and that of the seventeenth. The soul, vigorous to the very end, amid the decay of the body and the "gradual averseness to all food;" the clinging, without affectation, to the love of life to finish a cherished work;—" he did not beg," writes Walton, "a long life of God for any other reason but to live to finish his three remaining books of Polity; and then, Lord, let thy servant depart in peace;"—the calm, quiet, unexcited continuance in the usual rites and practices of a religious life, long familiar and become part of everyday life; the comfort of Eucharist and Gospel history; the employment to the last moment of the subtle and inquisitive intellect on its congenial trains of abstruse thought, relating to the deep mysteries of both worlds, seen and unseen, and rendered more real in the face of death—Anselm revolving the origin of the soul, Hooker "meditating the number and nature of angels, and their blessed obedience and order, without which peace could not be in heaven,—and oh that it might be so on earth!" —all these details bring together, at the distance of so many ages, the two great religious thinkers, who outwardly were so different. They make us feel that at bottom, in spite of all changes and differences of circumstance and custom, in spite of miracles told in one age, and the prosaic matter-of-fact of another, the substance of human affections and of religious trust is the same in both; and that to die as Anselm died, or to die as Hooker' died, is to die in much the same manner; with the same view of life now and to come, the same sense of duty, the same faith: the same loyalty to the great Taskmaster and Ruler, the same hope for the cleansing of what was ill in them, and the making perfect what was incomplete; the same submission to the will of God, the same loving hope in Christ.

Anselm was first buried next to his friend Lanfranc in the body of the minster of Canterbury, before the great rood which rose up in the midst of it before the choir. His remains were afterwards translated to the chapel beneath the south-east tower which now bears his name. There they now rest.

When he was gone, his contemporaries felt that the tender-hearted, high-minded, resolute old man who had comforted some of them and affronted others, was a man whom they might be proud to have lived with. His words, his wishes, his decisions, were received, even by those who had opposed him, as oracles which could not be gainsaid. His name, as was to be expected, passed into the roll of saints; but apparently the steps of the process are not clear. His canonization was demanded, but without effect, by Thomas Becket: the final ratification of it is ascribed to a papal bull some centuries later. It was addressed to Cardinal Morton, Archbishop of Canterbury under Henry VII. in 1494.[1] I have mentioned that the last abbot of Bec was M. de Talleyrand. The Pope who formally canonized St. Anselm is said to have been Alexander VI., Roderic Borgia. "In the visible Church the evil are ever mingled with the good."

But a very different judge had already interpreted the opinion of Christendom about Anselm. Before he had suffered the indignity of a canonization at the hands of Borgia, Dante had consecrated his memory, and assigned him a place with those whom the Church

[1] Crozet-Mouchet, p. 482.

honoured as her saints. The great singer of Christian Europe, in his vision of Paradise, sees him among the spirits of light and power in the sphere of the sun—the special "ministers of God's gifts of reason"—among those whom the Middle Age reverenced as having shown to it what the human intellect, quickened by the love of God, could do, in the humblest tasks and sacrifices, and in the highest flights: with prophets, historians, and philosophers; with theologians and jurists; with the glories of the great orders, St. Thomas Aquinas and St. Bonaventura, and with their lowly first-fruits. He sees him as one in those circling garlands of glorified spirits which he describes answering to another as the double rainbow, in their movements of love and joy:

> " As when her handmaid Juno summons, rise
>     Two arches of like hue, and parallel,
>     Drawn out on fleecy cloud athwart the skies,
> The outer springing from the inner one.
>     Like to the voice of that fair nymph that strayed,
>     Consumed by love, as vapours by the sun :
>   \*    \*    \*    \*    \*    \*
> Even so the twofold Garland turned to us, —
>     Of roses formed, that bloom eternally ;
>     And one with other corresponded thus.
> Soon as the sound of dance, and song, according
>     To such glad movement, and the revelry
>     Of light to light fresh brilliancy affording,
> With one consent were in a moment still,
>     Like eyes whose movements simultaneous are,
>     Opening and shutting at the mover's will ;
> From one of these new splendours came a sound." [1]

And when the poet makes the spirit of St. Bonaventura enumerate the twelve stars of the garland in which he moves, Dante, probably by accident, at any rate

[1] Paradise, c. xii., Wright's translation.

by an accident which suits the double aspect of Anselm's character, has joined his name at once with those who had stood for truth in the face of kings and multitudes, and with one who was the type of the teachers of children in the first steps of knowledge: the masters of thought and language in its highest uses and its humblest forms; with the seer whose parable rebuked King David; with the preacher who thundered against Antioch and Constantinople; with the once famous grammarian, St. Jerome's master, from whom the Middle Age schools learnt the elementary laws which govern human speech, and out of whose book of rudiments Anselm had doubtless taught his pupils at Bec:

> "Nathan the seer, the metropolitan
> John Chrysostom, Anselm, and he whose hands—
> Donatus—deigned the primer's help to plan."[1]

It is his right place:—in the noble company of the strong and meek, who have not been afraid of the mightiest, and have not disdained to work for and with the lowliest: capable of the highest things; content, as living before Him with whom there is neither high nor low, to minister in the humblest.

[1] Dayman's translation.


THE END.